Pilgrimage to Dzhvari

A WOMAN'S JOURNEY OF

SPIRITUAL AWAKENING

VALERIA ALFEYEVA

Translated by Stuart and Jenny Robertson

BELL TOWER

New York

Published by Bell Tower, an imprint of Harmony Books, a division of Crown Publishers, Inc., 201 East 50th Street, New York, New York 10022. Member of the Crown Publishing Group.

Originally published in Great Britain by Lion Publishing plc in 1992, and in the United States by Bell Tower in 1993. First published in Russian in 1989 and 1991. Copyright © 1989, 1991 by Valeria Alfeyeva.

Random House, Inc. New York, Toronto, London, Sydney, Auckland

Bell Tower and colophon are registered trademarks of Crown Publishers, Inc.

Manufactured in the United States of America

Library of Congress Cataloging-in-Publication Data

Alfeyeva, Valeria.
[Dzhvari. English]
Pilgrimage to Dzhvari : a woman's journey of spiritual awakening / [Valeria Alfeyeva] ; translated by Stuart and Jenny Robertson.
p.   cm.
Includes bibliographical references.
Contents: Dzhvari—Called, chosen, and faithful.
1. Alfeyeva, Valeria—Journeys—Georgia (Republic)
2. Alfeyeva, Valeria—Religion.   3. Authors, Russian—20th century—Biography.   4. Christian pilgrims and pilgrimages—Georgia (Republic)—Biography.
5. Georgia (Republic)—Religious life and customs.
I. Alfeyeva, Valeria.   Prizvannye, izbrannye i vernye.
English. 1993. II. Title.
PG3478.L448Z46513   1993
891.73'44—dc20   92-31832
CIP

ISBN 0-517-88389-9

10 9 8 7 6 5 4 3 2 1

First American Paperback Edition 1995

TO MY SON

Contents

Dzhvari

I see Thy bridal chamber adorned, my Savior,
and I have no wedding garment that I may enter there.
Make the robe of my soul to shine,
O Giver of Light and save me.

HYMN FOR HOLY THURSDAY

*F*ATHER DAVID TOOK us to the monastery.

We traveled a long way by car, and when the road stopped we walked across a green meadow toward a forest with a blue line of mountains in the distance beyond. The July morning was quietly swelling with light and heat.

Red-bearded, in jeans and a checked shirt, and carrying a heavy knapsack, Father David walked between me and my son across the grass, telling us how he had once been a novice in Dzhvari.

"My wife said, 'Why on earth do you want to go off to a monastery?' I said, 'Why not? Of course I want to.' 'Well, you can go then. I won't stop you.' "

So he left his wife and three children and became a novice. And that's when he saw demons driving the monks out into the world. He was tormented with thoughts of his family the whole time. He would wake up at night in a cold sweat, dreading that something had happened—he would have to go home before it was too late. So he set off with Father Michael, the abbot, to talk it over with his family.

"Father Michael said to Tamara, my wife, 'David will be a good monk. But how will you bring up three children on your own? Maybe you let him go on the spur of the moment?'

"In the church here in Georgia the rule is that a married man can be received in a monastery only if his wife doesn't object. Of course, she had just let me go on the spur of the moment, because she was annoyed with me. And, in fact, I shouldn't have left them. My eldest son was only four."

"Had you had enough of the monastery, then?"

"No, I always wanted to be back there, but I had to wait for ten or fifteen years, till the children grew up."

So here he was, a priest now, returning to Dzhvari for the first time since then.

The road led through a tunnel of ancient elm trees. At one time, in the old days, two-wheeled carts from the monastery and surrounding villages used to travel along it. Now the road was neglected, covered with last year's rotting foliage.

When even this road petered out, dried-up dirt tracks spread in different directions through the scorching forest, climbing up toward a pass.

After about an hour and a half we came out onto a narrow ridge thrown like a bridge across two gorges. To the right the gorge opened wide, stretching to the horizon. A kite circled like a blue speck far below, tracking the flight of its prey. Deeper down, a small river wound like a ribbon, sparkling, and seemingly still, dividing the slopes of the forest.

The gorge on the left was narrow and completely overgrown. Two poplars rose, like a hare's ears, from its opposite ridge, and below was a glade with a lonely farm and stacks of hay.

Father David said that the poplars were in fact called "hare's ears." There wasn't another house for miles, and the forests were so dense it was easy to enter them and never come out. A year before an old man who had been doing restoration work in the monastery had gotten lost and wandered for twenty days in the hills, finding no path or homestead. He had not been discovered until a day after his death. Another time a young deacon who was on his way to Dzhvari had fallen from this very ridge.

Mitya stood on a boulder above the precipice and looked down—a rather thin boy with sun-bleached hair, standing beneath the pure blue of the heavens. "What a pity he never became a priest," he said.

Father David looked up. "Don't you think a priest would have died too?"

He rested his knapsack against a tree trunk. Large drops of sweat streamed down his forehead. We had packed his knapsack together, filling it with fresh round loaves, sugar, tea, flour—and packets of meat soup for the monastery dogs.

While we were resting he told me how he had first seen Dzhvari twelve years before. He had been with a friend. They had walked all day, gotten lost, and, feeling tired, had given up all hope of finding the monastery when they came out onto the ridge. It had seemed dangerously narrow. His friend went off alone to have a look.

"It was September. The gorges were already filling with darkness. The sun was setting above the monastery, and the forest round about was yellow, red, and green. The rusty church roof shone like gold in the sunset."

As he spoke his face appeared hidden, until it lit up at some deep inner thought, so that we seemed to see the reflection of that sunset in his eyes.

"I'll ask on your behalf, Veronica . . . but I don't think it will help. You're an exception because you're with me. The abbot doesn't let anyone bring women. His own mother he admits only for twenty minutes. What kind of monastery would it be if you had mothers, sisters, and girlfriends all coming?"

I didn't know, but I was going to Dzhvari in the hope of being able to stay for a few days.

This has happened to me before: My whole life has been leading toward one almost unattainable desire. Now it seems it will never be fulfilled—life doesn't work out that way.

Father David went ahead, up a steep slope. Then he stopped and took off his knapsack for the first time in all that way. Looking down into the ray of light between the trees, he made the sign of the cross.

We went to the edge of the cliff and stood beside him. It seemed as though we were standing on the rim of a chalice encircling fathomless space filled with light. Above was the transparent blue, with swift clouds. The mountains sloped down to the center of this chalice, green hillsides, ledges, and yellow precipices. And there at the central point of the visible world, above the green of the glade, stood an ancient church of pale stone with a round tower supporting the pyramid-shaped dome above it. The church, which completed this space filled with heat, sun, and silence, was its shining heart, giving it sense and meaning.

"If you call from here, they'll be able to hear you." Father David cupped his hands to his mouth. "*Mamao Mikael* (Father Michael). *Mamao Mikael!*" A distant echo was all that could be heard.

The paths ran into narrow riverbeds, long since dried up. When the snows melt they are carried down here, cutting through stony bedrock and leaving behind fractured steps, which we descended, clutching exposed roots and tendrils, resting our elbows on both banks at once.

Finally we stopped beside a clear river, its water shallow here at the bottom of the precipice, where we washed. Ahead of us, still, was the ascent of the sheer slope opposite.

THE GATES WERE shut. We climbed along beside the wall, finding ourselves near the open terrace of the first floor of an old house, and from there we descended by way of a small stone stairway.

Father David went on ahead and we missed his meeting with the abbot.

When we went in we found three men in monk's clothing who had risen from the table and were standing there. The refectory seemed to be in semi-darkness after the brightness of day outside. The monk nearest to me was tall and lean, in a knitted waistcoat with a small cowl-like cap perched slightly askew like a ski hat. He smiled pleasantly and his close-set eyes looked me over with lively interest.

I bowed silently and approached him for his blessing. He blessed me but instead of holding out his hand for me to kiss, as the custom is, he touched my head lightly with the palm of his hand, blessing my son in the same way.

We sat at a table, the abbot at the head, and Father David beside me. Opposite me was a monk with coal black eyes and a thick beard, the hierodeacon, Benedict. The novice remained standing. He was small of build, dark-eyed, and with a black beard like the others. He wore a black cassock with a belt, and a *skufya*—a soft, conical clerical hat rather like a tea cozy.

A slatted table with two dark-stained, straight-backed wooden benches took up almost the whole refectory. An earthenware dish with thick pieces of Georgian bread—*lavash*—stood in the midst of dishes of tomatoes, cucumbers, and other vegetables. A wasp was buzzing about an open jar of preserves. Father David said something in Georgian. The abbot raised his eyebrows a fraction, and bent his head, looking at me in the same open pleasant way, but with gentle irony.

"A writer?" he repeated, as if translating what had just been said. "That's fine! You can share with others what you've discovered for yourself."

He was obviously searching for the right Russian words and intonation.

"Sadly, I've nothing to share." I did not return his smile because I was too nervous and the things we had to talk about were far too important. "I have found answers to all the questions, which separated me from my faith. I see that I could make a discovery, but I haven't yet."

The novice lifted the big pot and took it away to be warmed up.

"Thank God you have seen that. How many people today 'have eyes and see not, ears and hear not . . .' "

" 'And do not return that he might heal them,' " I continued (more or less) the text from Isaiah. "But to understand this is to come to the threshold of faith: conversion, healing should follow. What's the use if I know I ought to love people but don't know how? Or if I understand that prayer is talking to God, the very heart of our life, but I'm not used to praying?"

"You must thank God and rejoice," Father Michael answered quietly. "After all, a miracle has happened to you "

"Yes, a miracle!" I agreed warmly. "That's how we've been living this last year. We rejoice in God and thank him."

"Does your son share these . . ." he paused, "these feelings?"

"Yes, he does," my son said seriously.

Everyone laughed.

"And his father?"

"His father died recently. He was totally absorbed by the science of physics; he believed only in what was obvious to human reason."

The novice put the pot in front of us with some clean plates. "The soup will get cold again . . ." Father Michael stood up. "Please excuse us. Monks aren't allowed to eat with women. There's a mystical meaning attached to the monastic table. Enjoy your meal, and we'll continue our talk later. Things will have to change. Where are you going to hide? There'll be no peace. We have to begin life anew."

"That's exactly why we've come all this way to see you."

He paused in the doorway, the point of his cap scraping the lintel. He was silent for a moment, looking intently at us both; then he smiled and went out. Father David said the Lord's Prayer in Georgian: "*Mamao Chveno.*" Those were the first Georgian words I learned.

I poured soup from the bowl, first for Father David, then for us. Bean pods, little pieces of potato, and carrots swam in the greenish broth.

"Novice Archil cooked the soup," Father David explained approvingly when the others had gone.

"It's okay, the meal's been blessed!" Mitya replied.

The vegetable dish with slices of tomatoes and cucumbers was very tasty. Archil opened a tin of condensed milk. And after Father David had gone we had some more tea, because we were very thirsty and tired after walking so long in the heat.

Light streamed through the doorway and a barred window which looked out onto the monastery courtyard, overgrown with grass. We looked about us. In one corner was a narrow bunk. Beside the wall was a pile of mattresses and blankets, rolled together and covered, obviously ready for the next visitors. Three small icons hung above the table, a lithograph showing the Kazan Mother of God. There was a double candlestick covered with wax. Big earthenware vessels. Everything was simple, severe—and somehow familiar.

We went out into the shade of an awning above the

veranda, which was built on pillars. Beyond the shadow cast by the long grass, yellow hollyhocks burned like semitransparent lanterns threaded on stalks.

Dzhvari was huge. The curve of the roof, shining with new sheet iron, rose above the pines and the cupola floated among the clouds. The inside of the church was filled with scaffolding. Underneath, in a part separated from the sanctuary and its altar, Mitya saw a harmonium. He opened the lid and sent sounds ringing and echoing under the dome.

"An organ like this can be left for a hundred years without going out of tune."

He sat with his back to the sanctuary and began to improvise, with obvious pleasure. I made myself comfortable on the bare planks beside him. A ray of light shone through the window casement, illuminating part of a fresco.

Hierodeacon Benedict came and quietly crouched down against the wall next to the harmonium. He sat motionless, cross-legged, clasping his hands together around his knees. His dark eyes, peering slightly, seemed to be focused on something other than ourselves. The bridge of his nose was dented as if it had been broken; his dark, very curly hair was receding noticeably; his black beard curled slightly around an expressive face, full of character, but with a look on it that I couldn't understand. He wore a faded velvet robe that had once been dark blue or violet but had long since lost its color, and the braid of his undershirt stuck out under the collar. His boots had become stiff as boards, so that they crackled.

"Can you play what they're going to sing at my *panikhida?*" he asked suddenly.

"No. . . ."

"You've yet to learn about funerals. How old are you?"

"Nearly sixteen."

Father Benedict nodded vaguely as though he expected Mitya to have been older. They talked sporadically until Mitya got absorbed in his music—he could play for hours. Some time later I turned around and discovered that the abbot was sitting on a low plank of scaffolding; he was listening too, his cheek resting on his hand. Father David was standing beside him. Mitya noticed them as well.

"Go on playing, don't let us disturb you," the abbot said.

But of course everyone was distracted now. We stood under the scaffolding together, listening to Father Michael, who told us that the church had been built in the twelfth century in the days of Tsaritsa Tamara. One of her courtiers, a well-known prince called Orbeliani, took part in a plot against her. The plot was discovered, the prince was forced to become a monk and was sent here. Faith was strong in those ancient times. Although the prince had taken vows under duress, he decided he was bound to keep them before God. He built Dzhvari for himself, and it became one of the richest monasteries.

"And now, if you like, we'll show you his cell."

We followed the church wall along to an outlying building. Benedict brought keys and opened a heavy door. He rolled back a piece of flooring like a wooden trapdoor, revealing an opening to the cellar. We went down a wooden ladder and found ourselves in almost total darkness. The abbot lit three candles. In the flickering light, which cast our formless shadows, we made out a hole in the wall.

"Bend your heads and go in. Don't be afraid. What you'll see are the remains of previous monks."

Daylight failed to penetrate this underground cavity. Mitya shone his candle around the low ceiling and wooden partition along the wall where several skulls lay, and beneath them we caught the faint gleam of white bones.

"We'll look like that soon," Benedict promised gloomily, clearly enjoying his black humor. "We should come here more often, so that we don't forget. It would be better for me if I were to stay down here."

"So this is the prince's cell?" Mitya queried.

"It's a monk's cell," the abbot replied. "Monks need cells like these to escape from the world. How about you, Dmitri, would you like to make your home here?"

"Yes, I would," Mitya said hesitantly.

"That's bad. That means you're proud. Spiritual feats like that are beyond us." And I thought the abbot's face looked sad in the mingling half-light and shadow. "We ought to celebrate a *panikhida* here."

We came back out into the light and returned to the church. We couldn't see the paintings on the walls and ceilings beyond the scaffolding. Only Tsaritsa Tamara's round face and knitted brows, a crown on her head, the builder, with a model of the church in one hand, and the tsaritsa's son occupied the wall without scaffolding.

It was strange to imagine the prince who had fallen from favor standing here eight centuries before. How did he feel about this portrait of the tsaritsa? Was he angry? Or did he pray for those who hate us and revile us, in a spirit of peace and thankfulness because God had used the tsar's disfavor to reveal his higher will for him—this once-proud prince who had wasted his days in intrigues, banquets, and hunting?

The abbot explained that the paints were mixed with minerals and crushed precious stones, and so the frescoes had lasted almost a thousand years without losing their depth of color. All restorers did was to fix the paintings so that they wouldn't crumble away. They had been working here last summer and were due to return in two or three days.

Father David and I exchanged glances. When we had planned our journey to Dzhvari he said my only chance of staying would be linked with the arrival of these restorers: There would be two women among them—so another more or less wouldn't matter that much, surely?

"Up here," Father Michael pointed to the dome, "is the cycle of the Passion: the Last Supper, the Crucifixion. You can go there later. The restorers were overjoyed to find them, although they don't know how to make a connection between these Gospel themes and God."

"That's like all contemporary art. Father Pavel Florensky used to say that culture derives from 'cult' and has lost its roots," I said, and added, picking up on the word *later*. "Is it really true that we have a future here? Art is icon painting which has lost God. So too has existence and the family, the whole structure of spiritual life. The forms have been preserved, but the heart has dried up, like a nut. Its shell may be whole but inside there's only dust.

"In the past, on Good Friday, people would go to church with colored lanterns and take a candle home with them. The lamp in front of the icons was lit from this candle, and from that lamp the fire in the hearth. And so the house was consecrated, with the hearth and the food cooked on it, and the fields and fruits. The people too were consecrated through the heavenly fire descending to earth during the liturgy. All the significant events of life were blessed by God—through baptism, marriage, and the requiem for the dead."

"It was never as idyllic as that, of course," the abbot put in. "The sacraments don't work like magic. We're consecrated by faith, and it's possible to receive Communion and still bring judgment upon oneself."

"Of course, but there's never been such a desert as the one we're in just now, when thousands of people—hundreds of thousands even—not only don't take Communion, but don't even know what Communion is."

I had acquired the gift of fluent speech, and my words did not fall into a void. And then one of those miracles that sustain God's world took place. We stood at the very edge of the earth, in a church hidden in the mountains, with two Georgian monks and a priest: My son and I were aliens, but now we were being introduced into their world. I began to have the feeling we weren't foreigners, because all of us, including the prince-monk who had built the church, have a common homeland in heaven, and there we are already united by bonds no less secure than the ties of friendship.

"Many people nowadays, especially the intelligentsia, say they believe in God but they don't join the Church," said Benedict. "How do you explain that?"

"They don't really believe in God or in Christ. It's simply an incomprehensible feeling that there's something higher than ourselves, another world. But what kind of world this is, and what's included in the word *God*—that's an area of total ignorance."

I began to say that science had long since realized its limitations. It can't resolve the main problems of existence, can't even tell us how the world began, or discover the meaning of life or what caused it. But even if rationalism were to recognize the existence of God, it would make him something abstract, replace him with an impersonal spirit or an absolute ideal. That would impose no obligations on anyone, change nothing. It is much harder for a contemporary mind to accept Christ as God, to accept the mystery of the Eucharist, to believe that we receive his Body and Blood in the form of bread and wine.

"Do you accept this mystery?" Father Michael asked.

"Praise God, I receive all the sacraments of the Church now. I've devoted the last five years to becoming part of it: with my mind first, then with my heart, flesh, and blood. My whole life has become a sacrament now, a revelation of the Mystery."

The abbot was standing with his hand on the board

above my head, looking at me attentively with wise, smiling eyes.

"You're talking about great things. We're simple people here. We know only how to live in order to be saved."

I smiled back, feeling I'd said too much.

"I wouldn't know. We're both talking about high things, but you talk as one having authority and I'm like one of the scribes."

He was pleased that I saw this for myself.

The abbot and Father David went off across the yard, up the stairway to the veranda, and farther on over the hill—where the roof of the abbot's cell was visible above the trees. David was still Father Michael's spiritual son and he wanted to make his confession. Our own situation was being decided too. Mitya and I went for a walk, but soon came back and sat waiting on a part of the wall that jutted out beside the open gates.

Finally they both reappeared by the gate. The abbot knocked a stick against the front of his boots, the tops of which were barely covered by his old cassock; they probably didn't have one long enough for him in the monastery.

"Are you still waiting?" he asked with a smile.

"Yes."

"And what are you waiting for?" he inquired politely.

"To know if you'll allow us to stay."

He sat down on the jutting-out stone beside Mitya.

"How did you pilgrims manage to get here? Isn't anyone looking for you back there?"

"No, there's no one to look for us. Our whole family's here."

"That's all right. 'Where two or three are gathered together in my name . . .' "

" 'There am I in the midst,' " Mitya couldn't help adding.

We all smiled.

Father David was looking expectantly at the abbot as well. Obviously he still didn't know what had been decided.

"It's time to get ready for Vespers." The abbot got up. He stood opposite us by the gate and seemed to be deep in thought. "Well then, stay," he said simply.

"Praise God!" All the tension, anxiety, waiting were over. I got up involuntarily, crossed myself in front of the church, laughed, and tears came into my eyes. "Praise God."

ALONGSIDE THE CHURCH was a small basilica we hadn't noticed before. Archil opened it for the service. Severe, simple, of well-balanced proportions, it had a beauty of its own. It was built of light stone slabs under a triangular roof made of the same stone, with no superfluous features. The only ornamentation was an intertwining of stone along the portal; above it was a cross in a circle, and the narrow casement of the window was decorated in relief with the key of Paradise, which is often found on the eastern facades of old Georgian churches. While the builders had been putting up the high walls of the main church and crowning it with a buttress, while the artists crushed precious stones from the prince's treasury into paints for Calvary, the prince himself had prayed in this basilica no bigger than a small chapel.

Mitya and I walked around the church and found ourselves at the outbuilding above the cell of the first monk. The door was half-open and Mitya peered into the semidark.

"Come in, Dmitri," Benedict called. "We'll look for some boots for you."

We went in together. The outbuilding was used as a storehouse and was piled up with cupboards, boxes, baskets, stacks of old church magazines, pots and pans, and pieces of broken beehives. The hierodeacon pulled out a large pair of boots like the ones he was wearing himself.

"Why do I need boots?" Mitya asked.

"It's the traditional footwear for monks. So you'll wear everything as monks do. Okay?"

"Of course I want to," Mitya said, just as Father David had done, and turned to me, his eyes wide with surprise. He chose a pair of the smallest boots although they turned out to be size nine.

"It doesn't matter. I'll teach you to wrap your feet in strips of cloth and they'll fit all right then," Benedict said, reassuringly.

There were old clothes hanging in a cupboard and Benedict pulled out a shirt, a sweater with holes at the elbows, soldier's trousers, and, last of all, a very long cassock that a hunter visiting the monastery had sewn for himself. But he obviously didn't know how to make a cassock and produced something more like a surplice instead, with wide sleeves and a round opening at the neck.

"Ask Archil for one of those soft clerical caps like his. Then take all the clothes to the abbot to bless."

Archil fetched several caps. While Mitya was trying them on, the novice watched with a joyful smile, screwing up his eyes to hide the gleam of tears. We chose a cloth cap, four-sided, closely woven, like felt. The others were too big. With the clothes in one hand, the boots in the other, Mitya went into the church.

The abbot came out from the sanctuary. He was wearing a loose Greek-style cassock, without a waist, and with long wide sleeves. On his head, instead of the black cowl, which gives a monk a regal look, he wore a stiff cylindrical hat—the *kamilavka*—like those worn on Mount Athos.

Mitya stepped across the high threshold and asked for a blessing. I stopped at the threshold.

"God gives a blessing," said the abbot very seriously, making the sign of the cross over everything at once. "I want you to become a monk, because I think the monastic life is good." Mitya went away quietly to get changed.

I stayed in the church. Through the open door I saw Father Benedict ring the bell for Vespers. The straight angles of the door framed the blinding light of day, the green forest, and the hill beyond the green courtyard. Three bells, one big and two smaller, hung on a beam between the pines, and the old house with its veranda, the sound of the bells—I saw and heard it all with that piercing clarity, that pure joy, that leaves a deep impression and lasts for years, emerging later with a freshness that is already tinged with sorrow.

Father David, wearing a green chasuble, went into the sanctuary in order to conduct his first Vespers in Dzhvari.

Archil lit the lamps—there were only two—in front of the Mother of God and the Savior. Without its novice's cap his head—with its sunburned tonsure, his almond eyes reminiscent of ancient Eastern reliefs, and his black beard—seemed like that of an Assyrian warrior, except that he was holding a lamp instead of a sword and his eyes were gentle and meek. Benedict put on a robe like the abbot's and its blackness made his beard and eyes seem darker still.

My son appeared in the doorway dressed in his cap, a cassock tied with a cord, and boots. His eyes shone. I'd never seen such happiness in his face. The abbot, at the icon stand with Benedict, looked up. "Well, see here. Dmitri has become a real monk." Father David came out from the sanctuary, and they all smiled and started speaking in Georgian.

Vespers began. The abbot read None in an even, subdued voice. The church was just big enough for five people, and when it came to the censing Father David didn't have to go around the whole building. Standing in front of the royal doors, he censed all those praying and all three walls. If he had swung the censer even a little more he would have reached each of us with it, and even touched the walls, so he only lifted and lowered his hands lightly. The smoke from the incense wafted through the open door, vanishing as it went.

Quietly, with total concentration, in unfamiliar, sharp, guttural Georgian, the abbot, the deacon, and the novice sang, "Lord, I called . . ." and the ancient three-part singing filled the tiny church.

"Lord, I called unto thee, hear me, hear me, O Lord."

Mitya and I leaned against the wall. His slim neck shone white in the opening of his cassock. Tears filled my eyes. I had scarcely thought, five years before, when I had found out that there is a God and had baptized my son, that the whole of his life, like the whole of mine, would be poured into this deep channel with nothing held back. . . .

"May my prayer ascend like incense before thee. The lifting of my hands be an evening offering . . ."

THE ABBOT PITCHED a tent for us above the precipice. Archil used to live in it, but he had moved to the refectory. The tent had a table—a board fixed to a beehive box, and two beds—also boards fixed to boxes. The monastery used to have beehives, but the bees had all died the previous year from some epidemic and now the monastic way of life was being built out of their ruined homes.

The tent stood right behind some wire netting in the yard. Three paces behind, the ground fell steeply away. A little farther off, beneath a small wooden house which was Father Benedict's cell, dark gray layers of exposed ore descended like an amphitheater. Under them, in a narrow opening between the early green of the slopes, sparkled the river, cutting the monastery off from the world beyond. Violet flowers grew on the embankments and, higher up, behind Benedict's cell, the forest led away into the mountains.

Soon after the service Father David came up to say good-bye. He looked downcast and sad. Perhaps he regretted that we were staying and he was not. In my joy it seemed we had to stay; it could not have been otherwise.

"I didn't believe it was possible," Father David said. "You see, everything is given to those who believe."

"Everything—and more. When you told us about Dzhvari I'd never have imagined that this would happen."

When he had blessed us, as he was saying good-bye, he asked whether we knew what the name of the monastery meant. We knew that Dzhvari means "cross." Its full name, however, is "the Monastery of the Holy and Life-giving Cross of the Lord."

BENEDICT PULLED TWO mattresses from the stuff piled up in the refectory. After a considerable search he found two sets of new linen decorated with violets, which we took to our tent, together with the icon of the Kazan Mother of God, the candlestick, a lamp, a pottery jug for water, and a washbasin with a hinge, which Benedict fastened to a tree a little below our tent, where the slope ended in a triangular point. He suggested that Mitya should scythe the grass on the slope.

I made our dwelling habitable, spreading fresh sheets under cotton blankets which were also new, secretly rejoicing at the cleanliness and comfort of our unexpected shelter. I overheard a quiet conversation from the slope.

"What are you doing here?" That was the abbot's gentle voice.

"I'm cutting the grass." That was my son.

"Well, how's it going?"

"Not very well."

"Why's that, do you think?"

"Probably because I don't know how to do it."

"I think it's because you didn't ask for a blessing."

When I went out again, about an hour later, the mountains were submerged in soft semidark. The evening sky glowed behind the clear silhouette of the church, reddening the edges of the clouds, thickening and growing dark. Each bough, each leaf, stood out in the warm light.

The abbot and Mitya were sitting on the slope together. A little lower, the scythe stood in the grass, which still had to be mown. Father Michael had clasped his hands about his knees. There was a peace about him like the calm of evening.

I wanted to sit with them too, but as I came up the abbot rose slowly, picking up the scythe. "Have you settled in? Off you go to sleep. You must be tired." We didn't move and he added, with quiet satisfaction, "You see, we don't live like hermits here."

He blessed us, not making the sign of the cross or touching our heads, and went off to his cell. Mitya and I sat on the grass until the light faded. The mountains around us, Dzhvari itself, everything that had happened in this overcharged day was so unreal I could not get to sleep at first. I was going to have to get used to it all.

IT WAS STILL quite dark in our tent when the bell rang six times—a long metal clanging. It was cold. Dark shadows of the trees stretched across the mountain ridge on the other side of the precipice. Transparent light barely glimmered pale blue in dark coils of sky. Cuttings from the newly scythed grass, damp with dew, covered the path. We had no idea how the abbot had found time to cut it. We washed in cold water, watching the mist rising from the gorge. The bell rang for Matins at seven. In many churches Vespers and Matins are sung together but here the abbot was trying to restore the traditional pattern with all its meaning.

It was dark in the church. Only two lamps burned in front of the poor icon screen, which smelled of incense, old book bindings, lamp oil, and wax.

"Since you don't understand Georgian you must create the Jesus Prayer for yourself. For as many hundred repetitions as you get through at your first service, recite that number afterward. You too, Dmitri . . . Do you have a prayer rope?"

Mitya had recently been given a cord with fifty knots.

Father Benedict lit a candle stump and began to read. The abbot's voice echoed softly from the sanctuary. After the luxurious churches in town these quiet services seemed to have been given to me to teach me concentrated prayer. I twisted the first knot on my prayer rope. "Lord Jesus Christ, Son of God, have mercy on me." Up till now I'd read more about prayer than I'd prayed, just as I'd only read about the commandments without knowing how to keep a single one in its entirety.

"How many prayers have you counted?" asked the abbot, sitting on a low bench in front of the refectory.

"Three hundred."

"Why so few? And how do you say your prayer?"

I repeated the prayer.

"Why do you miss out the word *sinner*?" He bent forward a little, listening intently.

"Well, the words 'have mercy' cover everything, including awareness of guilt."

"No, no. You're explaining what you understand by it. What in fact is original sin?"

He took off his waistcoat and cap and without looking laid them side by side, obviously prepared to listen for a long time to what I had to say. His wavy hair was combed back, revealing his large forehead and sunken temples, and was tied in a knot at the back. His spare face with green, close-set eyes and a long, narrow nose, could no longer be called beautiful.

It was already baking hot and the dew sparkled on the grass.

How do I understand original sin?

Adam walked before God in Paradise. He had not yet done wrong and was still transparently open to the Lord's will. This meant omniscience, complete joy. Adam walked in the Garden of Eden and named the trees, the birds, and animals, because he understood the essence of each and the name sealed it. He held every seed in the palm of his hand and knew how it would grow. He knew the taste of the fruits. He could answer the birds. He understood the language of every creature and his loving heart embraced them all.

The Tree of Life grew in the midst of Paradise. Its fruit nourished Adam with the juices of eternal life. The Tree of Knowledge, Good, and Evil, grew beside it, but God commanded him not to eat its fruit.

This was the first commandment, a warning: "For the day you eat it you will die."

God gave Adam a wife like himself. Adam and Eve were perfect and their love in Eden was blessed and full of the life of the Spirit, mutually beneficial, finding its reflection in each other.

But the tempter, having fallen from this bliss and fullness at the very beginning of time, said to himself, "They don't know what death is, and so they're not afraid of anything. I shall go and separate them from God."

He started with Eve because she was a woman, and young, and he talked to her alone.

"God has deceived you and your husband," he said. "There are angels that know good and there are forces of darkness that serve evil—they are finite and bound.

"But Man is higher than every creature, higher than the powers of heaven and hell. Only he, like God, possesses the higher quality of spiritual creatures—freedom. Freedom makes him like God. But what's the use of having this gift if you don't know how it tastes? So here's fruit which looks and smells good. No other fruit in Paradise compares with it. To know God is totally different from being God oneself. God has deceived you because he's jealous. He wants to remain the only ruler of the universe. Taste, and you will be like gods, knowing good and evil."

Eve liked his clever talk, because he promised more than Adam. She was seduced by it. "Why should I do the will of God if I have no will of my own?" Eve thought, thus thinking herself equal with God for the first time and separating her will from his.

She looked longingly at the golden fruit, touched it with her palm, her lips, sensing a burning mystery, and all the fruits of Paradise became fresh to her. So as she bit into its peel the taste seemed extraordinary, sweet and bitter together, and sour. Eve gave the fruit to Adam and he ate, and they saw that they were naked. "Her flesh is enticing to me and arouses my desire as much as these apples," thought Adam.

"Adam, where are you?" God called in his loving voice.

Adam was ashamed of his nakedness and the lusts that he had not known while he was still innocent. His wisdom had been all-encompassing, his love total, but now he hid from God.

"Because you didn't listen to me, the land is cursed," God said, looking in sorrow at the best of his creation. "You will earn your bread with grief until you become dust again, because I created you from dust."

What had happened to Adam's hearing? He no longer understood the voice of the birds.

What had happened to his big heart? It had once

embraced every creature but now it had become empty and he had forgotten the names he had given the animals, the fish, flowers, grasses. Instead of joy there was only the desire for joy, in place of love, the desire for love.

What had happened to Adam's eyes? He no longer saw the living, merciful light that suffused the Garden of Eden, piercing every leaf and fruit.

The Evil One had promised to give more than God, only to take it all away.

God sent Adam and his wife out of Eden.

And in the East, at the entrance to Paradise, he placed an angel with a fiery sword to guard the Tree of Life and stop Adam eating from it, and so making his sin eternal.

And Adam knew Eve, and in this knowing there was sweetness and bitterness, insatiability and the foretaste of surfeit.

"Lord, do you hear me?" Adam wept, but there was no answer.

Then he knew the taste of freedom. He knew fear, and he knew death.

"THAT'S ALL FICTION, imagination," the abbot shook his head, disapprovingly. "We can't know how it was in Paradise. You mustn't spread the dry fruits of your fantasy out in the Garden of Eden. Nowadays it's fashionable to fillet the Bible and the Gospels into fables. The great secrets of religious life are reduced to a topic for literature, brought down to the level of fruitless conjecture.

"The Fall is one of the mysteries too. Each new

generation continues its downward path from the time when Man first fell. So far there's been no reversal of this. So-called progress only means that people plunge into material things more and more deeply, staying with the externals instead of looking within and turning to God. But 'the Spirit gives life while the flesh is of no value.'

"The Holy Fathers defined our makeup like this: spirit, soul, and flesh. Adam's spirit was nourished by God, his soul by his spirit, and his flesh by his soul. Now we've been turned upside down: Our spirit is nourished by our soul, our soul by our flesh, and our flesh by the material. The foundations have been damaged and the whole system's full of vice.

"We're born with a seed of sin, which grows as we do. It's in our desires and passions. We've come to faith and so we begin to understand it, but the greater part of our life has been spent without God. How much evil have we been doing all this time—and where do you think it has gone? It's in our flesh and blood, just like original sin. We have to cauterize the rest of our lives with a red-hot iron. The nearer we come to God, the more we feel our sinfulness. Yet you omit the word *sinner*! The Holy Fathers spoke differently. 'Have mercy on me, a sinner,' and, simply, 'Have mercy on me.'

"Oh!" he exclaimed suddenly, "they were holy fathers, yet they said, 'He has come into the world to save sinners of whom I am chief.' This isn't rhetoric! They went off into the desert, stood for nights on end, lamenting and wailing. One righteous *staretz* was asked, 'Why do you think you're the most sinful person if you pray more than all the rest, fast, and do

good deeds?' 'I can't explain the reason why,' he said,
'only I know for sure that I am the most sinful.'
Staretz Silouan of Mount Athos is one of the last
saints who actually lived in our own century; not one
wayward thought crossed his mind in all the thirty-
five years he spent in the monastery, but he used to
say, 'I shall die soon and my accursed soul will descend to hell.' And you're implying that. . . ?"

He gestured lightly with his hand, showing me
how trivial he thought my words had been. Mitya,
who had settled down on the bench beside Father
Michael, laughed.

"There should be weeping, a cry of repentance.
Sinner! Repentance is the whole way of Christian life,
the means is repentance, and the aim is repentance.
Those who strive toward a higher spiritual state—and
you can't seek it alone, especially without repentance,
without cleansing from all our passions—they are in
bliss. You don't really feel your sinfulness and so you
begin with Adam, not with yourself."

I sat beside him on the bench, moving the jug
toward the wall.

"The way I'm feeling just now is that everything
that used to fill my life has gone, but I haven't found
anything else so far. I'm like a jug that has been
emptied of water but hasn't been filled with wine
yet." To show what I meant I turned the earthenware jug over and rapped its base. "Empty—but expecting God to fill it . . ."

"That's something at least—but, oh, how little!
It's one thing to be aware of your own emptiness, it's
quite another to feel how wretched we are before the
Lord."

We heard Archil clattering dishes in the refectory as he laid the table. The abbot turned around.

"I got carried away. And why? This is all pride. How can one ever escape? If you're silent, that means you're being proud—and here I am, vowed to silence. You speak—and you're being proud again: How well I speak! How wise I am! We can't take a step without sinning, the merest word, the merest glance. Pray then, as we should all do: 'Have mercy on me, a sinner.' " He was about to get up, but suddenly remembered something. "Why do you close your eyes when you pray?"

I hadn't thought he'd noticed. "So as not to get distracted."

"How much of the day can you spend with your eyes shut? And if you open them, don't you get distracted? Learn to pray so that nobody else notices, and you won't require any special posture. Our great saints achieved a constant, uninterrupted Jesus Prayer. The person of prayer works and prays, eats and prays, talks and is still praying. The prayer has been formed by itself, even in sleep. Do you understand what this means? A person like that is always in God's presence, always available for God to use. It doesn't help if there's a separate time for prayer, and another one for a life-style which hasn't anything to do with prayer. There ought to be no division. We must direct our whole life toward God, just like a prayer. . . ."

He sat still for a while, clasping his hands around his knees. "So, Dmitri, do you think I actually manage to do everything I've just been talking about? Until I was twenty-eight I was an unbaptized bandit.

I'm saying all this for myself, like a lesson I've still to learn."

At twelve o'clock Benedict rang the bell for the meal. I ate after the brothers, and Mitya ate with them. We were entering a realm in which he had more rights than I.

I asked the abbot to give me a penance to carry out. He thought about it, and said no. "When a monk's received into the monastery he's allowed to rest for the first few days. Live as a guest just now. Look at the world around you. Go for a swim. Benedict will show you the way down to the river—only don't wander off on your own."

"But I'd like to contribute something. . . ."

"Please note that we don't insist on anything in the monastery. An act of penance which you've asked for yourself isn't a true penance, it's your own will and not worth anything." He thought for a bit, as though he wasn't sure whether to say any more. "What's more, you don't know our way of life well enough to be able to do anything really useful for us, and if you try too soon it will totally misfire."

"Surely it won't do any harm if I wash the dishes for you?"

"All right then, wash the dishes—that's not difficult."

After the meal Mitya came to find me and we went back to the refectory. A large bowl of vegetable salad was waiting for me, and fried eggplant in a covered pan.

"Who fried that tasty eggplant?" I asked when Benedict came through from the next room.

"Did you like them?" His eyes shone. "Sinful Benedict cooked them with God's help. You could learn to fry them like this too."

"I've only to do unskilled work just now."

"There's no unskilled work in the monastery. Everything we do is dedicated to God," he answered. "How about you, Dmitri? What are you doing?"

"I'm just sitting here with Mom."

"If you want, I'll teach you Khutsuri—that's old Georgian. All the liturgical books are written in it," Benedict said—and he appeared in the doorway with a closely written sheet of paper. It had the alphabet written on it in two colors, some letters above the others. "You'll be able to read at the service along with us."

While I cleared the table and washed the dishes at the spring beyond the gates, they sat together and Benedict drew large letters in an exercise book with a look of great concentration.

"Sister Veronica, do you mind that we all eat and you have to clear the table?" he asked, raising his dark head with a look that was both sympathetic and ironic. "You're not used to this, I'm sure. It's better for you to say so, to stop any grumbling."

"I can't say it's my favorite chore. But I like doing it here."

"That's good." He nodded.

"We felt at home the minute we arrived, as if I'd always been waiting for this."

"That's good too."

"I don't know. . . . What will we do when it's time to go?"

"There's a lot to do before then, you won't be going for ages yet."

We were free until September and so far the abbot hadn't given us a time limit. "This is one of those pitfalls, Father Benedict. It always seems like a long time, and suddenly you find it's all over."

I WENT UPHILL along the broad path from the monastery gates, a rocky path with ledges of loose stones, scree, and tire marks. Trucks and *gaziks*—as the cars made in the Gorki Car Factory are called—cross this way en route for one of the other mountain passes.

I wanted to see where the road led and to get to a point from which I could see farther afield. From time to time I turned aside into small clumps of trees, treading on dead foliage where purple and white harebells grew. A glade opened out a few bends of the road farther on, one we'd noticed from the north side of the gorge when we were on our way to Dzhvari with Father David.

Close up, the glade was lighter and more lovely than I'd thought. Hollyhocks lit up the tall grass with their little lamps and clover gleamed white and pink lower down. The path along the edge of the clearing rose more steeply into the mountains. A two-storied house with its own garden stood at the last bend— the only farm in the neighborhood. Several stacks of fresh-cut hay rose above the grass, like rows of tents. A chestnut horse was grazing among them, waving its tail.

A light heat haze blurred the outline of the trees.

Brown butterflies with white stripes on their wings were fluttering about in the blinding heat, wasting their brief summer.

Farther along the edge of the clearing the trees suddenly began to descend; the road went down steeply too, and above it rose a rock with a ledge jutting out at the center. Scattering loose scree under my feet, and grabbing spiky stalks, I scrambled up onto this ledge and sat down. It was an ideal lookout point. The rock above shielded me. Higher up were the glade and farmstead, and the road could scarcely be seen down below behind the trees.

Around me such a vast expanse opened up that I couldn't take it all in at one glance. The land rose in mighty forested folds and every glade, copse, every rock-face was clearly visible in the shining light. Chains of mountains stretched beyond the gorge that we'd seen from the ridge. Our tent actually stood above it. I could see yellow sandy banks like ruined towers at one point. I was at the highest point of the area and the distant ridges appeared to be at eye-level, descending right down to the shallow little river, with its ceaseless flow.

An eagle flew from the lower margin of the forest and hovered below me, its wings spread in massive span, soaring above the mountains in ever-decreasing circles. It could be seen so clearly that I made out the light feathers on the underside of its brown wings, and its head with the beak turned toward me. The eagle had noticed me too and I felt uneasy beneath its preying gaze. Then it turned into a black dot again, which I could scarcely see, its hovering lasted so long, and then the dot dissolved in the white of the sky. Cicadas chirruped. It seemed as if their noise and the heat filled the whole scene.

How greedily I had once tried to absorb the beauty of land and sea, to take it away with me, and yet my eye had never had its fill of seeing, nor my ear of hearing. It seemed to me that these heightened impressions had changed my idea of happiness, and if I were to look long enough something would open beyond the play of shapes, the hues of light, because none of this could be in vain. But that same unsatisfied longing still niggled away. Beauty promised and beckoned, but it seemed to exist independently of any connection with my life, not taking it into account.

A deserted, perfect, and idle world endlessly poured out its colors and lines, but I was rooted neither in its eternity nor in its perfection.

And so all the broken links were joined and the world received its highest justification and meaning. There were no more aesthetic delights, nor any gaping void beneath them—my soul was at rest. Light thoughts still came and went on its surface, but I wanted them to be still, my soul to become transparent like deep water when it is lit by the sun.

All my life I'd been going somewhere, urgent to understand, to write, everything made it seem necessary to learn more—so that, at last, everything would find its fulfillment. But perhaps I'd been going through the desert these last forty years, like the Children of Israel on their way to the Promised Land—and, behold, I had arrived! I had seen Dzhvari. I had no need to go elsewhere. I wanted to live and die here.

On my return I met the abbot, in the same faded cassock and boots, in his waistcoat and black knitted cap with a brown cross-stripe. He was sitting on a bench beside the wall.

"You're walking along as if this were Tver Avenue [in Moscow]." An inoffensive mockery sounded in the way he spoke. "Imagine two people viewing the world in a different way. One rides in a carriage and the other walks behind in the dust. You came riding here in your carriage. If you want to learn humility you must get out at the very least."

I sat on the bench, rejoicing at his directness.

"Do you want to change your life? Then start with the simplest things. Everyone here goes around in old clothes and boots, but you appear in an elegant white blouse, a white skirt, white sandals . . ."

I laughed, remembering how I had changed beside the river, putting on the fine cotton blouse with little flowers that I'd worn only once before, the previous Easter.

This man sees everything, I thought, and he doesn't care about elegance.

"So now . . ." he looked at me briefly, and turned away. "Look at the way monks dress. A young woman in a cassock becomes ageless. The bishop's garments emphasize the dignity of his office, not his male qualities.

"Every detail is hidden so that the essence comes out. There's no room for trivia in the spiritual life. All these little blouses, flowers, and hairdos are plumage for a wedding."

"Give me a cassock. I'll be glad to wear one."

"Indeed, you could put one on with pleasure—and pride yourself in it. That's the other extreme. But try a plain gray dress and head scarf—you wouldn't like that." He looked me straight in the eye.

I'd never worn head scarves because they don't suit me at all. It seemed pharisaical to make a woman wear headgear in church—and to wear a scarf here in the mountains in a soaring ninety-five–degree heat—I could scarcely think of anything worse! I mentioned this half-jokingly, but he didn't accept my light-hearted tone.

"It's written in the apostles' letters that a woman without a head covering brings shame upon her head."

"And in the ancient statutes it says a monk who has dealings with a woman deserves to be excommunicated."

"Well said! But no one keeps those ancient statutes anymore, and so real monks are a thing of the past." He lowered his eyes and his face took on a closed expression. "We never see an icon of the Mother of God without a head covering."

"Well, but men don't dress like the Savior," I objected meekly, not wanting to agree to wear a scarf straightaway.

"But, you see, you came here as an act of submission, yet you're insisting on having things your own way, quibbling about little details. I don't want anything from you. I'm telling you what I think is appropriate—it's up to you whether you accept it or not."

"I'll accept everything, Father Michael," I said, a

bit upset at the change in his voice. "I'll get changed tomorrow, and I'll wear a scarf, only I've never been able to get used to wearing one."

"Do you think I was born in this outfit?" he asked, lifting the edge of his cassock.

Well, his clothes seemed absolutely right for him, and I wouldn't have wanted him to wear anything else.

"You'll have to get used to it. You mustn't be a distraction because of your femaleness. Hair cropped short is very feminine." I saw him glance at my head as though he were stroking it, then he turned away: but I remembered that glance. A moment later his face resumed its usual kindly, slightly mocking expression.

"In general, then, once you've got out of your carriage, you'll have arrived, but to go farther you have to go on foot."

"Couldn't you wear lighter shoes in this heat instead of those boots?"

"The more free the flesh is, the more bound the spirit. Monks used to wear not just boots but massive iron chains; well, and they still do, only each monk chooses his own chains. Would you enter the Kingdom of God on light feet?"

A WAX CANDLE guttered low like a withering stalk. There was a dry heat inside our tent, a sleepy stillness in the courtyard.

Father Michael had gone to the patriarch's office for a few days. Benedict had disappeared after the meal. Only Archil was sitting on the stone bench that half circled the fountain. He was feeding the dogs, dipping the bread in a jar of pickled fish, giving pieces first to Muria then to Brinka, talking lovingly to them. Big black Muria gobbled his piece at once, while little white, shaggy-haired Brinka dragged hers along the ground and trampled it around with a look of childish delight on her doggy face. No one knew where she'd come from, but once she had turned up they looked after her.

Archil gave each dog its food separately, so there was no need for them to fight, and they lived peaceably. They'd even gotten used to monastic fasts, but tourists brought meat sometimes and it was given to the dogs.

The dogs knew they mustn't go into the church, and they lay on the grass outside during the services. Muria lifted his head and howled when Benedict rang the bell.

"Do you like dogs?" asked Archil. "Would you like to feed them?"

But I said we were going for a swim. I suggested that two bowls should be put beside the fountain, a big one for Muria, and a small one for Brinka. Archil nodded, but wondered if the dogs would be able to tell the bowls apart! We laughed, and Brinka jumped happily onto Archil's knee and looked at him hopefully

Archil's small body and dark, bearded face radiated kindness and peace. He never began a conversation himself, but always answered in a friendly way, though with very few words.

He smiled often, and sometimes his whole soul shone in that smile—such a carefree, meek smile, full of love, is found only in the pure of heart.

"Have you been in the monastery long?" Mitya asked.

"Only six months. I'm still just a young novice like you."

"I was under the impression that you'd been here for always," I said.

"I thought so myself when I came to Dzhvari."

"What did you do before?"

"It's difficult to explain." He smiled, a bit embarrassed. "I worked in the Institute of Marxism and Leninism."

That was the last thing I'd expected!

"I graduated in history. I was even thinking of a career in the Party, but luckily there was no way they'd admit me. Then I realized that you don't get anything on this earth if you've got nothing in heaven. Whatever you build crumbles . . ."

" 'Unless the Lord builds the house, they labor in vain that build it . . .' "

"Yes, yes," Archil agreed. "People look for the way to find bliss and happiness. But who can be truly happy? 'Blessed are the innocent who walk in the way of the Lord,' " he explained humbly. "Everything will be all right if you walk in the way of the Lord. He's shown us everything—the ways, the means, the goals.

"But I think people believe in the deceiver, like Adam and Eve did, instead of God. He promises ways that seem shorter, more direct. What will stop them if they are 'like gods' themselves? Who'll say, 'Don't kill, don't commit adultery.' And so anything goes. But try to grasp it—and there's nothing there. The Russian words *temptation, attraction,* and *charm* all come from the Slavonic root *lest,* which means a lie.

"But, someone will say, God planted the Tree of the Knowledge of Good and Evil in the middle of Paradise himself—didn't he realize people would choose this lie? They say things like that because they don't know where all the evil in the world has come from. Of course, if God had wanted to create us to be just like sheep he wouldn't have given us the ability to do evil. Man is raised above the rest of creation to the freedom of being like God, with the possibility of choice—to pray to God, or to crucify him. This is the terrible lot of human freedom: to go along the route of self-affirmation without God, to reject God—the way of the Prodigal Son—and then to understand that this way leads to the collapse and destruction of the individual soul and of the whole world. Only, will people understand this before they perish? Or will they perish before they understand it? These are the issues of our troubled times."

THE PATH WAS covered with grass and wildflowers. Benedict had showed us this way down to the river.

"Are you going for a swim too?" Mitya had asked him.

"No, I haven't washed for three months."

We laughed, thinking this was a joke; then we realized that Benedict was doing this as an act of penance, to mortify the flesh.

The water in the river came up to our ankles as it flowed swiftly over its stony bed. Its sparkle blinded us on the days when the sun was very strong. The river curved around the endless bends of the gorge.

After every sharp bend a fresh landscape opened up, totally enclosed except from above. Small trees stood motionless on the skyline. The gorge was so narrow that the bank was eaten away in places, and the trees grew right out of the water and up the wall of the ravine.

We stopped in a small inlet with a little waterfall. The banks here were almost vertical, rising up in shining layers that piled up jaggedly at the same angle like a bank of graphite, making a fantastic, geometrically exact sketch. Slivers broke off at the touch of a hand.

We got undressed on a stony promontory beneath a rock covered with burdock and went into the water.

Mitya leaned against a stone underneath the waterfall. Sparkling streams of water poured over his head and shoulders, falling away in tiny rainbows. His cassock and boots lay among the burdock and he splashed about, laughing, completely forgetting his novitiate. I lay on the shingly riverbed, feeling the joy of the water's movement and its transparent freshness in every pore. Then we changed places.

After a couple of hours we gathered our things together and walked barefoot upstream through the murmuring water. In a shady glade we found lots of millstones, left over from an old mill which had once belonged to the monastery. Farther on the gorge widened, but it was choked with boulders nearly to the halfway mark. The water foamed angrily over this "stone-fall." We had our last swim here and turned back with a wonderfully fresh, clean feeling.

※

FATHER BENEDICT CALLED to me from the refectory window. He was sitting in front of a large dish of faded green bean pods, shelling the beans; beside him was a dish of potatoes and eggplant.

I stopped in the doorway and he looked up intently, almost as though we hadn't seen each other for a long time. "I'm making a Georgian dish—*ajapsandali*. Would you like to learn how it's made?"

Mitya went to hang out the wet towels and I sat down opposite Benedict and began to shell the beans and toss them into the pan of water. My eyes soon got used to the darkness and I made out the deacon's face, pitted with pockmarks.

"Sister Veronica . . ." He looked up slowly, his sad eyes made gloomy by his very dark pupils and lashes. "Do you know how to cook?"

I had the feeling he wanted to say something more important and this was just a way to begin. "No, not at all. One of my relatives lives in the room next door to us. She's quite lonely—she took on the cooking as a labor of love. I'm sorry now that I didn't learn anything from her."

"Never mind, we'll teach you. Do you know what real monastic food's like? There should be no taste, color, or smell."

I peeled the potatoes and eggplant while he sliced the purple onions into even rings.

"Veronica," he tried again. "I happened to see you at the river today."

He put his knife down. "If I'd known you were

going for a swim I'd never have followed, you may be sure, but my horse had wandered off, as usual. It went across the ravine—and suddenly I saw a woman bathing. I was very upset."

"Haven't you seen women swimming at the beach?"

"Well, yes, I used to go to the seaside, but you view things differently after you've spent a long time in a monastery. It's not your fault, nor mine, but here, you know, our struggle with all the passions becomes stronger. I ought to confess this. We think it's better to tell each other right away if there's any little shadow. If you don't, it just builds up. I'm glad I've told you because I want to be pure before you." He smiled. "When a man comes to a monastery the demons cook up all sorts of different temptations— and here's another one. If you don't mind, would you wear your scarf?"

I hadn't put it on, of course, that morning when I'd gone to the river, so I went straight to my tent and tied my blue silk scarf around my head.

Father Benedict's glance showed me he approved of my submissiveness.

That awkward moment over, he began to talk freely. I wanted to put a cloth on the table. He chose a green woven one and we covered it with a clear oilcloth. I was sorry I hadn't picked any harebells the day before to put on the table.

"We don't often have flowers, maybe at festivals: a single rose in front of the icon screen. Everything in a monastery should be severe and strict. The more beauty there is, the more temptation too."

I took this as a last joke on the theme of our previous conversation. But the nature of this conversation struck home. I hadn't expected such openness and directness between people. There seemed to be no cunning in Benedict's words.

Above the cliff, a little below the monastery was a clearing with an old garden bench on iron legs. I went out after Vespers to sit there and watch the sunset. Soon Father Benedict appeared, followed by a young woman with bare legs.

He led her to me. "This is Lorelei, Sister Veronica. She's a leading actress in one of our theaters, just back from a successful tour in England. Lorelei's here with some friends. We'll have supper, then you two can eat together."

Lorelei's appearance, not least in such a remote place, was even more unexpected than her name. Her chestnut hair flowed over her shoulders and was bound around her forehead by two braids joined in three places with rings. Her short striped blouse with thin shoulder straps looked more like a vest and scarcely covered her bosom, which was not concealed by any undergarments. Her blouse barely touched the waist of her long fine-mesh cotton skirt. She was carrying high-heeled sandals and a short wrap.

Benedict smiled guiltily and left us. Lorelei sat beside me on the bench, tucking her toes with their pearly nail polish under her.

"Just call me Lo. . . ."

Forced to wear a head scarf and buttoned-up dress, I probably reacted more jealously to her frivolous clothes than I would otherwise have done. After several polite exchanges I observed, no less politely, that it was indecent to come to a male monastery with a bare bosom. She mechanically put her hand across her breasts, but replied quite airily, "It's not important. They see something more interesting in me. Judging from the old frescoes, our ancestors went around in semitransparent clothes like angels."

"I don't know about our ancestors, but our contemporaries have lost that angelic purity—I'm sure you know that quite well."

"Oh, but I've been coming here for ages. I've known some of them since they were children. Benedict studied art at the same college as my daughter."

"How old are you?" I asked in surprise, trying to exercise some restraint. This strange conversation hadn't left the realm of social nicety so far.

"Forty-six," she replied, rather unwillingly.

I'd thought she was no older than twenty-eight, and so I'd presumed to comment on her appearance. Looking more closely I discovered that her hair was tinted, but she was beautifully preserved.

"How old is Benedict?"

"Twenty-nine."

That was another surprise! I'd never thought about his age, but I'd assumed we were the same age—that meant his balding head and his beard had aged him by fifteen years.

Our conversation hadn't upset Lorelei and so I continued. There in the world, I gestured beyond the edge of the ravine, and especially among actors, her style of dress wouldn't surprise anyone. She scarcely raised her eyebrows, as if my suggestion hadn't flattered her.

"But they won't notice it here," she interrupted. "Monks are—holy."

What rubbish! But I couldn't tell her so. "Human-kind encompasses the whole spectrum from animal to God," I said. " 'Be perfect, as your Heavenly Father is perfect.' That's the essence of all the commandments. But it's too high, totally beyond our human strength. There has never been a higher ideal in the world, or a nobler moral code. Most people aren't capable of Christianity and therefore say it's unattainable."

"Don't you think that's right—that it's unattainable? Who can be as perfect as our Heavenly Father?" she asked, intrigued.

"Even Christ's disciples were amazed and asked, 'Who then can be saved?' His reply was, 'It's impossible for man, but for God everything is possible.' Monastic life is a spiritual feat aiming at the Heavenly Father's perfection. It goes beyond the bounds of human strength into the realms of mercy."

"But you're idealizing them!" She raised her hand to stop me. "There's no painting, no acting without the spark of God. Everyone brings it in their own way, serving the cause of good: The priest brings it to the pulpit, the actor to the stage—and nowadays it's the actor who attracts a bigger audience."

I'd heard all this many times in the circles of the self-styled creative intelligentsia. The conversation became impossible: It was in a different language, so that words like *good, truth,* and *love* could have completely opposite meanings. I remembered a playwright telling me that he'd written a drama about

Christ. He didn't believe in God, but somehow thought God had spoken through him. I wanted to ask, "Why God? Why not a lesser demon of vainglory?" But that would have been impolite. And the playwright didn't believe in demons, though they are even closer to the seat of our being.

Even when the people I was talking to were serious and believed in the existence of God, we had no common language because we couldn't agree on how he exists. I'd spent the last five or six years just trying to find out the answer to this question, getting used to Christianity and its two-thousand-year-old culture. It was only as I went down into the depths that I found out the extent to which this is an unknown area to us contemporary, thinking people, or as one writer who is now abroad put it—the "educated generation." I realized that in fact unbelief comes from ignorance.

"Do you ever go to church?" I asked Lorelei.

"Very rarely. Our work has ideological overtones, and if they saw . . ."

"Yes, of course, and there's no need to . . ."

She let the point go, although the usual answer is that there's no time to.

I see now that faith and unbelief shape two different ways of life, two separate characters, each the opposite of the other. Alexander Yelchaninov—a wonderful man—received his schooling here in Georgia. He became a priest in Nice and died of cancer in Paris. It was a terrible death, he was shouting in his sleep. But during his waking moments his nearest and dearest saw tears in his eyes only once—when Holy Week began and he couldn't go to church. Yelchaninov left his notes, which were edited and published by his relatives. Nobody understood the human soul like this priest, to whom thousands came for confession, revealing their most intimate, secret thoughts. He wrote that a gifted person can be like a spring of water constantly bubbling up—so that there is no place left for God, no silence in which the voice of God can be heard.

LONG WHITISH CLOUDS drifted up behind the mountain, and the sun was setting beneath them, full circle. Lorelei threw her shawl about her, covering her breast and shoulders, carelessly, as though she hadn't been paying close attention to our conversation, but she looked more serious now, and suddenly seemed older.

"Doesn't art lead to God? Doesn't talent come from God?"

"Why? Lucifer was endowed with God's beauty and wisdom, but he fell and became the chief angel of darkness. Religion and art can lead in opposite directions. Religious life is the way to moral perfection, to awareness of one's deepest self, getting closer to the original pattern God wanted us to fit. Acting, writing, more often than not means putting on a mask: It is a falsification, a game that confirms us in our proud self-sufficiency. But this game assumes such importance that we're all too ready to see God at work in every aspect of the arts. . . ."

"Benedict said you're a writer yourself?"

"I really don't know anymore. But yes, I am, though I haven't written much, and I've been doing more reading than writing lately. I lost interest in literature when I saw that the Holy Fathers know us much better than all the artists who make themselves the guides of the human soul."

"What do you do now?" Lorelei asked with interest.

"I'm thinking about what I should do."

"Have you been thinking for long?"

"Yes."

The more anyone tastes religious life, in the liturgy or in prayer, the less they need to create an external world. On the contrary, meaning is found in silence. It was, after all, through silence that Rublev painted his icon of the Holy Trinity with the help of the Holy Spirit—in the same way as King David wrote the Psalms and Simeon the New Theologian wrote his *Divine Hymns*. . . .

Do we need other forms when literature has ceased to be pagan, but hasn't yet become a prayer? Are the forms that reflect our way to God, our troubles, our first discoveries of heaven, still remote and impossible? Once I asked a priest what I should do. He opened the Gospel of John and read, "And so they said to him, 'What must we do to carry out the works of God?' Jesus answered, 'This is the work of God, that you believe in him whom he has sent.' " That's what I live by. But I don't know how to live in the world.

The sun sank into a purple-blue expanse. Peace poured over the darkened mountains. Oh, if only my words could sink into peace, dissolve into silence . . . and in this silence I would learn simply to be before

God; not to discuss him, but to observe him and hear his voice. Why then would I have to write?

But I don't know how to be silent or to pray, and so I speak and write and my words are in vain.

FIVE EMPTY WINE bottles, their tops wrapped in foil, stood on the table between the pots and the dish Benedict and I had spent all day preparing, between the glasses and watermelon rind.

Benedict was sitting on a low stone wall with two of Lorelei's actor friends; they were talking in heightened, cheerful voices. Lorelei poured herself some wine and offered me some but I refused. She didn't drink hers either. She didn't like our food. "What can this be?" she wondered politely, barely tasting it.

I told her the Georgian name and she said that of course she knew the dish, she just hadn't recognized that this was *ajapsandali*. But all the same, she didn't eat it.

Soon she joined her friends, two carelessly elegant young men who looked young enough to be her sons. She sat down gracefully in front of them, spreading her white skirt. One of them was doing tricks with his cravat and playing cards, which he'd obviously brought with him for this purpose.

Benedict was well and truly drunk. He looked at me and came up to the door. "It would be shameful to make you clear all this up. We'll help you," he promised, without waiting for me to answer. Just then Mitya appeared in the clearing in front of the church.

"Come here, Dmitri," Benedict called. "Our visitors want you to play the harmonium."

They all went off to the church, talking loudly, while I wondered, with some annoyance, whether to wash up or not. Why should I? The monastery's not a place for actors and conjurors to hold their orgies. They didn't disturb me that much, but I was mortally offended by Benedict.

Perhaps I should wash up, so that the table wouldn't be a reproach to the deacon once he'd sobered up the next day. Besides, it would be good for my pride. While I was wondering, things resolved themselves, as they so often do. It was completely dark by now, and there was no lamp by the well. However, the church was lit and I heard the sounds of the organ. I felt unhappy that Mitya was entertaining these people—all these conjuring tricks and improvisations on sacred songs. I sat on the grass in the dark outside the tent, wondering where they'd all spend the night.

Around midnight Mitya came up "They're going now."

"Where are they going in the dark?"

"Their car's on the old road, an hour and a half from here through the forest. Father Benedict was more than willing to go with them.

'I said, I don't think you should go so far at night.'

'Do you think I'm dwunk, Dmitri?' he asked, speaking Russian with his Georgian accent."

"What do you think yourself?" I asked.

"I think they're all a bit dwunk," said Mitya.

"Archil, too?"

"No, he sat with them, but he didn't drink. He

went off straightaway so as not to get mixed up in it."

Soon we heard shouts on the other side of the precipice and saw the flicker of pocket flashlights— the expedition was trying to get up the slope on the other side of the river.

On our very first day Mitya had asked the abbot's permission to read evening prayer in the small church. So now we got the keys and unlocked the door, which could be barred from inside by a beam jammed into a metal handle. The candle flame, with not a breath to stir it, looked like a stiff petal of light. Not a sound issued from the thick walls. Mitya recited the prayers by heart. His cassocked figure cast a shadow along the wall.

I couldn't concentrate on the prayers. When we'd finished saying the office, Mitya suggested that we should pray for the Hierodeacon Benedict, in case anything should happen to him on his travels. I'd never even thought of praying for the four of them—my Christian love didn't extend that far.

AT MATINS ARCHIL read the office in Georgian. Mitya and I read the psalms in Church Slavonic. Father Benedict was sitting in front of the lectern, his head resting on it. He was dozing, but shook himself every time we had to stand for the Glorias, got up, crossed himself, then rested his head on his hands once more. Twice he left the church rather unsteadily and disappeared into the refectory for a while. His pockmarked, ruddy complexion made him look older than his years. He looked apathetic and depressed. The hair on his temples was like black down. Somehow he got through the service and disappeared without a word to anyone.

I glanced into the refectory as I passed by. The table was laid and spread with a clean plastic cloth. A huge earthenware jug of springwater stood in the middle, wiping out the memory of the bottles. Archil had obviously gotten up early before the office and had made the refectory presentable.

Mitya and I forgot all about having a swim. We went off to the river, where I told him about my talk with Benedict the day before. Mitya took off his cap and cassock, had a wash, and started studying the "Thrice Holy" in Khutsuri.

We got back for the beginning of Vespers. Benedict was leaning against the wall with his hands folded, talking to a plump elderly woman bulging out of a loud polyester dress. She was talking in strident tones, waving her arms. He replied with a broad, rather flaccid smile. He glanced at us briefly, averting glazed and bloodshot eyes. He looked terribly shabby in his cassock, a bit as if he had on a faded dressing gown showing the dirty borders of his undershirt.

A little later we asked him if there would be a service. "Are you sure you're ready?" he asked with a wry smile, pouring some water from the jug into a mug. He clearly wasn't ready himself.

"What's wrong, Father Benedict?" I asked, trying to ease the uncomfortable atmosphere that that smile of his indicated. "You don't look very well."

"Well, *you* look great," he replied in the same unpleasant tone. "And why not? You've come here for a rest and you spend the whole day at the river."

"Has your work in the monastery made you tired?" I tried to make a joke in spite of myself. He looked at me dourly and went out without answering. I didn't want to offend him. I guessed this hadn't been an isolated incident; it was a weakness of his. All the same, he began the service around seven o'clock.

The plump woman brought half a dozen other women and three children. They'd come across the mountains for Vespers, and Benedict tried to make up for his lack of sobriety by being very polite. He fetched benches and sat everyone down in two rows, as if they were in a village hall. He read animatedly, sometimes raising his voice, sometimes muttering, but whenever Archil made a mistake Benedict told him off loudly.

The women felt uncomfortable, whether from the general atmosphere or because they weren't used to sitting down during services. They hushed the children noisily and kept getting up, taking the children out, coming back in, pushing their bags of food under the benches. Once, the deacon gestured so wildly that the broad sleeve of his gown knocked over a candlestick, adding to the commotion. Another time he began the litany, which only a priest should say; but realizing his mistake, he started singing loudly, beckoning to everyone to join in.

The plump woman sang in a piercing voice, looking around at Benedict with a glance that expressed compassion and a willingness to help. She glanced around at the other women. "Well, there you are, what tough luck! We've found one monk in the monastery and he's blind drunk."

Trying to comfort the deacon, she turned her back to the icon-screen and, raising her fat arms, started to take off a medallion that hung around her neck on a black cord. There and then she tried to put it on Benedict, embracing him with a generous gesture. Benedict bent down. He took the medallion and began to put it on Mitya, so we were left with a peasant woman's cheap little medallion of St. George and the dragon as a memento of this distressing service.

Half an hour later the women began to leave, but not all at once, in case they offended anyone; they went off separately to make it seem as if they were leaving by chance. One would look around at Father Benedict, rustle around under the bench, pull out her bag, and make for the door, watched by the others. Then the next one would shuffle along the bench— until in the end only one woman was left. She hovered between me and the door, anxiously clutching a bag bulging with leeks. Her friends who were waiting at the door kept waving to her, but she ignored them and went on frenziedly crossing herself.

"Nina!" They couldn't wait anymore. Nina looked around. Waving one hand while the leeks waggled in the other, she shook her head and continued to cross herself even more determinedly.

"Nina! Ni-na!" they shouted, as loudly as if they were still in the forest but rather awkwardly because they were disturbing her eager prayer.

Mitya and I watched with great interest to see how long Nina would hold out. Only Archil went on reading the psalms in a meek voice. At last Nina hurried away. The women headed for the gates, chattering loudly, no longer bothering to keep their voices down. They'd barely gone when Father Benedict finished the service.

"The abbot's not here and the prayer isn't going the way it should," he concluded in Russian, looking at Archil. "That's right," the latter agreed quietly.

At that moment a *gazik* drove through the gates.

"There's the Father Abbot," Benedict said in a crestfallen voice and went out to meet him, looking like a man condemned. We locked the church, then followed him. The deacon had gone out through the gates without a backward glance.

Father Michael was wearing his cassock; his prayer rope hung around his neck. He turned around and we were as pleased to see each other as if we'd been apart for a month. He blessed us and, still looking pleased, nodded toward the vehicle from which Archil was already hauling a bucket of tomatoes.

"Look at all the things I've brought you. . . ."

The bad moods had disappeared. The abbot was back and the whole community cheered up. We all began to unload the tomatoes, cucumbers, and potatoes, dragging them to the kitchen under the awning above the veranda, making separate piles of pears and rather bruised peaches on the table.

Father Michael, smiling broadly, unwrapped a large cheese and pushed it toward me. "Smells strong, doesn't it? It's homemade, that's why."

I couldn't resist taking a bite. "What was my sin called, Dmitri?"

"Gluttony," Mitya answered, looking lovingly at the abbot.

"You don't understand. Gluttony's when you want to eat a lot to satisfy your stomach; and if you want to please your gullet you're satisfying the demon that possesses it. Every single desire has its root in a different sin. Oh, how hard this Christian life is! Checkmate whichever way you go!"

Well-baked loaves were lying on the table along with green and red peppers, bunches of parsley and dill, sharp-smelling herbs. Jars of honey, each as big as a glass, and three large watermelons completed this still life. We never had such abundance again!

"See how many good things God has sent us!" Father Michael rejoiced.

I didn't fully understand his joy. We simply enjoyed this bustle of domestic activity; it was like a short holiday. The abbot opened a cardboard box and, squatting beside it, began to hand out presents for the office—notebooks, pads, and pencils. I'd actually forgotten that once, in front of Benedict, I'd regretted the fact I had no notebook with me. Father Michael pulled glass funnels for the oil lamps carefully out of another box.

"You can't buy these. I had to order them specially from a factory."

He climbed a wooden ladder and fastened two rings for the lamps to the wall. Archil poured in kerosene and we trimmed the wicks. A pale flame glowed in the dusk. The glass misted over, but soon cleared. I remembered how I'd seen kerosene lamps being lit long ago, just after the war. The abbot hadn't even been born then, and I was only eight.

The men gathered for supper. I went out to get water for tea. Father Benedict was sitting on the bench beside the pine tree in front of the well. He seemed rather restless. An overflowing basin stood under the stream of water. "I'm just giving my horse a drink," the deacon explained.

I dined after the brothers. Mitya kept me company, drinking a second glass of tea. Father Michael opened a bag of shelled Greek nuts and a three-liter jar of preserves, offering us some. "I'm sure you've never tasted preserves like this. They're made of figs. My mother sent them. She knows my weaknesses. Don't forget to close the jar when you've finished, or ants will get in."

We mixed the nuts with honey and drank tea with the preserves. The figs shone like amber. It was already dusk when Mitya and I took the dishes out to the well. Father Benedict was still sitting in the same position, and the basin was still standing under the stream of water.

"The basin's full now," I pointed out.

"Ah." The deacon gestured with his hand. "Archil forgot to give the horse a drink. Well, never mind. She won't die of thirst."

Kerosene lamps burned in the refectory. The warm night darkened beyond the windows. Peace prevailed as usual in the monastery.

THAT NIGHT A deafening crash shook the earth. A fine rain was falling, then there was a growing rumble and an avalanche of water burst from the sky.

"Get up, Mom!" I heard Mitya call distantly through the roar. "It's a flood!"

There wasn't really any point in getting up. Water

was soon dripping through the collapsing roof onto the table, drenching the pillows. Shivering in the dampness, I got up and started to put my clothes away, half pulling back the curtain around my bed. The darkness hummed and burbled. Water flowed past our tent in torrents, flooding around us with a cold roar, seething and splashing. Lightning flashed, silhouetting the huge black outline of Dzhvari: one long roar, and then darkness swallowed it up—again and again. A pale blue fire lit up the drowning world. The cross on the high dome flashed. Pine branches shivered in the momentary blue.

"We'll be swept over the ravine in this tent."

"Just like it used to be on board ship when a sailor died," Mitya added cheerfully. "They wrapped him in canvas and threw him overboard."

The canvas billowed up about us and water flowed in underneath. I shoved clothing and footwear under the mattresses and wrapped myself in a blanket, rummaging for my watch in the dark. Lightning flashed and the hands lit up. It was one o'clock. We had six hours to get through before morning.

"You'd think someone would be worried about us, in case we'd been washed away."

"Oh, come on, Mom! Stop fussing! They're not going to stay awake all night thinking about a woman. That wouldn't be decent. And if we were washed away it'd be too late to worry. We'll see everything all right when it's light tomorrow morning."

So we lay in bed, wrapped in blankets, under canvas on the edge of a precipice—at night, in the mountains, on the edge of the world—and chatted, sure

that nothing bad would happen to us. "You are protected now," an old friend had said to me when I'd
only just come to faith and had started to pray. And
it's true. I felt I was protected and I haven't been
afraid since then.

Lightning flashed right above the gorge. Water
flooded between our beds but didn't rise to the height
of the mattress. By morning we fell asleep, wearied
by the crashing and the incessant water, the blankets
pulled over our heads.

DAWN GLOWED IN a dull mist, which curled up
from the gorge, spreading in layers above it, hanging
in patches about the pines. Mist clung to the mountain ranges as though daylight could not penetrate
the thick shroud. The pines were dripping and every
needle glistened like a string of shining beads. The
wet grass along the path to the basilica came up to
my knees, drenching my legs.

It was dark and still in the church, as always before
the service. A candle guttered, casting a circle of light
on the beautiful ancient lettering of the liturgical
books. The silver threads that were sewn into the
black cover of the lectern shone: a cross in a crown of
thorns. Benedict's slow shadow moved along the
wall.

"Will you read, Dmitri?"

Mitya read the "Thrice Holy" in Khutsuri. Archil,
half turning, looked at him, his long lashes shading
his moist eyes. Then the hierodeacon uttered the six
penitential psalms. "Lord, hear my prayer and listen
to my supplication in thy truth. Enter not into judg-

ment against thy slave, for no living thing will be justified before thee. The enemy pursues my soul, has trampled my life into the ground, has forced me to live in darkness as those long dead. My spirit is weary within me, my heart is in confusion. I stretch out my hands to you. My soul is turned to thee, like a thirsty land. Hear me early, O Lord, my soul faints . . . Do not hide thy face from me lest I be like those that go down to the grave . . . Teach me to do thy will, for thou art my God. May thy blessed Spirit lead me into a land of truth. For thy Name's sake, O Lord, quicken me. For thy truth's sake lead my soul out of sorrow."

They sang "More Honorable Than the Cherubim," and Father Benedict knelt down as usual. His shoulders were bent beneath his surplice, his downcast eyes were fixed on the flame of the lamp in front of the Mother of God.

Upat'iosnessa, Kerubim -ta-a-sa . . . Da ag'matebit uzestaessa Serapim -ta-a-sa . . .

The cadences of Old Georgian chants, which cannot be transcribed musically or put into words, sound like the broken cry of a longing soul that pierces the heart like a sweet pain, and if the soul can grieve thus, then surely within this very cry is the promise of consolation.

Father Benedict's prayer came from the depth of his heart—that "broken and contrite heart" that God would not despise. The Prodigal Son must have wept like this when he'd wasted his goods and had become wretched and lonely. Destitute and starving, he returned to his father and said, "I have sinned before heaven and in your sight and I am no more worthy to be called your son." He was sorry for himself too: His heart melted in repentance and he was happy even if he had to die at his father's gate. Did he really believe that his father would embrace him, weeping? "This my son was dead and is alive again, was lost and is found."

Upat'iosnessa, Kerubim -ta-a-sa . . .

Father Benedict's face in the dim lamplight was beautiful and inspired.

LATER THAT MORNING the restorers arrived by truck with all their equipment. I saw them in the distance, then we met by the well—two men and two women. The older woman, Eli, short for Elizaveta, was around fifty, a doctor of art history. The younger was under forty, and a smoker. Both wore trousers. The restorers were quartered above the refectory on the first floor. They would live and eat independently of the monastery.

The first change brought about by their arrival was that the abbot, after consulting with the brothers, stopped ringing the bell, so as not to waken the restorers too early. In monasteries one of the brothers acts as watchman, getting up before the others and rousing them, going around all the cells with a candle. He comes to the door and says, "By the prayers of our holy fathers, O Lord Jesus Christ our God, have mercy upon us." The brother in the cell gets up, opens his door, and lights his candle from the watchman's candle. In big monasteries where fifty or sixty brothers have to be woken, the watchman has to get up very early. He usually lights all the lamps in the church as well. Here in Dzhvari, with three brothers and two lamps Benedict suggested appointing Mitya as watchman. So in order to waken Mitya they gave us an alarm clock, and Mitya began to worry that he wouldn't wake up in time and would let the brothers down.

I HEARD THE clip-clop of hooves on the upper road and then the rider appeared, dressed like a cowboy. His russet horse raced past the bench in front of the well, almost bumping into Father Michael. The horse neighed and reared up on his hind legs. The abbot, sitting resting his hand on the back of the bench watched with a smile as the cowboy tethered his horse and lit a cigarette.

A few minutes later, tourists appeared. The abbot hurried away and the area in front of the well was soon filled with boys and girls in jeans, shorts, sleeveless dresses, knapsacks, and transistor radios. The State Travel Bureau had included visits to Dzhvari as part of its tourist plan, and horse riding was included at weekends. We'd already spotted the group on the other side of the river. The cowboy in his Stetson hat rode in front on a stallion, bridled in, which picked its way very carefully down the sheer slopes. Farther back was a scattered line of people on foot, leading their horses by the reins. They mounted once they reached the old road in the shade of the elm trees and dismounted again at the pass. Beyond the farmstead was an encampment of tents with stalls for the horses.

Saturdays and Sundays tended to be the most disrupted days at Dzhvari. Apart from that, tourists visited about twice a week, leaving their mark in the surrounding glades in the form of empty jelly jars, bottles, melon skins, and a litter of other rubbish.

Archil usually took this noisy crowd over the monastery—the abbot and Benedict disappeared from sight. The tourists took photographs of themselves in front of the church, in groups and in pairs, embracing, and dropping melon skins and the empty boxes that held their films. An old woman asked the guide if the monks minded these visits, and the guide replied, clearly denigrating the monks, "Why should they object? The monastery belongs to the state." The lively visitors looked into our tent, and rang the monastery bell until Archil ran up to tell them to stop.

The world came crowding in on Dzhvari from all sides, even during services. The church door opened out on to the clearing where wire netting replaced an older stone wall. I viewed these raids from the standpoint of someone closely connected to the monastery.

A girl was perching on the cowboy's knee. Close up, he turned out to be quite an old man, hiding his bald head under his idiotic hat. Bare shoulders and arms, bare legs, short skirts, embraces, flirtations, songs in bad taste sung to a guitar—it was one thing after another.

I saw Archil come out each morning afterward with a brush and a rake to sweep up the litter from the clearing. I saw how the services were disrupted when tourists strolled into the church and gawked shamelessly at the monks. The females stared at Archil and Mitya when they came to the well in their monastic caps.

"Can we borrow seven glasses?" a smart young

man asked me. He was wearing an Ossetian cotton cap—and he'd already chilled his bottles in the spring.

"Wait a minute, I'll wash some for you."

I asked Archil if I should give them dishes, and he nodded. "If they ask for something and you have it, you must always give it to them."

"Doesn't it matter that they'll be drinking wine and the hieromonk will be having tea out of the same glass afterward?"

Archil looked sad. He hadn't liked that question, and I felt sorry too, but the monastery property seemed sacred and I was sad to carry it out into the world.

"You can wash the glasses thoroughly with soda," Archil advised.

"Well, couldn't they clean the rubbish away themselves?"

"They are guests." Archil looked at me reproachfully. "It's not right to ask them to clean up. There's a Georgian proverb that says that an unexpected guest comes from God."

We've got a Russian saying too—that an uninvited guest is worse than a Tartar! (That's a relic from the Tartar invasions, but I decided not to quote it.)

The tourists took the glasses, came back for two more and didn't appear again.

"Are we going to drink our tea from wineglasses or metal glasses?" I asked Archil as I set the table.

He thought for a bit. "Perhaps we'll use those glass jars," he said, trustingly.

As it happened it was quite nice to put tea bags in small jars, and it would have been a bit much to have used the glasses. Archil went off to the spring to wash the jelly jars out with soda.

"Besides," he recalled on the way out, "yesterday we drank Bozhomi wine and ate meat that the tourists had brought. And we had watermelon on Wednesday as well."

Mitya had told me about the meat. Nobody in the monastery eats meat, but if tourists bring some they receive it gratefully, place it on the table, and offer it to their guests. Father Michael had offered some to Mitya, who had refused. The meat was fatty and he didn't like the look of it; what's more, he felt ashamed to take some in front of the abbot and Father Benedict, and there were no knives or forks. Father Benedict suddenly reached out and took a piece. Holding a bone in his hand, he ate the meat. He glanced at Mitya and asked, "Dmitri, do you think it's worse to eat a piece of meat or to condemn your brother?" "I think it's worse to condemn your brother," Mitya had replied, looking away. He pretended not to understand Father Benedict's question. Archil had sat with his head bent.

The abbot had taken a vow long ago not to eat meat himself, even if he offered it to others. He looked at the three of them and, as he got up from the table, concluded, "Well, here we all are, quite content: Oh, how abstemious we are! And as a result, Benedict has won and the three of us have lost."

The nine glasses we had lost to the tourists were less important than being judgmental and critical but, all the same, I asked the abbot when Archil was listening, "Should I give out our crockery anymore?"

"Have we any left?" he asked with interest, raising his eyebrows.

"Not for tea," I said.

"Well, don't give them any tea things then," he answered.

BRINKA AND MURIA were rolling in the shade, tongues hanging out. I remembered that Archil had asked me to feed them, even, at my suggestion, putting out two bowls beside the well. I'd poured soup into them once, but the dogs didn't touch it. The soup must have been sour and they wouldn't eat it. What was I to feed them with? We ate vegetables and potatoes and had to cook food separately for the dogs.

Father Michael came downstairs with his scythe. He had taken off his waistcoat and cap, and his pectoral cross swung on top of his cassock. "Brinka!" He whistled, and Brinka flew to him, rolling at his feet among the burdock, his shaggy fur getting covered with burrs and looking quite pathetic.

Leaning his scythe against the wall, Father Michael sat down on the bottom step and carefully pulled burr after burr out of Brinka's coat. He pushed Brinka and she rolled onto her back, panting and yelping, and suddenly started to race round the clearing, barking loudly with joy. Father Michael pretended to catch her, but couldn't. When he picked up his scythe I asked if I could have a look at some of the monastery books. "Of course! You can do whatever you like." His eyes were shining after his game. "As the Apostle said, everything is permitted, but not everything is expedient."

He showed me a room next to the refectory and opened the bookcase, which took up a third of the wall and was crammed with books from top to bottom, mostly in Georgian. I started to take them down, one by one. They were covered with dust. Some had costly leather bindings; others weren't bound at all. The illustrations were austere yet magnificent, the texts were written in ancient script on thick bluish gray, yellowed paper.

The most intense time of my life had been spent among books. This is where my religious awakening began. The Hindus say that truth will find you when you're ready for it. It won't delay a day or an hour—it will knock at your door. And that was certainly the case with me.

My book of short stories had been published. I had received a large fee. I had stopped working for money. I would never put my work to any illegal or underhand purpose. I'd settle on a sofa under the window and friends called with books borrowed from libraries, or old catalog stock.

As a student I had read Schopenhauer and Nietzsche and believed in the Hegelian Absolute Spirit that is found in the world. Later I read the Existentialists and I began to feel that all the eternal questions have their roots in religion. I wanted to get to know all the religious systems that had ever existed in the world, so as to find Truth. The *Bhagavad Gita,* the *Dhammapada,* yoga, Buddhism, Zen, Anthroposophy, Berdyaev: the pile of books kept growing.

They were all foreign and because they were so expensive I couldn't afford to buy and read them at the rate of two or three hundred pages a day. My life at that time seemed to be a state of constant discovery.

All the same, I didn't find Truth. It found me. When I began to read the Church Fathers, and again, in the light of what they said, the Gospels, a fountain of knowledge that had previously nurtured my reason now welled into my heart—so deep that everything else was lost to sight. Knowledge became a means of grace.

Father Michael pulled a crumbling folio from the bottom shelf. He sat down on a bench in the corner and leafed through it intently.

"Which of the Fathers have you read?" he asked.

So, in all good conscience, I began to tell him. When I got to Simeon the New Theologian the abbot nodded and I felt encouraged. I wanted to tell him about the contemplation of Divine Light, which I'd read with such delight, glimpsing a great height that was slowly being unveiled, so far beyond my reach that it filled me with tears.

But the abbot interrupted. "This is terrible . . . it's terrible that you've read the Holy Fathers."

I fell silent, waiting for what was to come. "Surely you've learned from the Fathers that we should read only the things that correspond to our own spiritual level and mode of life. How can you read Climacus, a monastic classic, living in the world as you do? This only widens the gulf between what you know and what in fact you are," he said, laying his folio aside. "You tell me you hadn't taken even the first steps on the Christian way . . . How dared you read

about the contemplation of Divine Light? The saints
fasted, prayed, mortified the flesh, lived in the desert,
fought with demons all their lives, and you snuggle
on a sofa and think you can enter their revelations."

This wasn't offensive because it was the truth, and
I knew it myself, but I had no option. I had had no
religious teaching at home, at school, or at a university. I was thirty-eight before I ever met a Christian
believer. I didn't think I'd entered into the contemplation, only that I'd learned about them when I
might never have done so. Long ago a child would
go fasting to Communion, and take part in the Easter
Vigil, standing in church with a candle. Boys would
drive into the forest in a cart with their father and cut
down young birch branches and pick flowers to dec-
orate the church at Whitsun. Children would go to
confession and listen to "The Peaceful Light of Holy
Glory" . . . But Russian homes today have the metal
discs of loudspeakers instead of icons, and instead of
prayers all I heard in our communal apartment were
curses and drunken songs. Praise God for books in
which I found out that someone had seen the Divine
Light. It meant that God had given me a basis of
knowledge and destiny which I had to live out.

"So, live, take your first steps—don't bury yourself in books. What have you just dug out of that
shelf?" He came up to me and took a beautiful edition of Maximus the Confessor out of my hands.
"Well, what are we talking about?" He weighed the
book between his hands. "I don't forbid you to read
Maximus the Confessor. I want you to come to understand for yourself that it's better if you're not allowed to read this."

I followed him to the bookcase to see where the book was put.

"Why are you staring like that—as if I'd stolen bread from your mouth? Take it then . . . but I'd like you to put it back in its place yourself, tomorrow, if not today."

"I won't be able to read all this by tomorrow. . . ." I looked at the book and saw that there were almost eight hundred pages, but he didn't see my joke.

"You're still hoping you'll read another hundred books and become like Simeon the New Theologian."

"No, I'm not." I gave a sigh of relief, clutching Maximus the Confessor with both hands.

"Why don't you take in anything I say? This is nothing but intellectual greed: Some people stuff their rooms with furniture, others pack their heads with knowledge which they don't need. How simple it is to understand! Christianity isn't what you know. It's a way of life."

"I've been telling myself that for two years. This is the last thing I'm going to read. I'll begin a new life after this."

"Why haven't you changed your clothes?"

"But I have!" I was wearing my head scarf and a long-sleeved cotton print dress.

"None of this is enough."

"I've nothing else to wear."

"We'll find something for you. A black kerchief and a long worker's overalls. No sandals, please. Put on clogs."

His face assumed its customary sardonic expres-

sion as he spoke. This smile wasn't personal, however. From the way he was speaking I guessed that he
wasn't supposed to speak seriously to a woman about
religion. He'd gotten carried away by our talk and
now, suddenly aware of this odd circumstance, he
was secretly laughing: look how I've been chattering!
I wasn't offended by his laugh.

He closed the bookcase and sat down on the windowsill. I stood opposite, leaning my shoulder
against the wall. Beyond the grating sparrows were
rocking on long-leafed sweet corn.

"How difficult it all is, to find the right level . . .
Recently I was on Mount Athos. The monks there
have very long services. They even use sleep time.
They sleep for only three to four hours at night, but
doze all day. As long as you're taking part yourself
it's all right, but once someone else takes over you
doze off. But I thought, isn't it better to sleep a bit
more and not doze all day and not be much good for
anything else."

"Of course it's better," I agreed.

"Aha, and how much do you sleep?"

"Me? Quite a lot. I always needed a clear head to
take in what I was reading and to be able to write.
Why should I deprive myself of sleep when I need to
think straight?"

"An interesting life! And has it never entered this
clear head of yours that it's possible to work with
other parts of you than your head?"

"No, it never seriously occurred to me."

"We're not tadpoles. We have bodies equipped to
do heavy work. Physical weariness sometimes brings
a greater state of peace than can be found in any

book. Haven't you noticed that when you are tired you don't feel irritable? All extremes are bad. It's bad, you see, if you work in a factory and use up all your energy earning a living. But just using your brain is not good either. Harmony is broken. The royal way is the midpoint between the extremes . . . And 'know thyself' is not an intellectual concept. It's not about abstract knowledge. So we've each to find our own level—of sleep and food, reading and prayer, work and contemplation. In fact, you generally needn't read as much as you pray."

"Then I'd hardly read at all."

"Or you'd pray much more. Spirituality is a special kind of energy. It becomes apparent in our desire to pray, when the soul turns not to the world but into its own innermost depths, to God. . . ."

He got up absentmindedly, wanting to do something with his hands. He began to scrape wax off the sleeve of his cassock. Benedict looked in, but said nothing and stayed in the refectory.

"I don't know, I don't know. . . ." Father Michael said softly. "Is it worth saying all this to you? How far will you go? If you simply went along to church and lit a few candles at festival times, I could have a talk and let you go in peace. But you want more. A fine way of carrying on, in fact. You got as far as Simeon the New Theologian."

"I don't know how far I'll get. I don't even know how I can go on living, where this road of mine is leading. I only know that I don't need anything else now."

He looked straight at me. "This road leads to monasticism. . . . The sooner you understand that, the better." He got up and began to sharpen his scythe. I sat on the window ledge watching him scythe the row of cornstalks nearest our tent, leaving a flattened pathway behind him and the shorn stalks of holly- hocks whose yellow lights fell on the grass and went out.

We endured another stormy night. Nobody wor- ried about us. When I said we'd hardly slept, Bene- dict simply asked if I'd thanked God for the experience.

"Yes, when it was over and we were safe."

"No, no, that's not what I meant. You must give thanks during the trial."

"Is that what you do?"

"I have to, in case it gets any worse."

That evening, thunder rumbled again in the distant hills. The air became overcharged and rain fell in big drops. After the service Father Michael came up to me and said, "You can transfer to one of the cells." He sounded quite indifferent, although he knew how pleased we felt. Not only did the tent leak, it also reminded us of how short our stay in Dzhvari really was. A cell was quite another matter. Once we were settled in, we felt we'd already become part of the community.

There were three wooden cabins on stilts in the forest beside the church. They were built on stilts so that the floods wouldn't wash their foundations away. The abbot's house with its perpendicular roof was hidden among the trees not far from the two- story winter house. Benedict's cell was on the cliff behind our tent. It had a flat roof bound around with tarred felt and between them in the forest was another small cabin we hadn't known about till now. The Hieromonk Hilarion had lived there for a short time. He'd left three months before, for medical treatment in town and, according to the abbot, wouldn't be coming back.

"Our life doesn't suit everyone. Hilarion needed people."

The abbot blessed our transfer to Hilarion's cell. The cabin seemed roomy after the tent. It was on stilts like Benedict's cell, with a flat roof and two windows—only a sheet of transparent plastic had been put in the frames instead of glass. An iron bed frame stood by the wall opposite the door. Ten half-burned thick candles and dripping wax were stuck to the rusty bedstead. Hilarion obviously used to read by candlelight, because there wasn't any glass for the lamps. In one corner, on a beam beneath an icon of the Mother of God, stood a lamp, long since extinguished. A stole hung alongside and a black cover with a Calvary scene sewn in red, like the cross worn by monks who have taken their final vows.

Benedict helped us move the second bed and table from the tent. They were broad and low, and a bee-hive box was attached to the table; two more went under the bed to keep it firm. We placed the table end-on to the door, with Mitya's bed along the wall under the window, and hung his cassock and clothing on a hanger behind the door. It was already dark when Mitya and I dragged our mattresses, blankets, and other things across to the cell, lighting our way with torches and making a narrow path through the damp grass of the hillside.

Rain was drumming on the roof, but we were

warm and dry. We closed the shutters and lit two candles. We sat on little wooden benches by the table, surprised that everything had worked out so well for us this summer.

"Could you stay here forever?" Mitya asked, trimming one of the wicks.

"Yes, but only with you."

"Well, I can stay, but you can't."

"I know, but I've never felt so much at home."

I'd longed for silence and solitude all my life, but had lived among strangers in hostels or communal apartments. So here we were, Mitya and I together, my next-of-kin and the only person I feel really good with, and all around us were the forests, the mountains, the rain.

In the morning I returned to our cell from the church, still feeling deeply moved by the service. The path led between the trees down the hillside above the monastery yard, past the belfry with its three green bells, past yet another scarcely noticeable little spring—out of which water flowed into a small basin, where frogs filled the yard with noise each night.

Gentle, red-tinged clouds shone above the dome of Dzhvari and sunlight pierced the pine branches above the roof. The cupola of the church was in front of me. It always reminded me of an umbrella, half-open above the round tower under it with its twelve window casements. For someone standing directly opposite the church, the two middle windows were in line, with the sun's rays striking through the tower. The windows were carved with archlike relief work, as if for a festival, preserving the ancient decorative style. The whole church was faced with layers of light sandstone and each layer had its own peculiar lettering; and the whole thing hung together in a living way, which I had come to love.

I loved Dzhvari, and these mountains, the gorges around my cell, the brothers, and Mitya so much that I wanted to thank God for everything in deep prayer. I had never spent days so filled with light, gratitude, and prayer.

One day Mitya, Archil, and I went to Tbilisi. The abbot sent Archil on a special trip—to learn how to bake the holy bread, the little round loaves that are used at Communion and are given out afterward. Up till now they had had to be ordered, to arrive in time for the liturgy each Sunday, and we decided it would be simpler to bake them ourselves. Mitya and I also had to pick up some of our things from a relative of Father David's. When we had all come to Dzhvari Father David had told us we had no hope of staying, but I had brought a few things just the same. Now, having gotten settled in our cell, we wanted to bring the rest.

We left in a fivesome—Muria and Brinka ran in front, keeping us company. We went up over the dry riverbeds, which had been in flood a few days before. The dogs ran about ten yards ahead, waiting for us, tongues hanging out, wondering why we were going so slowly when they could go so much faster.

"Ask them to meet us tomorrow in case we get lost," Mitya said to Archil.

"We must go with the Jesus Prayer and we won't get lost," Archil replied.

We halted at the familiar ridge, startling some gray

lizards. Snakes are often seen here too, crawling out to bask in the sun, and so I decided it was better not to stop. But Archil said there was no need to be afraid of snakes since we'd left the monastery with the abbot's blessing and had made the sign of the cross over the path ahead. Without his cassock, in a black woolen shirt (despite the heat) and black trousers, small, narrow-shouldered, and with a head that seemed too large, Archil would have looked defenseless if it hadn't been for the shining quality of his faith that made him seem taller and stronger. Everything went well because we were with him.

Once we reached the main road we caught a bus at once. The three of us settled in the backseat and the dogs ran behind for a long time—not to catch us up, but showing their keenness until they couldn't go any farther. The roar of traffic, exhaust fumes, the noisy crowds, and the heat of melting tar overwhelmed us: After Dzhvari the city seemed an unbearable place to have to live.

AUNT DODO MOVED a table onto the balcony, set out bottles of green mint water, beans, salad, and greens. I watched through the half-open door. I sat down with David's wife Tamara, talking about a topic that interested us both—him. She told me, not without secret pride, that he'd studied at the Geological Institute and was a leading specialist, a great socializer, quite a man about town. Suddenly, however, he had gone off to do repair work in a cathedral, undertaking all the menial work, and after that had worked as a laborer in the monastery. Tamara began to think that her life had been ruined by some abbot or other. She even began to dream about him—wanting to pull out his beard!

From Estonia, a slightly built woman, Tamara was blond, brown-eyed, with a friendly face framed by fashionable glasses with tinted lenses. She looked too young to be a mother of three, a bit affected, but with a hint of humor. She seemed just as proud of David's socializing as she was of the fact that he almost became a monk.

I knew that he had been preoccupied by the thought of death even as a young man. More often than not people try to pretend death doesn't exist and won't affect them, and so they don't ask questions, unaware that the shadow of eternal night falls on the withering flowers of day, although I find it difficult to imagine joys which we may delight in forever. David, however, belonged to the minority who need a higher definition of existence. His meeting with Abbot Michael wasn't a mere coincidence, as indeed nothing is.

It was here on neutral ground at Aunt Dodo's that Tamara had met the abbot for the first time. David had come from Dzhvari with him and she ran up "like an enraged lioness."

"I used to think in my stupidity that people became believers because of some lack or other. I saw that the Father walked uprightly, a strong, tall man. A wise one too . . . I saw that he knew everything about me and I was angry because he saw right through me. He spoke peacefully, softly. 'David will be a good monk,' he said, 'but will you be able to bring up good children on your own? Perhaps you acted on the spur of the moment? Take your time, think it over.'

"They could have given him the tonsure and that would have been the end of it. He would have been a good monk. I sat timidly, like a little mouse under a spell, not a lioness anymore. I still couldn't believe that this man had given me back my husband."

"Well, let's say I came back myself," Father David put in at this point, suggesting that we should go and sit down at the table. David's younger brother Georgi came in from work and we sat around the table together till late in the evening.

This little family opened a new world for us. Georgi, Aunt Dodo's son, was really David's own brother because of the unusual love that joined these relatives. Twenty-eight years before, David's mother was expecting her third child. Her gentle sister Dodo and her husband were childless and Dodo shed many tears, asking God for a son. When it was discovered that she wouldn't be able to have a child, David's parents decided to compensate for the cruelty of nature with kindness and gave their newly born son to Dodo, filling the chalice of family happiness for Auntie Dodo. When Georgi grew up and learned who his real parents were, he didn't feel upset—at any rate, not from the way he told me his story. Quite the contrary, he even felt he'd been unusually lucky. Each of his friends had only one mother, but he had two, both of whom loved him very much; one because he came to her as an unexpected, late gift, and the other because she tore him from herself in a sacrifice of love. David felt just as much at home with Aunt Dodo and his brother as with his own family, and so he had brought us here on our first day in Georgia.

We ourselves had become acquainted in the cathedral where he had begun doing menial work. He'd been ordained and served as priest there. We knew his name only through other friends. We had sat on a bench outside the cathedral and talked about God until Vespers began. After the service, Father David came out to us, still wearing his cassock and cross. "Let's go," he'd said. We didn't ask where to. So far in this short religious life God in his great mercy had sent only his best servants along our path. We'd got used to the fact that it was worth listening when we met a priest—everything would turn out well. So we came to Auntie Dodo's and visited her every day after that, until we left for Dzhvari. Georgia was a miracle for us, as well as a holiday, and it still is.

Auntie Dodo showed us what *ajapsandali* is. We ate this spicy dish and nonmeat pies, which are eaten when there is a church fast. After our journey through the heat we drank six cups of tea with cherry preserve. Auntie Dodo kept smiling and pouring more tea with a quiet joy. That day, as always, we all had a good time together. We talked about the faith, about spirituality. Father David told us that we could not even begin to imagine how physically difficult it is and what total self-giving it requires to be on duty for a whole week in church, baptizing, marrying, singing the liturgy—but what a peace descends afterward.

Georgi, a film critic and cinema expert, comparing his work with his brother's, asked me whether I thought secular art could help the cause of good. I said that the cinema does not deal with serious things as a general rule: It certainly isn't part of its function to control our behavior. If I were a man and felt there was hope of becoming a priest I would give up art without a moment's thought. Any human occupation is of doubtful value, but a priest unites heaven and earth, God and mankind in the mystery of the Eucharist. "So from man to priest is like from earth to heaven," I concluded, half-jokingly.

"From man to being a real Christian," Father David corrected me. "It's very difficult to become a real Christian. It means total commitment, spiritual battle, sacrifice."

EARLY NEXT MORNING, Mitya and I walked along the green tunnel of old elm trees. Our feet made no sound as we tramped over a damp covering of last year's leaves. Only the birds shrieked and chattered. The sun cast trembling pools of light through the foliage. We had left with Father David's blessing, and we made the sign of the cross over our road. We were enjoying our walk so much that we missed the turning, got lost, and finally found ourselves at the other end of the gorge from the monastery. But we trusted God to lead us out and he did.

COMING BACK TO Dzhvari felt like arriving home— we'd missed it terribly. Everything was in its usual place, only they'd made a sheaf of grass cuttings in the yard that smelled of dry hay.

The abbot himself had fried a panful of potatoes

for our homecoming. Benedict suggested that I should prepare something for the second table. It was high time for me to learn how to cook, so I asked the abbot once more to give me this as a penance. This time he agreed, though he seemed very unwilling to do so, and I couldn't understand why.

I went to ask the women restorers how to make beet soup. I found Nona on the first floor. She was the younger of the two, with slightly puffy features and dark eyes under swollen lids, a cigarette between her fingers. She was surprised that I didn't know how to do such a simple thing, but she explained it all clearly. So for the first time in my life I spent hours in the kitchen and I enjoyed myself. I boiled beets, carrots, onions, cut potatoes and cabbage, picked dill. In the end I had a huge pot of borshcht, which seemed quite edible. I took chopped tomatoes and spicy sauces from all the jars I could find and so we had salad for our first course and fried buckwheat porridge for our main dish with onions and vegetables.

During the meal Benedict smiled at me for the first time in the last few days. "You just didn't cook for us before, did you?"

I told him that I hadn't known how to cook, but I'd learn now. The abbot pulled at his lower lip and said that one can be proud of anything—even of not knowing how to cook—a strange affair—but the food I'd made was just ordinary monastery cuisine. I already knew that real monastery cuisine has no taste or smell, but I didn't take offense because it was clearly untrue. It was just that Father Michael was determined not to praise me in any way.

To reinforce this, after the meal he carried out his

threat and brought me a flannel overall and told me to put it on. It was old and worn out like Benedict's cassock, with white paint stains on the back. On the other hand it matched my shoes, which were worn out with rough walking, their soles half torn off.

"Excellent. That's just what we need." Father Michael smiled. "You look ugly now. What else can we think up for you? Look, these glasses make you look intelligent. Let's knock out one lens and paint the other white. Don't mend your shoes. Tie them with a piece of rope."

Well, nothing mattered anymore: If I had to wear an overall, that was all right, and so was a bit of rope.

Vespers was moved to 9 P.M. because of the influx of summer tourists. I managed to get something to eat and wash the dishes. Before the service began, Father Michael in his cloak and high cylindrical *kamilavka* came up to me and gave me a black head scarf. The moment he stopped with a chilly smile and outstretched hand I felt as though a hot wave had struck me. The significance of what was happening struck me in every fiber of my being: my skin, my nerves, my heart. The abbot was defending himself against me with this scarf, as he had been with the dirty overall and with his irony.

When we came out after Vespers a warm thick mist enveloped us with the sweet soothing smells of grass and forest. The starry sky shone above the black earth and the outlines of the trees and mountains. The shining Dragon with its triangular head hung over us, its tail twisting the vault of heaven in two. A star fell low, flashing like a burning firework thrown from above.

Archil lit the lamp in the refectory and we gathered around the flame. Guram, one of the restorers, came in too. He'd stood through the service for the first time, crossed himself when everyone else did, and was now continuing a conversation he'd begun previously with the abbot.

"Tell me how the bread and wine becomes the Body and Blood of Christ. I can't understand this at all, and so receiving it . . ."

Darkness was pouring in through the open door and the window grating and it filled the room. Benedict, Archil, and Mitya sat at the unlit end of the table, while I sat on a couch in the corner. Guram was leaning against the doorpost. Only Father Michael was sitting beside the lamp, leaning his hands on the table, his eyes cast down. The lamp threw shadows across the hollows of his eyes. Moths fluttered against the funnel of the lamp and their shadows flickered about the ceiling in circles.

"This is a mystery, which therefore is not to be understood with the intellect," the abbot replied, making an effort to overcome the silence. Guram waited and no one else spoke. "Remember, in Luke's Gospel, the Virgin Mary asked the Archangel, 'How will this be?' How should she give birth to the Son of God? And the angel replied, 'The Holy Spirit will come upon you and the power of the Almighty will overshadow you.' That's all we may say. The Holy Spirit comes down to create the flesh of Christ in Mary's womb, and so during the liturgy he changes the bread and wine in the cup into the Body and Blood of Christ. How? This is where the secret lies."

His voice was hushed, and hearing him speak, I

felt the mystery being poured out on us that night with its mixture of darkness and light, and in us ourselves, in our ability to see, to think, to breathe, to suffer, to long for love, to long not to be burdened by any earthly possession.

The secret of the creation of the world, of the birth of the first and every subsequent human being, is in the bursting of shoots from a poppy seed and the ripening of an ear of corn. Superficially it seems we can explain the world because we can follow the mystery, name it. We can catch birds in a net, but never the mystery of life.

Mankind, like Pilate the Procurator of Judea, constantly asks: "What is truth?" And, like Pilate, we shrug our shoulders and turn away from the living Truth who stands before us, condemned by us to be crucified. But Christ answered this question at the Last Supper; he answered it as no one before him had the right to do: "I am the Way, the Truth, and the Life." This is the heart of the mystery from which the world is woven.

Father Michael had said that in order to believe in God and receive this truth you must offer your entire being—your heart, will, understanding, mode of life. What can understanding do by itself? It can only penetrate our ignorance, clear away anything which hinders our faith: knowledge which is partial and self-satisfied hinders our faith, but knowledge which has embraced our whole being brings us back to it.

I'd never seen such a look on the abbot's face, except perhaps when he came out of the royal doors. He looked up and in his eyes I saw a quiet flame burning from the very depths of his spirit.

We ask how . . . what . . . but any analytical knowledge, even theology, is only a dead formula of the Living Truth, a means to an end—which is God himself, the Alpha and Omega, the beginning and end. Contemplation of him, communion with him, pleasing him, joining our lives to his Eternal Being is our aim from first to last.

Human life is not independent of other forms of being. We are only creatures, participants in life itself. God is Eternal Life, the Source of Life that nurtures us, the Tree of Life growing in the midst of Paradise. We are simply small branches on that tree, and if a branch is cut off, it withers. Without God we become severed branches, as Adam did once he had stopped eating the fruit of the Tree of Life. We are dying a slow death. But we cannot be grafted back onto the trunk and receive its quickening sap by reason alone, only in our entirety, body, soul, and spirit. So it is the sacraments that give us an unseen mercy in simple, visible forms. "I am the Vine, you are the branches . . ." is not merely a symbol; we pray and take Communion in order to receive this real strength.

Theological awareness becomes a means of grace and of creative life only in the Church and its worship. There is no Christianity without the Church and its sacraments. When the Holy Spirit comes down on you and the power of the Almighty overshadows you, you will learn everything you need to know. So you will experience life in God for yourself, and not need other people's reports.

LATER, IN MY cell, when Mitya had already gone to sleep, I sat at the table with a candle and read through the chapter in John's Gospel where Christ speaks of himself as the eternal Bread of Life.

He had just fed five thousand people with five loaves. The people searched for him, wanting to make him king. "You seek me not because you have seen miracles but because you ate bread and were filled. Do not seek food which perishes, but food which lasts until Eternal Life which the Son of Man will give." But they demanded new signs, remembering the manna that fell from heaven in the desert at the time of Moses—they expected bread and a miracle. Jesus said, "Truly I say to you, it was not Moses who gave you bread from heaven, but my Father gives the True Bread from heaven. The Bread of heaven is he who comes down from heaven and gives life to the world." They answered, "Lord, give us this bread always." Jesus answered, "I am the Bread of Life; he who comes to me will not hunger and he who believes in me will never thirst."

Farther on he utters words that they could not understand. "Truly, I say to you, whoever believes in me has eternal life. I am the Bread of Life. Your fathers ate manna in the desert and they died; the bread which comes from heaven is such that you may eat of it and not die. I am the living bread, which came down from heaven; if anyone eats of this bread, he will live forever; and the bread which I shall give is my flesh, which I shall give for the life of the world." The Jews then disputed among themselves, saying: "How can he give us his flesh to eat?" So Jesus said to them: "Truly, truly, I say ...

unless you eat of the flesh of the Son of man and drink his blood, then you will not have life in you. He who eats my flesh and drinks my blood has eternal life, and I will raise him up at the last day. For my flesh is food indeed, and my blood is drink indeed. He who eats my flesh and drinks my blood abides in me, and I in him. As the living Father sent me, and I live because of the Father, so he who eats me will live because of me. This is the bread which came down from heaven."

Many of his disciples said, "What strange words! Who can hear this?" and went away. Then Jesus said to the Twelve, "Do you want to leave me too?" Simon Peter said, "Lord, to whom can we go? You have the words of eternal life. But we believe that you are the Christ, the Son of the Living God."

I'd read these words so many times, but I hadn't taken them literally. Now I understood completely: These words had been fulfilled in the Last Supper. "And when they had eaten, Jesus took bread, and having blessed it, broke it and gave it to them, saying, This is my body. He took the cup and gave thanks and gave it to them and said, Drink of this, all of you. This is my blood of the New Covenant, poured out for many for the remission of sins."

The priest says this during the Eucharistic Canon as part of the liturgy, after the Thanksgiving and the Secret Prayers. "Take, eat, this is my Body which is broken for you for the remission of sins. Drink of it, all of you. This is my Blood of the New Testament, poured out for you and for many for the remission of sins."

When the deacon has crossed his hands he raises

the Holy Gifts above the altar as an offering of love
and thankfulness to God. In the Secret Prayers, the
priest asks for the Holy Spirit to be sent down upon
them. The same words are pronounced and we receive the same gifts from the Holy Chalice as the
disciples received from Christ's hands. So it is not the
priest, but the Person who was present at the Eucharist two thousand years ago who hallows and blesses
the Holy Gifts.

The Holy Spirit comes down and the Last Supper
is reenacted as each person receives the Body and
Blood of the Lord's New Testament. This moment
is the meeting point of Time and Eternity, the central
focus of all being, uniting humankind with God: We
ascend with penitence and love to God who comes
down to us with forgiveness and loving kindness.

I WAS STILL reading when Archil called from outside the door. He said he'd seen a light in the window. One of the women restorers was not feeling
well and the other had asked me to come.

Archil didn't know their names. I recalled a story
from a life of a *staretz* who'd died not long before. A
monk came to him for advice: How should he answer a woman who offered to help him? "What did
you say?" asked the *staretz*. "I said, the Lord save
you." "And what did she say?" "She went away but
she came back again." "Has she been doing this for
long?" "Yes, about three years." "Is she young or
old?" "I don't know: I didn't look at her."

Eli stood in the darkness beside the veranda railing
wrapped up in a shawl. They had had guests that

evening, and Nona had drunk a little wine. Then she fell down suddenly, went into a seizure, and was unconscious for about two hours. Eli didn't know what was wrong. She was frightened Nona might die.

Nona was tossing around on a mattress that lay on the floor, groaning through gritted teeth. This was terrible! Eli was clearly expecting me to help and I was scared stiff of the dark force that was breaking Nona in two.

A light was still burning in the refectory as I went back down to find Archil. The medicine cupboard had a thermometer and aspirins. I asked Archil if the abbot was asleep yet. The abbot was still awake and came at once. He crouched down beside Nona, talking to Eli in Georgian for a couple of minutes.

"We could wake the men and send them for a car," said Eli.

"No need. We just have to wait," the abbot said, calmly. "This will pass."

"What's wrong with her?" Eli asked timidly.

"I don't know, but no evil can happen here." He said no more, but we both felt calmer at once.

The abbot and I went back to our cells. We came to the place where the paths divided, stopping at the pool for a moment.

A scattering of stars still twinkled above us. A thick mist dripped through the treetops. The frogs were croaking and the shining yellow sickle of the moon swam in the still water. I couldn't see the abbot's face, only his cap stood up black against the starry background. He was pulling at a small leaf and I smelled the sweet smell of birches.

"This is a punishment," he said quietly. "One must accept it and endure it."

"Punishment for what?"

"Did she not drink wine?"

"Only a little . . ."

"It doesn't matter whether someone has stolen a lot or a little. We may sin in our thoughts—that counts too."

He scrabbled among the pebbles beside the pool, threw one in, shattering the moon's reflection. I felt that was a bit much. Christ himself changed water to wine. Or did Father Michael mean something else?

I WENT BACK to Eli. Nona had fallen silent, and we stood by the railings looking at the sky and the monastery yard. Moonbeams fell on the church dome. The black pine trees swayed silently, hiding, then revealing, the stars.

"Do you like Father Michael?" I asked.

Eli was silent for a moment. "Very much," she said. "After all, you know, we lived here all last summer. They've changed quite a lot since then. Benedict has become more spiritual, Father Michael less shut in. Last year they wouldn't talk to us at all."

"Do you ever go to church?"

"No. . . ."

"Don't you believe in God?"

"Yes, but I'm fifty-two. It's difficult to change the way you think."

"Why? We're not too late for anything. Do you remember the parable about the workers at the eleventh hour? The owner of the vineyard gave them all the same amount of pay—those who'd worked from dawn, as well as the ones who came at dusk."

"I've never understood that." Eli smiled. "Do you think it's fair?"

"It's more than mere justice. It's mercy. Justice rewards measure for measure. As the Old Testament says: 'an eye for an eye, a tooth for a tooth.' But our evil is completely swallowed up in the mercy of God, like a grain of sand in the ocean."

"What about good?"

"Yes, good as well. We can't earn anything, you see. It doesn't matter whether we begin in the morning or toward night. We don't get anything as a reward, but freely, as a gift . . . Like the Holy Gifts, like life itself."

"But haven't you just begun yourself?"

"No, it's not like that at all. I used to feel sad that I'd begun so late. I regretted the last forty years. Now I know that I found faith because of them. I had to feel thirsty, you see, for all that time, before I could begin to look for satisfaction."

"Do you think you won't ever lose your faith now?"

"I'd rather lose my life. What would I do without faith—without God?"

MITYA AND I began to see each other less and less often, only at the services or in the evenings. I was busy in the refectory nearly all day, peeling, cutting, frying, cooking, and then I had to wash the dishes at the spring. Archil was very glad that I was doing his work. He'd do anything, he said, except women's work. I laughed at this, and in his turn he gave me his ready sympathy.

To tell the truth—why not?—we had less and less food every day. In the cellar beside Prince Orbeliani's cell was a bag of potatoes, and on the ground were piles of beets and onions, which I had to grope around to get. In the cupboard was tea, vermicelli, flour, and preserves. Sometimes the restorers would bring us jars of Bulgarian salad or peppers, or a blue bowl with yellow peaches, or two or three fresh round loaves. They got a delivery once a week.

Mitya, however, spent all day with the brothers. At the services he would say by heart "Heavenly King," "Thrice Holy" right up to "Our Father" and then the Fifty-first Psalm, all in Khutsuri. He lit the censer and handed it over. He liked to be in the sanctuary. It was quite small, separated from us by a linen icon-screen. The abbot moved in total silence there, while we could hear every whisper and rustle Mitya made. If Mitya took too long in the sanctuary Benedict laughed a bit jealously and said, without meaning to, "Don't make such a noise, Dmitri!" Once, after that, the abbot left us in the middle of the church and told us a parable about a king who came to a certain hermit. They got talking and the king stayed overnight in the mountains. However, in the morning he didn't find anyone in the cell: The hermit had left him forever. That's why you've got to be wary of privileges and try to avoid them. Mitya didn't enter the sanctuary after that.

Sometimes they had choral singing practice around the harmonium. Mitya would play and the brothers sang, while the abbot leaned on the organ, smiling.

Benedict leaned against the wall, his hands behind his back, looking as though he couldn't care less. Archil harmonized with Benedict, keeping his eyes fixed on him as he sang: He looked strained and rather frightened. The abbot insisted that Mitya should indicate if anyone sang a false note. Sometimes it would be Benedict, sometimes Archil, because they couldn't read music, not having ever sung before coming to the monastery. But Benedict was bolder than Archil. They'd been trying to master "The Cherubim Hymn" for the liturgy, but no one could get it right.

Mitya and I always shared our impressions of the day, and I learned details of monastic life that I wasn't allowed to see myself, for example the abbot often sat at the table before the others and seemed to be taking a long time over his meal. Mitya often sat beside him: he noticed that Father Michael poured half a ladle of soup into his own plate, placing a spoonful of the second course in with the soup, drinking it with tea. This was no food for a grown man, but as he came out he would say, "Well, there you are: I came first, left last, and I've stuffed myself as usual. That's what Climacus says about an unsatisfied belly. It expands from excess but complains of hunger all the time."

So I learned about these little quirks of monastic life. In the past they were allowed to station a monk at the gate for a whole year and he had to bow to everyone passing by and say, "Forgive me, I'm a thief and robber." But to say of yourself that you're a glutton and lazybones, or that you hadn't washed for three months—this is medicine against pride as well. What is a monk's role in fact? To pray, to fight evil thoughts and pride. As long as you're filled with the awareness of your own worth, like a Pharisee you remember all your virtues, your talent, your wit, beauty—and the way to God is closed to you; there is no place for the Divine at the level of pitiful human ideas of self-worth.

But when you learn to feel with your whole inner being that you can do nothing without God, that you cannot add a single cubit to your height, that you cannot save yourself from a single sin, then you call from the depths of your being, and God will come and fill your every imperfection with his abundance because of his love.

And here's another of the abbot's secrets that Mitya discovered unexpectedly. "Father Michael is always seated in the sanctuary when I go there with incense. Once I happened to drop my pencil. I bent down to pick it up and through a chink in the royal doors I could see the heels and thick soles of his shoes. An hour later I dropped the pencil again, and again I could see him through the chink. He hadn't moved: He'd been on his knees for the whole service."

Once Mitya was in the abbot's cell. It seemed a bit bigger than ours, with one window looking out onto the green slope; there was a table under the window and the bed was a broad plank perched on beehive boxes. Another beehive box served as a bookshelf, and a funeral veil was hanging in a cupboard—a constant reminder of mortality. In one corner was a beautifully painted icon of the Mother of God lit by a red lamp. There could be nothing simpler or more severe. "This cell is dearer than anything else in the whole world to me," said the abbot. "All I need to do is build a veranda around it and I'll be fenced off completely. Then they can tell the visitors the abbot's asleep."

Mitya sat on the edge of a hard bunk. Father Michael was on a low bench beside the wall. Being a tall man, he couldn't help looking at you from top to toe when he was speaking to you and so he tried to stoop if he was standing, or to sit back on his heels, leaning against the wall.

He spoke about the monastic life being a distinctive calling. "If a man has the taste for it, it means that God is calling him. Many rise in the hierarchy of the clergy, but only a few become monks. 'Sit in your cell and it will teach you everything,' the saints used to say. You must learn to love solitude, silence, the depths of prayer—after all, we're talking about the spirit here, not what passes for such. . . ." When they left the cell, Father Michael looked back at his cabin on stilts. "If I had the good health of monks long ago and could bear heat, and live on grass, I would go far, far away into the mountains and live alone."

Mitya's eyes shone when he talked about Father Michael. "He says if anyone discovers you've got a certain good quality it becomes worthless in God's sight because you've already been rewarded on earth. If you've done something good and talked about it, you've done it in vain."

We still recall how ingloriously Mitya's job as watchman ended. Even on the second day Archil had to wake us up: Our alarm was forty minutes slow. "If something good has happened, it's better to attribute it to someone else," the abbot said. "But if it's something bad you must take the blame yourself."

"How can I blame myself if my clock's gone slow?" Mitya laughed.

"Well, perhaps you forgot to wind it up."

The next morning the clock was slow again and Mitya took it off in triumph to show the abbot.

"Are you trying to prove you're right?" Father Michael shook his head. "Well, you're not right for that very reason." So Archil became watchman once more. He woke up without a clock.

The abbot told of an experience he had had when he was a novice, which showed how dangerous it is to blame someone else. His cell-brother had cut out excellent woolen insoles. His own shoes let in water and he often used to borrow Father Michael's. Once when Father Michael put on the shoes he noticed that the insole was much smaller than it should be. "What have you been up to? Have you changed our insoles? No, indeed I haven't," the cell-brother said. "What do you mean, you didn't change them? Look for yourself. The insole's much smaller now. Or perhaps you cut the sole to your own measurement?" "I haven't cut anything." Father Michael was very upset. They'd lived together for a whole year and to start cheating about such a trivial matter . . . He threw away his insoles and cut new ones. The rains came and the shoes got soaked. He put his soles on a radiator to dry—and noticed that these had gotten smaller as well. Then he realized that it was because they'd shrunk—and he had quarreled with his brother because of them.

"Who's to blame," he asked with a smile. "The soles?"

"Yes," agreed Mitya cheerfully.

"No," said the abbot, "in a mystical sense we're all guilty toward one another, even when we don't think so. If we look more deeply into ourselves, we'll find the blame all right, and so the Church has Forgiveness Sunday at the beginning of Lent, when everyone asks each other's pardon. We have repentance, confession that washes away our guilt, whereas in the world this guilt is allowed to grow, like electricity in the clouds, and is discharged at a communal level by a quarrel, or at a global level by war."

Father Michael had growing authority over Mitya's soul and I sometimes felt envious. Perhaps the abbot envied me a little on account of my son, because we were together and each of them was alone. The word *monk* comes from the Greek *monos*—alone.

Once when I was at the spring, Mitya called me for the start of the service, and came to meet me looking very upset.

"Why aren't you coming? You must watch the time or I'll have to call you and Father Michael will look out from the church and tease—'Watch out now, there's a young novice in a cap and cassock standing in the monastery yard shouting Mom. . . .'"

I was used to thinking of my son as a boy, but now I saw he'd become a young man, who would soon turn sixteen. In his pointed cap he looked taller and more solemn. His tender, clean features had taken on a new definition. His brows had darkened. When he and Archil gathered hay in the meadow behind the church, or led our horse out, he could have passed for a young monk to a casual observer.

The abbot said something half-jokingly to me. "It's time for your son to go his own way. Leave him with us, and you go to the convent. There's one not far from Mtskhety."

"But you let us both live here. You can't take your present back—and my son still needs me."

"A son always needs his mother, but sooner or later he has to leave."

"Well, better let it be later. And, do you know, a certain writer said to me that he'd been married several times, but the woman who was spiritually closest to him was his mother."

"Of course a mother can be closer to her son than a wife, but she ought not be closer than God, and it's the same for the son vis-à-vis his mother. 'He who loves his father or mother more than me is not worthy of me; and whoever loves his son and daughter more than me is not worthy of me.' It seems to me that you love Mitya more than you love God."

"It's just I don't make any distinction between these two kinds of love. . . ."

"That's what I mean. It's time you did."

I didn't agree, but this conversation made me very sad.

SOMETHING HAD HAPPENED to Benedict. We didn't see him drunk anymore, but lately we'd hardly seen him at all, only at services and in the refectory. If we met on the path he stepped aside and let me pass without saying anything. Or he looked through me with cold eyes. I wondered if things were tense between the abbot and him as well.

Once, Mitya went into Benedict's cell. Benedict had promised to show him how to carve crosses. The deacon was carving the Virgin Mary out of wood for the patriarch's name day. They sat and talked for a bit but Benedict wasn't concentrating and said, "Forgive me, Dmitri, just now I'm in a state of grace with the Most Holy Mother of God and you're putting me off." Mitya got up to go, but Benedict said, "Suppose she got upset and left me because I'm not keeping my promise."

He was carving the crosses from juniper, apple, lime, and pear. If you boil a flat piece of pear wood in cooking oil it becomes a rich dark brown. I had seen pear wood pectoral crosses that looked very old, and soon after our arrival Benedict promised to carve Mitya and me a cross each. He showed us quite big crosses too, decorated only with round Georgian letters, and sometimes he would set a light wood crucifix in a darker wood.

"What do you do with them once they're ready?" I asked.

"I get money for them. People give what they want."

"Roughly how much?"

"Anything—thirty rubles, even five hundred sometimes."

I said quickly that he shouldn't make one for us. Thirty rubles wouldn't be so bad, but there was no way we could pay five hundred. I didn't want to make Benedict feel he had to give me such an expensive present.

Anyhow, I think that if you have to buy a cross that costs the earth it's not holy. We'd already been given expensive presents, everything we needed: a Bible, a New Testament, a prayer book, and a bronze crucifix. Three icons followed: the Savior, the Mother of God, and St. Nicholas. We got everything when we needed it; we began praying and we were given a prayer book. We began to understand the liturgy, the Church's yearly festivals, and we were given a lectionary. God will send me a pectoral cross if ever I have a right to wear one.

All the same, a couple of days later Benedict brought a vise, sawn pieces of wood, and several fretsaws. He fixed the vise to the beehive box beside our cells and carved a small cross in a few minutes, but his face was strained and switched off. Mitya and I tried too, but my fretsaw cut askew. "This isn't a woman's work," said Benedict disapprovingly. That's what they've always said about everything I've done—from chess in my teens to theology now. "You're too curious," the deacon went on in the same cold voice. "You want to find out about everything . . . that's not helpful if you want to lead a spiritual life. It was curiosity that made Eve eat the forbidden fruit."

I suppose there was something in what he said. But I think something else had upset him too.

THE ABBOT FULFILLED my previous wish and showed me how to make a prayer rope.

Mitya didn't want to learn: You have to complete seventeen operations in order to tie one little knot, winding the thread around your fingers, drawing it into cross-shaped loops, passing one loop under the other—I didn't think I'd ever remember how to do it.

"I get lost myself, even now," Father Michael admitted, trimming the thread on my hand with scissors. "It'll take me another week to explain it all over again . . . and in a month's time you'll be making prayer ropes for us. Look, Dmitri, your mom's more capable than you, though she doesn't think so."

I went wrong and had to begin all over again, and so I suggested I should note down my "technology" so as not to be working in front of the abbot. Mitya and I had a good laugh. "Well, for example, how would you describe this?" Mitya asked cheerfully.

"I won't write the design, just the steps. You bend the thread in two, tie a knot, and twist it across your forefinger and middle finger." I told him what I was doing, I wrote down my "technology" all the same, had a look at it later, and next day I made a prayer rope, adding a little cross and tassel from the same white silk braid (we couldn't find any black braid in the monastery). The prayer rope seemed perfect: The knots were even and set out regularly.

I really liked this task. Complicated work can take us away from God, whereas simple work is all right, as the *startsy* would say.

Mitya ran to fetch Father Michael. "She's already made three knots and wants to boast about it. . . ."

The abbot did not betray any feeling when he saw the prayer rope. "Everything has to be done without passion, not to be praised, but for the glory of God. You had to ask me three times to teach you. That's not right. One may express one's desire once, then you must leave everything to God's will. You have to make a prayer rope peacefully, with the Jesus Prayer, then it's holy right from the start, whereas you've woven your passion and pride into this prayer rope."

Just the same, he blessed the prayer rope and I sent it to Father David.

WE SAT IN the shade under the awning and looked at an old photograph album. Sixteen years ago there were two *startsy* in Dzhvari who'd come from Mount Athos—Ioann and Georgi—and they've left their traces; there's something tangible even today. They lived in the two-storied house. The dismantled hives come from their apiary. The apple trees that have gone wild are from their orchard. These old monks couldn't run the place by themselves, but people who came to pray helped them pick grapes and bake bread.

"How do we gauge the state of this or that national church?" asked Father Michael, looking at a faded photograph. "It's not the magnificence of its arch-priestly services, nor the number of parishioners who come at festivals with their candles; it's defined by the monasteries. Again, not the monastery's wealth, or the number of monks, but by what these monks are like, the level of their spiritual life."

Another old photograph showed a tall, white-bearded *staretz* wearing a little cap and round glasses. This was Father Georgi. He was very thin, in a short cassock, a knitted waistcoat like Father Michael's, and worn shoes. He was squinting in the spring sunshine and his glasses sat askew across his nose. Round about, trying to squeeze in beside him, was a bunch of poor folk who were obviously not used to having their photograph taken. The men were wearing boots and military trousers, the women woven scarves pulled low over their foreheads. Their abandoned rakes were lying in front of them.

"However much you looked at his face or heard his voice . . . we could live in his house, pray in his church, but we could learn nothing of his secret life. Hieromonk Gabriel came to us too," the abbot went on. "He'd been a novice in Dzhvari at the end when Ioann had died and Georgi was left alone. Gabriel used to say, 'There is a monastery only where there is love. Let there be two monks and Christian love between them, and you've got your monastery.' Then people won't come in vain. Every tree gives its fruit in due season. Our only concern should be to keep the commandments and pray, and as for giving us food: God will look after that himself. But do we really live like that?"

"Did he talk about Father Georgi?" I asked.

"Yes, he did. He said he was the only saint he'd ever met. He told us about a miracle. . . . Father Georgi wouldn't allow it to be mentioned in his lifetime, but now we can. Several years before he died, his side ached so much that he couldn't get up. Once he was lying praying in his cell when the Mother of God appeared to him with two of the Apostles and he thought, 'This is terrible. The Mother of God is here, and I can't even get up.' She smiled and placed her hand on the part that hurt. It was like lightning burning. He had never felt such pain, but the next instant the pain went and never came back."

In the next photograph, both the *startsy* were sitting on the veranda, drinking tea, just like us, with bread and honey. "He belonged to another world even in his lifetime and he was led not by his own will but by the Holy Spirit, and so everything was wonderful: his words, his deeds. It happened that Father Gabriel was in Tbilisi on monastery business and suddenly, he told us, he seemed to hear a voice. 'Go back to Dzhvari as quickly as possible.' He thought, 'How can I go back when they've sent me here to buy things, and I've not managed to get anything yet?' Nothing worked out, and wherever he looked, he just kept on hearing, 'Go back to the monastery at once.' So he went as quickly as he could, not even taking the things he had managed to buy. In he came and Father Georgi was lying on his bed holding his prayer rope, looking up at the sky through the open window. 'Why have I come?' thought Gabriel. 'What shall I tell him?' But Father Georgi said, 'Thank the Lord that you've come. That means the Mother of God has heard my prayers. I'll go tomorrow . . .' 'Where's he going, when he's so ill,' Gabriel wondered. 'What does he want to go to town for?' 'I'm not going to Tbilisi,' Father Georgi said. 'I'm leaving you bodily, but my spirit will stay with you forever.' Father Gabriel didn't want to believe this. Father Georgi said, 'Get ready today and tomorrow you'll celebrate the liturgy and give me Communion.' He took Communion in the morning, taking the bread with warm wine. As it happened it was the Feast of the Beheading of John the Baptist, and on that very day Father Georgi had been received into the higher, more ascetic form of monastic life. Gabriel asked, 'Should I get anything ready?' 'No,' he said, 'I don't need anything else. Go and rest.' But Gabriel disobeyed, not wanting to fall asleep in case Father Georgi needed anything. Father Georgi lay still, looking upward and praying with his prayer rope. Suddenly Gabriel fell into an unusually deep sleep, even though he was still sitting up. He didn't know how long he'd slept—perhaps only five minutes. He woke up, and Father Georgi was lying holding his prayer rope in the same way as before, but his soul had already departed. . . . No one had come to the monastery for a long time, but it so happened that two Russians arrived. They sang his requiem and dug his grave beside Father Ioann, under the pine trees near the sanctuary of the main church."

Two granite grave stones lie there now, and under them rest the ashes of the last two Georgian monks who had been to Mount Athos. The monastery is still nourished by their spirit. They taught the monks the strict, poor life-style of a hermit, hallowed on Mount Athos by centuries of tradition.

"The *startsy* often know the time of their own death," said the abbot. "Sometimes they're honored with visitations from on high or are transfigured in the spirit at the moment of their death. That's why Father Georgi didn't want Gabriel to see his last moments—that's what I think."

Father Michael liked to talk about St. Macarius the Egyptian who struggled with demons all his life without ever yielding. So he died with one foot already across the threshold of Paradise. Then the demons clapped their hands and shouted, 'Glory to you, great Macarius. You have conquered us.' He turned around and said, 'Not yet,' and stepped across. The struggle for a human soul goes on every hour, every moment, and it can all be lost right at the last moment.

"So you've come and felt that this is a special sort of place, that the very air's suffused with grace. In fact, many people don't receive anything. When I was a novice, I knew an abbot who liked to say that in the last days there will be people who will be permeated with wood resin, which is impervious to grace, so whether it's resin, spirits, false earthly wisdom, or simply lies, it's all the same because 'the devil is a liar and the father of lies' and a murderer. This new falsification of existence is indeed death before death. But our *startsy* help us even yet with their grace-giving prayer."

"Is that why you said that nothing evil can happen here?"

"I think so."

Had Father Michael been praying at the graves of the two *startsy* when Nona had felt unwell? She fell asleep soon afterward, slept all night, and got up next morning feeling well again. Eli and she often came to Vespers after that, standing at the open door, without actually coming into church, both wearing trousers and uncovered heads—but standing there for the whole service.

"Two years ago Father Gabriel came here. The bees had just swarmed and he said, 'Wait a minute, I'll help.' 'What could you do? Have you never seen a swarm of bees? It's a black whirlwind, and then buzzzzzzz. . . . They're off, and there's no way anyone can catch them and they never come back.' Father Gabriel went off to the graves and prayed. We looked and—buzzzz! They were back in their hives."

"Did Father Gabriel keep anything of the spirit of the *startsy*?—Is he a good monk."

"No one has the right to judge whether we're good or bad monks. Man looks on the outward appearance but God knows the heart. Gabriel said, 'If you and I speak about God and there's no love between us, all our words are empty.' I think that if they had beaten Gabriel, he would still have shone with love."

FATHER MICHAEL HAD spent ten days on Athos with a Georgian church delegation. He brought his flat *kamilavka* from there, his Greek-style cassock—which is shaped like a cross when you unfold it—a woolen prayer rope with a big cross tassel that can be used to sprinkle holy water. He brought back the custom of not wearing a cross even during services, whereas he wore a *paraman* quite openly. Consequently, Athos-style, he didn't allow his hand to be kissed during a blessing, and more often than not gave his blessing without making the sign of the cross, but simply saying, "God bless." But these are all external gestures, and his prayer life was hidden from us as deeply as the spiritual life of the *startsy*.

Some time in the future, when Dzhvari has grown and strengthened, Father Michael would like to go to Athos, to the Iverian monastery. "It's great there," he said thoughtfully, and his face took on a faraway look, as though he were already there in his thoughts.

Somehow the monks from the Iverian monastery

managed to come to Georgia as well. The patriarch gave Father David the job of meeting them, and he, of course, took them to Dzhvari.

Several photographs existed as souvenirs of their visit. We saw them standing at the doorway under the carved cross; they stood out clearly because of their cylindrical headdresses. Two were older, thickset and strongly built, alike in the massive cast of their faces and their bushy beards. The third was still very young, with thin-framed glasses and a slender face. In front, crouching down, were David and his brother Georgi. In the second photograph Father Michael and his Athos monks were sitting at the table in our refectory, only the table was liberally spread with snacks and bottles of wine. Tall candles stood burning in the candlesticks, making them look like flowers. Father Michael's gaze seemed absorbed and remote, as it had done when he talked to us about Athos.

Mitya asked for a copy as a keepsake. "Take the lot," Father Michael waved his hands. We were glad, and chose several: one of them sitting at the table; two group ones with the Athos monks; another with Father Hilarion (whom we never saw), the abbot, Benedict, and Archil (whom we were so glad we knew) with his beatific smile, and three landscapes—a close-up of Dzhvari and two others.

These were the best days of my life and when I left I clutched these photographs like straws; I needed anything I could get as proof that those days in Dzhvari had really happened, although they were long since over.

"We'll send you something too as a memento," Mitya promised.

"A memento for monks?" Father Michael laughed, looking at me. "We'll try to forget you the day after you leave."

MY JOY IN Dzhvari was no longer as bright as it had been in the beginning. It had been clouded by alarm and foreboding that you can't put things off forever. Sometimes I went into the big church to look at the wall paintings and fix them firmly in my mind. I climbed up to the lower platform of the scaffolding, where an angel with red wings barred the entrance to Paradise. At this point the frescoes were in a poor state. The colors had faded, but a deep blue river still flowed and unseen leaves shaded its banks. A little farther, the righteous Noah who had survived the Flood stood beneath the rainbow of the Covenant, surrounded by birds and animals.

The frescoes showed how we ascend to God in love and faith and how God comes down to us. What Adam lost through lack of faith, God's chosen ones give back by their unquestioning faith. And so Abraham received the call to go to the Promised Land, and went, not knowing where he was going, and he was willing to sacrifice his only son. As Mount Sinai was wreathed in smoke, the Lord descended amid thunder and lightning to give Moses the commandments for Isaac's descendants. King David danced before the Ark of the Lord: his triumphant hymn of praise raised him above the earth in a fiery whirlwind of love and his red garments flew about him.

As I stepped across the gap at the ends of the boards I came upon the sanctuary where Guram and his assistant Shalva were removing tracing cloths from the huge figures of the prophets. The long cloth was fixed to the wall with a plaster mold. The figures were outlined with colored ink, and the ones that had been muddied and stained took on a plasticity, a graphic clarity.

The nine prophets, mighty pillars of the Old Testament faith, supported the arch of the apse above the altar. Isaiah, Jeremiah, and Ezekiel were depicted with their various revelations of God—the wrathful Judge and the all-forgiving, merciful Father, devouring Fire and limitless Love: God, hidden in darkness and in light inaccessible. All their revelations were prototypes of the greatest mystery—the Incarnation, the mystery of Jesus Christ, the Son of God.

The whole earthly life of the Savior was shown on the upper part of the north wall, where the church narrowed and a shallow niche was carved by the two windows. These narrow niches heightened the effect of the vertical composition of the frescoes. I was impressed by three of them.

One showed Christ washing the disciples' feet. The men had just been arguing about who was greatest in the kingdom of God. Here they were sitting one above the other around the sides of the oval niche, each on his own wooden bench. And Christ, their Lord and Teacher, so soon to die, leaves them a picture of true love, humbling himself and serving them. He stands, a towel wrapped round him, a jug in his hand—bending over Peter, a tiny figure in the bottom right corner of the fresco.

This is how the artist saw the mystery of God's descent to man.

The frescoes were placed from the birth in the cradle at the bottom, which was the beginning of the way of the cross, to the ascent to Calvary and the Crucifixion shown at the top, because his incarnation was also the self-limitation of the eternal, almighty, and limitless One—in the temporal, the weak, and the fleshly. As we follow the frescoes we see how his voluntary kenosis became ever deeper, and his cross became heavier and heavier: the suffering of the Infinite in the finite—which led to his sacrificial death, his utmost self-giving and final suffering.

"The Last Supper," as a composition, repeated the same vertical oval: the disciples sitting around the table, the figure of Christ, still wrapped in a towel, seated at the head, now at the top of the oval. The Savior completes the apostolic group, closing its circle, but is already noticeably at a remove and raised above them. At this ritual table he breaks and blesses the bread in an ancient priestly action, but he adds the words of the New Covenant to the traditional words of thanksgiving: "Take, eat, this is my Body broken for you. Do this in remembrance of me." The ancient ritual of the sacred table becomes transformed into the liturgy; the Last Supper, hallowed by his presence, becomes the first Eucharist.

"Gethsemane" was the third wonderful fresco of the Passion cycle. The disciples are closely grouped together, having fallen asleep, heavy with grief, leaning against each other. Above them Christ kneels alone in the garden—a small figure, no bigger than the disciples, wrapped in a dark cloak, his head bowed to the ground. Christ is depicted in profile, but as in ancient Eastern reliefs his eye is elongated by the dark circle of the pupil—the only seeing eye in the fresco. "My soul is sick unto death. Stay here and watch with me." I could not escape from his gaze, but I was still not able to watch with him.

MITYA HAD TURNED sixteen. When I congratulated him on his birthday I thought sadly that sooner or later he would pay dearly in his own way of the cross for all these days at Dzhvari and everything he was being given in the Church. All the same, I wished him the thing he most wanted for himself—that he become a priest.

"What should the clergy be like?" one Russian archimandrite asked in his lectures on pastoral theology, and answered, "Those who are ordained should be true to their calling, and the religious should be religious."

After Matins Archil read Mitya a poem in Georgian that he had written himself. His face shone as he shared this birthday present with my son. But Mitya had to translate it, and we only understood one word: *Elia,* Elijah. Archil probably wanted Mitya to become like the prophet Elijah, who had sent drought and rain upon the earth, brought down fire from heaven, slaying the false prophets, and was taken up to heaven in a fiery chariot. But, a true Georgian, Archil also wanted Mitya to become like the most holy and most blessed Katholikos, patriarch of all Georgia, Elia II. Somehow he didn't manage to explain this and Benedict began to say mockingly that the poem was stupid and didn't rhyme, that it was written without the abbot's blessing; and, what's more, monks don't celebrate birthdays, he said, taking the paper away. Archil smiled guiltily, but when Benedict went away he brought Mitya three flat pieces of polished juniper wood to make a cross, and a pair of socks. He would have given everything he had, but he didn't have anything else at all.

A little later on, Georgi appeared on the path, carrying a traveling bag with sweet pies and cakes baked by Aunt Dodo for Mitya and the brothers. The three of us had tea in our cell. Georgi had shaved off his beard, which made his face look younger. It shone with contentment. When we'd met before he'd seemed a bit depressed.

"Has something good happened?" I asked.

"Yes." He nodded. "I'm working at the patriarch's office."

That's how things happen. I've been thinking and talking about my role for five years, but I'm no further forward. What can a woman do in the Church? Sing in the choir and light candles? A week ago Georgi was a cinema critic, now he and a friend—a historian who had joined the patriarch's office a year before—were about to visit all the churches and monasteries in Georgia, whether they were still in use or had been neglected and abandoned. They were planning to take photographs and draw up a detailed description, traveling on horseback with a tent, or by car and on foot wherever they could. Mitya and I felt very happy for him.

Georgi was a spiritual son of Father Michael and this change in his fate had happened with the abbot's blessing. "Well, your arrival hasn't gone unnoticed either." Georgi smiled.

Several more young people appeared in Dzhvari with Georgi, and Father Michael sat on the grass under the pine beside the church like an apostle surrounded by his disciples. Only the disciples were dressed for summer, in modern clothes, and Father Michael was in his cassock, boots, and waistcoat as usual. The same ski cap perched to one side adorned his high forehead: the climate and swift passage of time had no power over the abbot. The sounds of the harmonium echoed from the church.

Two days before, Mitya had come in late. He looked anxious and told us how the abbot and he had been sitting in the refectory, thinking what they could give the patriarch as a present from the monastery for his name day.

"Benedict is carving the Virgin. . . . I wonder what we could think up? What about you, Dmitri, do you want to give something too?"

"Me? But I've got nothing suitable."

"Well, could you write some music for him, perhaps?"

"I don't know . . ."

"Did you like the patriarch?" the abbot asked—and this was a trial by ordeal. "What did you think of him?"

"I liked him very much," Mitya confessed candidly. "I thought I was meeting a living saint."

"That's right," said the abbot.

Father Michael pulled a magazine, *Vine Cross,* from his bookcase. It had a poem that an archbishop had dedicated to the patriarch: "Our nation rejoices at your life, because you led us in Christ's way. . . ."

"Try to set this to music. Only you must forget all

about yourself. Don't let ambitious thoughts come in. If you think, wow, what a clever boy I am! Here I am composing a song, what a surprise I'll give them!—then it's better to write nothing. But if you hear music that will fit these words—I don't know where you'll hear it: in your heart, in the air—let it pass through you like something that doesn't really belong to you. We have to do everything for God, to his glory, to live just for doing his work, without expecting any fruit. Whatever the fruit may be, sour or sweet, won't depend simply on us. We only plow and sow; fruit ripens according to God's will."

Mitya sat at the harmonium the whole of the next day, drowning the sounds of the restorers working on the upper tiers, and managed to make a rough copy of the hymn for a six-voice male choir. He was waiting for the abbot to be free to listen to it. Father Michael approved of the song, to Mitya's joy. "There's a real Georgian feel about it, that's wonderful. I was afraid you'd compose something pompous and Italian. When did you manage to get such a feel for Georgia that its spirit breathes in your music?"

When we first arrived in Georgia we had gone to about five cathedral services that were celebrated by the patriarch. We had never heard anything like it before; it was like the choirs of Zion performing ancient church songs. You couldn't mistake them for anything else; it would be impossible to imitate.

Everyone would have to greet the patriarch after the Sunday evening service in the cathedral; so Mitya had all night to transcribe the music.

Even though the visitors were still there, Benedict and Mitya wrote assiduously before and after supper, spreading the pages of music out on the table. Benedict wrote the text in a beautiful round script and drew an ancient Georgian cross on the cover in ink. They began the late office at ten o'clock, once the visitors had gone. Mitya didn't go with the visitors because we planned to receive Communion next morning, which up till now we had usually done together.

How our little basilica was transformed at this night service! You waited all week for these moments when Father Michael's head appeared in the gap above the royal doors, which looked for all the world like a window display made of cardboard. Then the swing gates opened and you saw the sanctuary in all its poverty and shiningness.

Night already filled the long window with its broken cornerstone. The abbot, dressed in a shabby chasuble and stole, was censing the altar, up and then across. The altar smoke curled upward blue-white, and the smell of incense spread through the church. The sanctuary was so small that the abbot scarcely fitted in the space between the royal doors and the altar. He only had to take one step back to cense the altar and the holy place was completely revealed.

There was no celestial place and a stone ledge of the wall served as an altar, covered in red with silver embroidery. Seven candles and yellow lamps were lit and two more tall candles burned at the edge of the sanctuary, making the whole altar very bright in the semidarkness of the church. Two crosses stood on the altar, with the New Testament between them in an embossed binding.

"Glory to the Holy, Consubstantial, Life-Giving,

and Undivided Trinity . . ." The abbot uttered the opening invocation quietly.

The monastery choir—Father Benedict, wrapped in his old cloak like a black toga, Archil and Mitya in cassocks—replied from around the icon stand. "Come, let us worship God our King. O, come let us worship and fall down before Christ, our King and God. . . ."

Mitya read the psalm of introduction in Khutsuri, blessing the Lord who created this wonderful world by his great wisdom. The doors shut like the gates of Paradise. The choir responded to the Great Litany with the prayer of penitence: "Lord, have mercy." In the evening, as they enter with candles, they always sing one of the most beautiful and ancient prayers: "Gladsome Light of the Holy Glory of the Immortal Heavenly Father, Holy and Blessed, O Jesus Christ! At the going down of the sun, having seen the evening light, we hymn Father, Son, and Holy Spirit, God. . . ."

The service was conducted in Georgian, but I recognized it all. Sometimes I followed the Old Church Slavonic or Russian text and the words of the prayers and psalms echoed in the depth of my heart as though they had been given life by its very beat.

Afterward came Matins, the six penitential psalms sung with only a dim light: "God, you are my God, from early dawn I seek you; my soul thirsts for you, my flesh longs for you in a dry and thirsty land where no water is. . . ."

Now I know, Lord, why you made our soul so limitless and deep that nothing on earth can fill it. Beyond every joy is the desire for a purer joy, behind every love is the desire for a higher love. In our being is an unquenched and unquenchable longing for you, the unending joy and eternal love, the end of our every desire.

The all-night vigil always ends toward 2 A.M. and we go to confession afterward. I left the church first and Mitya closed the heavy door from inside. I sat in the dark on the ledge of the wall, leaning against the rough warm stone and saw the countless multitude of stars burning above me like candles. The midnight service continues there, choirs of angels sing the Gloria, "Glory to God in the highest and on earth peace, goodwill toward men. We praise you, we bless you, we worship you, we glorify you, we thank you for your great glory."

Because of his great glory the sun will rise tomorrow, the flowers will open their petals, and the birds will sing. The day will open like a new page of the book of Genesis, the book about the Absolute, written in an accessible language about the relative.

The timeless vocabulary of this book is infinitely richer than ours. Not only colors, smells, sounds, whatever we can absorb with our senses, our very feelings and thoughts, their movements and changes, but also people, animals, trees, stars, mountains, and rain—these are the living words that the Living God spoke for us. What does a poppy mean in and of itself, or a cornflower with its blue crown? The grass of the field, which is here today and tomorrow has withered, is just like ourselves. The whole world, taken by itself, is transitory, fleeting, dying, nothing more than dust borne by the wind. But just take a flower as the word of God turning toward you as a sign of love, and you take the world as a gift, un-merited and great. Your heart is filled with gratitude and responsive love: "Praise him, sun and moon, praise him, all stars and light, praise him heaven of heavens and the water which is above: let them praise the name of the Lord, for he spoke and they came into being: he commanded and they were created. . . ."

And what is sin? Sin is whatever separates us from God, our guilt in the face of his love. Forbidden fruit, eaten for its own sake, doesn't satisfy. Love, apart from God, will not be able to bear a load of excessive expectations, won't slake an unending thirst.

How eagerly I used to seek every source, hopeful at first, but then knowing, as time went on, that it is just quenching your thirst in a dream; afterward you wake up with a dry throat. Jesus spoke to the Samaritan woman about this: "Whoever drinks this water will thirst again, but whoever drinks the water I give will never thirst."

But "Let the one who is thirsty come, and let the one who wants take the water of life freely." And so ends the Book of Revelation.

One candle was still burning, illuminating the Gospels, the cross on the icon stand, and Father Michael, who was sitting in front of it. I stood beside him, leaning against the wall, and caught my breath as always before the first words of confession.

"Why are you always so upset, breathing so heavily, as though you were sixteen?" he said, turning to me with his ironical smile. "Do you still think you can manage with your own strength? You must stand before God quietly, aware you can do nothing, and pray for him to help you. For with God nothing is impossible. Cast all your care upon the Lord and he will care for you."

He was reading prayers in Georgian: Christ stood there unseen receiving my confession. I bowed over the lectern, placing my head on the Gospels. The abbot covered my head with his stole and placed his hand firmly on top.

Afterward we talked about monastic life, about God, about love.

"The soul no longer receives anything temporal; I try to achieve the absolute, even in my relations with people, to go out to the unconditional—to spiritual closeness."

"There can't be spiritual closeness between man and woman, it's all mixed in with passion, don't you think?"

I began to talk about the two people closest to Mitya and me, one a priest, our spiritual father, the other a hieromonk whom we visited last winter when he'd just been given four neglected parishes. He celebrated the liturgy in a monastic style, omitting nothing, every day in unheated, icy churches. He had to be deacon, psalm-reader, and choir. The edge of the chalice froze to his lips during Communion.

"Every day?" Father Michael shook his head in disbelief. "Like Father John of Kronstadt?"

Then there were religious rites—baptisms, Communion for the sick, funerals . . . He thawed out at home over a hot cup of tea and began to smile. The parishioners gathered around his simple table. He poured out such love and light on everyone that you saw a living picture of Christ in him that made you want to kneel in front of him.

"A married priest, one's spiritual father—I don't know, perhaps. . . . Well, have contact with him. Leave the monks in peace, however."

Father Michael sat up straight, throwing his head back and leaning against the wall, watching the melted wax of the candle ooze under the thick petal of the flame. There was no longer any irony or levity in his smile; instead I noticed a deep secret sorrow.

A vein pulsed in the hollowed temples of his high forehead, and his eyes reflected the motionless candle flame. His beard, streaked with gray, hid the smile that lay forgotten on his lips. The silence between us was filled with unseen currents of darkness and light. I wanted to speak—we had never yet talked about intimate things.

"When I was with this hieromonk I understood that the monastic life is a daily feat of love which is far beyond me. Grace begins when one's own strength becomes totally used up."

"You can't understand a thing about the monastic life. Nothing. Has it never occurred to you that these long services, three hours' sleep in the entire twenty-four, strict fasts: This is the price of such a spiritual communion?"

"No."

"Not its only price, of course . . . but once you're a nun you'll see what it costs to live without passions."

And he said that when you enter a monastery with passions that you haven't overcome yet, they'll torment you with a force that is ten times greater. Everyone has their unsubdued passions. In the world it may seem that nothing troubles you because you can fulfill every desire, but once your vows are taken the struggle gets worse. This is the soul's struggle for eternal stakes. That's why it's better for a monk to be ill all the time. Not only do his desires pursue him but visions of old desires, recollections, and dreams. And what if a live passion, not just a vision gets him?

"I understand. . . ." I interrupted a pause that was lasting too long. "When you know nothing's ever impossible, but you keep on experiencing this torture . . . that's desperate—a high-risk act."

"What do you mean—a high-risk act?"

"Walking a tightrope right under the Big Top."

He smiled and slowly raised his head onto the lectern; his brow rested against the crucifix, He shut his eyes. "Oh, it's too much!"

Poor thing, I thought, poor dear thing, and in my thoughts I stroked his wavy hair, already thinning on the crown and gathered in a knot at the nape of his neck. I knew I would never caress his hair in reality and this is the same "never" that we were talking about.

He lifted his head with a degree of effort, but straightened immediately and gave a short laugh.

"You still don't understand anything, do you? What we're talking about—well, to you it's just a story. The spiritual closeness you were talking about between a monk and a woman—that's just self-delusion. The greater the understanding, emotion, that desire you talked about to get on your knees— the more repressed, the deeper, is the longing for full

closeness." He spoke evenly and his voice was muf-
fled. "So men and women have always been saved in
separate ways. That's why we don't admit women to
the monastery. You shouldn't feel totally safe here
either."

I remembered Father Benedict's sullen look, how
he always seemed to be averting his gaze. But I
thought the abbot's alarm was premature. I'm sure I
would have been the first to know if any danger
threatened.

"What do you mean? There are other women living here, and they're not afraid."

"They're other women, as you say," Father
Michael replied, trimming the burned wick which
was nearly drowning in the pool of wax. "They're
alien to us, whereas we, you and I, have a life in
common which draws us together." He made two
slight movements, putting one hand over the other,
but leaving a slight gap between them. "You have
come too close."

Personally I didn't think it was too close, as I was
not alarmed by the closeness. My purpose in wanting
to draw still closer was so that the relationship between me and my spiritual father, who was my age,
might become simpler, as if in the family. Two more
days would pass before our mutual openness defused
the tension between us—and this was possible because in Christian love there should be "neither male
nor female"—it transcends sexuality.

It was around four o'clock when I drew back the
bolt that locked the inside of the church. The same
warm starry night surrounded us. A lit lamp lay on
the refectory windowsill: it was Archil or Benedict

indicating to the abbot that the brothers were thinking about him although he had been drawn away from them. Father Michael took the lamp along the path to my cell, lighting the way for us both, stopping a few steps away to wish me good night.

Mitya was asleep, breathing evenly as a tired child sleeps. Only two hours were left before Archil would waken us, only three hours until the liturgy. As usual I didn't believe I could last out until Communion.

THE CANDLES AND little lights shone faintly above the altar in the sunlight, swimming in the yellow lamps from the seven-branched candlestick. A thin sunbeam danced through a crack in the icon-screen, shining from a cloud above the head of Christ, a poor attempt to portray the Savior walking barefoot upon the earth.

Dressed in his green chasuble, filling the royal doors, the abbot raised his voice in thanksgiving to God, just as Christ himself began the mystery of the Eucharist with thanksgiving at the Last Supper with his disciples. Once, two thousand years ago, Christ came, the very heart of the mystery, but giving us his heavenly kingdom for all time in his life, death, and resurrection, and his Church has been left on earth to give meaning to the life of the world and make it spiritual.

When the time was clearly right, Eternity descended in the shape of the Holy Spirit—the Holy Gifts are transformed into the Body and Blood of Christ. The heart of history coincides with the heart of our everyday life: "He who eats my flesh and drinks my blood remains in me, and I in him." This is the heart of mystery: this "I in him" isn't anything abstract or relative, it means a real incarnation of Christ in everyone who receives Communion, in our bodies and in our blood. He is incarnated in us in order to save us, to be crucified again for our sins and to rise in us. Therefore we bless and thank him, and the choir sings "Hosanna in the Highest, blessed is he who comes in the name of the Lord, Hosanna in the Highest."

The abbot repeated the words of Institution: "Take, eat, this is my Body which is broken for you for the remission of sins. Drink of it all of you, this is my Blood of the New Testament which is poured out for you and for many for the remission of sins."

He took the paten with his right hand, the chalice in his left, raising them in the form of a cross above the altar: "Yours, of your own, we offer to you, on behalf of all, and for all. O Lord, we bring the bread and the wine to you, chosen from your innumerable gifts to us on earth as a grateful offering on behalf of all and for all."

Then the abbot in the Secret Prayers asks God to change the bread into the Body of Christ and the wine into his Blood by the power of the Holy Spirit. . . . And the change takes place, as the Savior promised.

. . . The priest standing with arms raised in front of the altar is the highest image of man, the symbol of his predestination. He receives the world and everything in it from God as a sign of his presence, as a gift—and hallows them and returns them to God as an offering of gratitude and love. The empty flesh of the world which can never satisfy man's hunger in and of itself is transformed in this universal Eucharist. It becomes the means of communicating with God. Life is transformed into eternal life in him.

"Receive me, Son of God, as a participant in your Holy Supper today, for I will not reveal your mystery to your enemies, nor will I give you a kiss like Judas, but like the thief I acknowledge you: Remember me, O Lord, when you come into your kingdom. Let my communing of your Holy Mysteries, O Lord, not be for judgment or condemnation, but for the healing of body and soul."

The abbot said these words in Russian, because Mitya and I were the only communicants and, crossing my hands on my breast, I followed my son to the Holy Chalice. "God's servant Veronica receives Communion for the remission of her sins and to eternal life. . . ." I kissed the silver base of the cup after receiving Communion.

There was a clearing on the hill behind our cell with forest all around, and Mitya and I went there after the liturgy, sitting well apart so as not to get in each other's way. I spread one of Hilarion's old sheepskin jerkins under a birch tree and stretched out, resting my hands under my head. Mitya and the monastery disappeared from my sight in the long grass.

That's how it's always been. Tension mounts before Communion. After the midnight vigil, the canons and prayers for Communion that sometimes end in the middle of the night, after Confession and the liturgy, I struggle to the chalice with my last reserves of strength. And afterward I have no strength left, but it doesn't matter because everything has been fulfilled.

A dreamy silence spread within me and around me. I saw the pure blue of the sky and little white clouds through the branches and shiny foliage. The sun shone overhead and when I closed my eyes it burned through them with a tender, reddish light, and each blade of grass, each three-leafed clover was suffused with the sun. I looked at the network of veins branching across transparent green oval leaves with their indented edges, and the lilac crown of the tiny flower whose star-shape could be so easily missed in the grass. The forest ant dragged a red pine needle with a drop of pitch on its end. The wind rustled through the birches, and everything fell silent in its hidden thoughts.

Snatches of thought, words from the previous day's talk with the abbot came into my mind, hindering me. "Lord," I thought, "free me from every word. Let me dissolve in your blessed peace, even if it's only for a moment. . . ."

IT WAS TIME for Mitya to go. I half got up and glanced around for him. He was lying asleep in the grass in his cassock and boots, his cheek resting on his cap; his face was radiant and pure. A moth covered with blue pollen hovered above him, settling on his shoulder and flying off.

The gifts of the Lord are unsearchable. I still suffered from my own sad childhood, while my son had grown up, and our deep relationship had taken the place of all forms of kinship, surpassing them. I

would never be able to give body and soul so completely to anyone: if only this would last till the end
of my days. . . .

Immediately after the meal a *gazik* rolled up. It
turned out that Eli and Nona were leaving with
Mitya. They planned to come back together in the
same car two days later. Mitya was cheerful. He'd
swapped his cassock and boots for a white shirt, velvet trousers, and sandals. He waved his folder from
the footboard. The door slammed shut. A cloud of
dust whirled from the wheels, settling again on the
rise of the road. Brinka and Muria chased after them,
barking.

Benedict turned around and went off to his cell,
pulling his knitted cap over his ears. I suddenly realized I was left alone, and I felt anxious, for the first
time since the abbot's hints. I was tired after my
sleepless night and I lay down in the cell straightaway, dropping the hook on the door and even testing it to see how secure it was, but sleep didn't come.

I remembered all the small details of the last days,
beginning to realize that something was happening
that I hadn't noticed, because there had been too
much else to think about.

For example, to start with, I ate in the refectory
after the brothers, but sometimes I didn't manage to
get the dishes done before Vespers and it got too
dark, so I asked the abbot whether I could have dinner in my cell at the same time as they had theirs. "If
you like," he'd said, shrugging his shoulders indifferently. So it happened that I was carrying a pot of
borshcht with a plate on top with bread, watermelon,
and an open jar of cherry jam—and Benedict hap-

pened to meet me on the path. He made way for me, looking at my plate as though he were admonishing me for the sin of going off to eat in secret. He didn't say anything, and nor did I. However, he said to Mitya next day, "Your mother's making progress." "What progress?" Mitya was interested to know. "She's taking food to her cell." "Yes, that's so as to get the dishes washed more quickly and the cooking done." "But she's doing it without the abbot's blessing. . . ." "No, it's with his blessing."

Benedict could hardly begrudge me the borshcht, which I'd only just cooked for everyone in a big dish shaped like a bucket, or the piece of melon. He could hardly suspect I was hoarding food in the cell against a rainy day. It must have been some kind of hidden irritation or resentment.

Then there was the time Georgi and his friends came to Dzhvari; while one of them was helping me stack the dishes he began to say something derisive in Georgian to Benedict. They were obviously talking about me, and in reply to my questioning glance, the young man explained, "I was asking Benedict what kind of Georgian he was, taking money from a woman who asked him to carve her a cross."

I don't know who he'd heard that from, the pair of us had hardly said a word before or since.

"I didn't ask him."

"So it was his idea?"

"I told him to mind his own business," Benedict said evenly, but with cold hostility, looking at me with an icy stare.

Was there something about me that made Benedict keep disappearing all day?

There were three days when I felt that his relationship with the abbot had grown tense. Then Archil went away, Benedict didn't want to do the cooking, of course, and the abbot couldn't bring himself to allow me to get closely involved with them—perhaps because they'd had a quarrel about Mitya and me. Or had I offended Benedict when he'd been drunk? But this was all too insignificant to explain the hostility with which he looked at me.

I really didn't want to think out the consequences of all these "either-ors." Whatever the reason for the upset, I had to find an explanation or think about leaving. These days in Dzhvari were the best of my life, and I'd have given up the next few years if only to prolong them.

I must have been dropping off when Archil called me from outside. The restorers had handed in some mushrooms, which needed to be fried.

"Perhaps I could fry them later, Archil, for your meal?"

"Fine," he said and went off.

I just couldn't get to sleep. I kept looking at the time, afraid I wouldn't manage to cook the mushrooms—never having done so before.

After I'd had a wash and put on my faded old work gown and head scarf, I decided all my worry was just a silly dream and I had to get things sorted out between Benedict and myself. I hadn't done anything bad to him and so I needn't expect anything bad in return.

A big bag of mushrooms stood by the spring, smelling of autumn, moldy leaves, and rain. I tipped them out onto the wall: orange cap boletus, yellow chanterelle, lots of russula mushrooms with purple and red streaky skins, and one other kind—with membranes lining their little caps—which was barely edible.

"We've got to cook for the restorers too," Archil told me as he looked through the colorful pile.

As I was walking past the balcony I noticed Guram and Shalva sitting at the table with two young women, talking and laughing.

"Perhaps we'll share the mushrooms—but can't those women fry them for themselves?" I suggested. There was only half an hour left before the monks' meal and there was no way I could get supper ready for eight in time. I'd taken on the cooking thinking it would just be for the brothers, but the restorers and their visitors was another matter.

"They're just girls, not women." Archil sounded a bit offended for some reason. "They just happened to call by today—and stayed on."

"What do you mean, Archil? It's all the same to me."

"What's more, we're not inviting them over to our place," he interrupted. "Monks don't sit and eat with women. You just happen to be lucky."

"But the russula mushrooms can't be fried, and there won't be enough of the others to go around."

"Even a little is nice when it comes from a kind heart. . . . Do you know what I mean?"

Yes, I got his meaning, and my heart sank. There seemed something odd about this sudden unjust outburst, just as in Benedict's behavior, and I felt depressed.

"But I'm telling you, you just don't fry russula mushrooms. . . ."

"Why not?" Archil was getting upset too. "I'll help if it's too much for you. It's Christian love, to do good to others."

"You might as well try to fry cucumbers, but do what you want with them."

A sillier subject to quarrel over would be hard to find, but I'd really offended Archil. My hands were trembling as I washed the mushrooms, chopped them up, and sprinkled them into hot oil. Archil came up when they were almost ready and told me, off his own bat, that he had thrown out the russulas.

"I could have done that as well out of Christian love."

"They looked worm-eaten."

I asked him to try the mushrooms but he said that they probably needed to be fried a bit more.

No one came down for supper at six o'clock. Archil went to fetch the abbot but he came back alone.

"Where's Father Michael?"

"He's not feeling well," Archil said, with some restraint now but still showing the same total lack of interest as Benedict. "He'll come later."

The table was already set, the vermicelli soup and fried potato and onion were getting cold. The mushrooms were still being cooked. I wanted to serve them hot, but when I lifted the lid I saw that they'd really shrunk, so I put a tablespoon aside for myself and put out the flame under the pan. Then Benedict came into the kitchen for some matches: I knew he smoked, although he tried to hide it from Mitya and me.

"Father Benedict, I'd like to have a word with you."

I shouldn't have made the attempt when I was feeling so distraught, but now I'd started I had to go on. Father Benedict only gave an unpleasant smile as he rattled the matches and went on into the refectory. When I brought the kettle in a few minutes later he was sitting next to Archil. Benedict looked sullen. "Did you want to have a word with me?"

I didn't know what to say. "Well, not just now while you're eating," I said, and went off to have my own supper in my cell. I could hardly swallow the frazzled mushrooms. I remembered how happy I'd felt that morning in the sunny glade, with Mitya asleep. And now I would have liked to cry, but all I had in my unkind heart was emptiness and a feeling of oppression.

When I came back to do the dishes Archil showed me a plate of mushrooms, half the amount that had been in the pan. "We didn't eat them. We left them for the restorers. Mushrooms are a delicacy here."

"They must have dried up when they were cooking," I guessed.

"No, it's because you grudged giving them to the visitors," Archil said, half-jokingly.

I hadn't begrudged them, but it didn't matter anymore.

Before Vespers Father Michael was sitting in the refectory, wrapped in a quilted jacket with a woman's silk shawl underneath. I asked whether he had a temperature and suggested a Vietnamese ointment called Golden Star.

"There's no need. Keep it for yourself," he replied mockingly, looking around at Benedict, who was cutting something with a scalpel and didn't lift his head. Then, because he'd sounded harsh, he added: "I said a monk should always be ill. . . ."

The plate of mushrooms was still sitting in the middle of the table as a reminder and a reproach. We could hear women laughing upstairs.

AFTER VESPERS THE abbot, Benedict, and Archil started talking together in Georgian. I asked for a blessing and went away. Weariness and depression had laid me low and I fell asleep at once.

Next day, waiting for Benedict to leave the table, I went out to the path. I was still feeling upset. It was obvious that he was avoiding me, and it was demeaning and unpleasant to be cold-shouldered.

Benedict stared right past me. He had a glazed look as though he hadn't slept. I asked how he felt about Mitya and myself being in the monastery, whether we were getting in his way. He answered, evasively and unwillingly, that the presence of women in monasteries is always a temptation.

"So do you want us to leave?"

"It doesn't matter what I want. You're here with the abbot's blessing, so that's his affair. In any case a monk should have no will of his own."

While we were standing on the slope the abbot appeared beneath us, coming along the path from the monastery through the glade, heading for Benedict's cell, his head bowed in thought. He caught sight of us and turned back. He looked around, paused, turned around again, and started climbing up the slope. Benedict spotted him and went to meet him.

ARCHIL WAS SITTING on the steps of the outhouse in front of the open door of the storeroom with a large pot at his feet. He was trimming pieces of wax with his knife and arranging them on the grass: The abbot had suggested that we should make candles out of these odd bits. Three days before he'd given me the job of cleaning the wax, but I hadn't had any time, and now I began to feel that Archil was doing this just to show me up.

"Archil . . ." I hurried up, a bit out of breath. "Does my being here in the monastery bother you?"

"Not personally," he said. He seemed to have expected this, and had decided to challenge it. "Monks must have solitude. You understand this yourself. Perhaps it would be better if you prepared the food over by the fountain."

Well, I thought, that's all I need. All that remained was to wait for Mitya. I had asked destiny for several days in Paradise, but now the expiration date had come up.

I cleared the table and did the dishes at the fountain. Father Michael, still with his quilted jacket slung across his shoulders, was sitting beside Archil with a growing pile of wax on the grass. I didn't meet his eyes, but I felt he was watching me.

In the morning I asked if I could leave the monastery after the meal. I wanted to go into the mountains, to look at them again before I said good-bye—

and now I was waiting for the abbot. He appeared, looking rather strained, went on through the refectory into the neighboring room, but reappeared in the doorway.

"Were you planning to go off somewhere?"

"Yes."

"Where to?"

"I want to be alone."

"So that's how it is . . ."

"If you'd be able to have a talk . . ." (I said "able" knowing he wouldn't want to talk to a woman.) "let's do so, as there seems to be very little time left."

"That means you've felt something. . . ."

"Of course! And how!"

Father Michael sat down on the bunk beside a small table and I sat on the edge of the bench, resting my elbow against its back. He opened a service book, leafed through it, found an eraser, and began to rub out pencil marks in the margin—unlike me, he had a job to do. "What do you want to talk about?"

"Well, first of all I want to talk to you as a confessor. You've been watching Mitya and me for quite some time. You see us as we are. Let's talk about our faults."

He smiled, raising his eyebrows, and inclining his head a little. His expression, gestures, intonation had become so familiar I couldn't understand why I'd ever thought he was ugly: Now I liked his every feature, his short brows, small eyes, long nose. I even liked the way he knotted his hair at the back of his neck and the long fingers of his broad hands. In fact, as I looked at him now I saw tenderness in the light of my departure.

"Our defects are an inexhaustible theme. Wherever you look there are faults on all sides. Take this little book—I stole it from the library. I decided they didn't need it. Shall I say more? Or would it offend you?"

"Maybe."

"Well, as you wish." He glanced briefly at me, mockingly, as though he were sizing me up. "You're a terribly proud person. God can forgive everything: theft," he bent his head slightly and added, "lasciviousness, banditry . . . but pride—this is like a copper wall between us and God. 'God resists the proud and gives grace to the humble.' There's such pride in your every look and gesture. What is there to be so proud about? Who do you think you are—the most virtuous Christian?"

I laughed. "You're joking."

But even that wasn't enough for him. "Perhaps you're the most beautiful woman?"

This was a real slap in the face. I'm not beautiful in the least. I could never forget it and in my younger days I always thought of beautiful women as those on whom Fate had smiled. I'd read recently in Yelchaninov, "Blessed are the unlovely, the untalented, the unsuccessful—they do not have to contend with the chief foe, pride." This is just like "Blessed are the poor in spirit, blessed are those who weep . . ." The only problem was, as the abbot said, there's nothing a person can't take pride in: If you're not beautiful you are proud of your intelligence; if you're not intelligent you take pride in your job and your wealth; if you're not wealthy you take pride in poverty and you can take pride in joy and even sorrows.

"You had an old gown put on you and you washed the dishes—but there's no humility, even in that. It's as though you're playing a part, like Cinderella—only a Cinderella who knows her golden carriage is waiting outside the gates." While he was talking he continued to rub out the comments in the book. "What are you actually busy with just now? Are you reciting the Jesus Prayer?"

"No. . . . I'm busy in the kitchen."

"Ah—you can make the prayer in a grotto, but not in the kitchen. In the monastery, food should be prepared with prayer. In fact prayer has gotten to be our most important activity. Everything else is secondary. And what is it you're always writing? You sit in your cell and write in a notebook. Perhaps you're planning to write a novel about monastic life?" He'd obviously observed me more closely than I'd thought.

"I can't write about monastic life. I'm not a nun."

"I think you intend to, just the same."

"Do you think I'm lying?"

"No. . . ." This argument puzzled him for a moment. "In my opinion you don't tell lies at all," he said, with some surprise and quite a bit of respect.

"I try not to lie. I don't think it's worth it."

"There you are, there's a reason for pride. So, what are you writing? Long letters?"

"I wrote down what you told us about the *startsy*."

"Why? All the same, that means—perhaps unconsciously—you're getting ready to write." He shut the book and tossed it onto the bunk, obviously feeling confused. "How do you think you'll get close enough to their life—it's so different from yours.

You haven't a clue about them; it's the same with contemplation, however much you may read about it. We find it funny when you quote the Holy Fathers. It's just like children holding a book upside down, running their finger along the lines and pretending they're reading. 'The spirit is only reached by the spirit.' Until you live the monastic life you'll achieve nothing, however hard you try. That is, you'll see the cassock, the boots, the hole in the icon-screen . . ." His voice became more even. "Decide for yourself, once and for all. Do you want to write about Christianity or live in a Christian way? If it's to live, then give up everything before it's too late and enter a convent."

"I want to live rather than write. When we leave Dzhvari I'll miss this other life, and I'll be searching for a way into it. If I don't find it, perhaps there'll be nothing for me except writing—I don't know how to do anything else."

"And do you know how to write?"

"Better than I know how to live a Christian life or to pray."

"So go and learn to live according to the commandments, and pray, otherwise I'm afraid that faith will just become another hobby—you'll be discovering a new world."

"For me salvation lies in faith. I don't even mean eternal life—I don't know how to exist in our modern world without faith."

"That's fine, if that's really the way it is."

"I hear that the soul comes alive and rises from the dead. Writing won't bring it to life. But I won't enter a convent. I've got a son."

"Let him go his own way."

"He does already, but he still needs me."

"You see, we're going over old ground. We've talked about this already. You ask my advice, but you don't carry it out. 'A son always needs his mother.' When I went back to Tbilisi to get my internal passport and be registered in the monastery I didn't even look in at my mother's."

"Perhaps you don't love her. . . ?"

"There you are, that's just what she said too. Do you think your son is better than anybody else's?"

"Well, isn't he a good boy?"

"Dmitri? Oh, you'll see how proud he is, what a high opinion he has of himself. People like that make bad monks, but they can become bishops and run the Church. You see, God isn't enough for them: They need an audience. If he goes on like this, you'll be a hindrance to him in a couple of years."

"Then I'll go away too. . . ."

"He's sixteen. He's written an anthem. What ought he to have done then? He should have handed it over to the abbot, and that's it. But he took matters into his own hands. He worked out who he should approach so that his anthem would get to the patriarch."

"He only thought that was the right way to go about it."

"Do you see what you're doing arguing, rejecting, blocking what I want to say?"

"I'm just trying to make it better for him." This rebuke seemed unjust; it left me feeling like the way I had when Archil had gone on about the mushrooms.

"There's no use trying to soften it when you want to hear the truth. On the contrary, you should agree and say, 'Yes, and here's another incident like that.' You find it easier to stick to your own opinions. So what else do you want to talk about?"

Everything had come off the rails and my feeling of resentment about the way Archil and Benedict had treated me was still simmering in the wake of all this confusion. "You judge us from such a height," I said.

"That's the way you wanted it."

"That's what I want. But here's Benedict telling me only today that a woman means temptation. So how do you evaluate that from your dizzy height?"

He lowered his eyes. "Like it or not, that's how monks view women."

"But if they don't see Christians in half of the human race, not even people, but only temptation . . . and what a dirty word that is! How do you put that together with God and Christian love?"

"You forget that there is a devil. . . . You underestimate his role." Now Father Michael's face was closed like a house with shutters fastened. "You seem to think that Christianity is some kind of festival with willow branches and candles. But Calvary came after the entry into Jerusalem. Who wouldn't be a Christian if love like this were given for nothing? The higher a man tries to rise, the more evil he has to conquer both in himself and in the world around, and evil takes its revenge. This is a bloody war, not unto life but unto death. So the stakes are high: The fate of the soul in eternity. And woman can be a snare in this war; even human nature itself."

We sat opposite each other in silence and Benedict came in, measuring us with a disapproving glance. The abbot smiled ironically, like someone caught in the act and taken unawares, as he got up to meet him.

I SAT SLUMPED against a hayrick. Hollyhocks were still shining like little lamps above the fresh green of the meadow. Dragonflies flashed transparent wings against the transparent blue. Bumblebees buzzed about. Everything around was flooded with a blinding golden light. The trees, their twigs, and every leaf on their green tops stood out in sharp relief against the sun. A horse snorted as it clumped heavily along, its ruddy coat shining in the sun, driving flies off with its tail. Beyond the trees on the precipice and ravine the distant outline of the mountains could be seen in a whitish heat haze. Cicadas chirred, heat poured down, the day was full of light like the blessing of God.

Where would I find the strength to leave Dzhvari? Everything had finished too quickly, cutting the ground from under me.

Someone might come out into the glade and I didn't feel up to meeting anyone. I got up and went along the path through the forest toward the old monastery winepress where the monks had once made their wine. You could still see the tops of the vats dug into swampy ground, choked with duck-weed. I went beyond them, along an overgrown path toward the precipice, and lay down. The river murmured far below me and the trees stood motionless about me. I had no strength, no bitterness, no thoughts. Tears were streaming down my face and I did not want to keep them back. There was a sweet smell of pine needles and dry leaves warmed by the earth. An unseen bird chirruped among the bushes and its pure high call found an echo in my tears. Through them I saw the stalks of grass and the yellow line of the precipice across the bank, the clouds above—and then my tears dried up.

A deep peace descended such as I had never felt before. My whole past, words, tears, everything sank into it. The only thing that remained was the here and now, transparent to light and to God.

The river was still murmuring below. A butterfly with gold and black patterns on its underwings swayed upside down on a bending stalk; the stalk itself, the fingers of my hand, let the sun filter through to dapple the grass. I saw the pattern of the lines on my palms crisscrossing, interweaving: the line of life, of sorrow, of love. Yesterday God had entered this weak flesh and he still lived in it, looking through my tearstained eyes at the butterfly's wing, the pattern of the bark, at the day and the forest that he himself had made. There was neither barrier nor distance between him and the world. Lying on the grass, I felt God within me and I was filled with light and gratitude for his presence.

Sometimes I spoke words to him that cannot be repeated, at other times I was silent, but in this silence I was told things that made my former life seem so empty, overwhelmed as it had been with a flood of words—my own and others'.

Three or four hours passed in this way, and if the nineteen days I'd spent in Dzhvari had been the best of my life, then these hours were at the very heart of those days.

The sun was setting as I went barefoot along the stony riverbed, carrying the silence within me, afraid it would spill out and disappear. I so wanted to depart from the monastery along that river and never return again. It would be more than I could bear if I were to meet anyone and have to say unnecessary words. There were just three hours left before it got dark and I would go back and sleep. Next day Mitya would return and we would leave. So until darkness fell I stayed sitting on a warm stone by the path from the river to the monastery, leaning against a tree trunk, my hands clasped around my knees.

The cicadas fell silent. It became cool and frightening. The stars appeared in the pale sky, which was filling with a deepening blue. It was good to see the moon appear above the hills, lit up with phosphorescent light. It was eleven o'clock when I came out onto the glade with the hayrick, bathed in a green light. The trees and the hayrick cast dark shadows and the black horse wandered along, still snorting loudly. A cry came from the monastery. "Aahhh!" This cry produced an unpleasant echo in me: It meant they were looking for me and I could expect still more reproaches and explanations.

I went along the upper path without meeting anyone, but two figures stood beside my cell, and from his height and his cap I made one out to be the abbot.

"Who's there?" he almost shouted as I came up, "Who's that?"

I came up quite close, to avoid replying, but answered nevertheless, "It's only me."

"Where were you? Did you meet anyone?"

"No."

The abbot went off quickly toward the house. "The restorers and Archil are out looking for you," Benedict explained.

Above the monastery, red rockets shot up and went out one after the other. I felt ashamed that all this firing and alarm was on my account, but somehow it didn't seem to matter anymore.

"Have you any matches?" Benedict came into the cell with me and lit the candle on the table. "Thank God you've come! Otherwise it would have been like the time when that deacon went out late and never came back."

There was neither alienation nor hostility in his voice. The abbot called Benedict, who went out and I followed. We were now standing in front of the open door and I could barely see their faces.

"Where were you?"

"I told you I wouldn't be back for the service. . . ." I had a real physical difficulty in getting the words out and so I spoke quietly.

"You haven't had a bite all day. Come on and have some tea." He lowered his voice a bit too, but was still excited.

"I'm not hungry."

"Has something happened? What's up?"

"No, nothing's happened."

The whole day long had been spent saying farewell to Dzhvari and its inhabitants. I'd shed my tears for them and here they'd returned and were right beside me. I had a strange feeling that I'd already left, that I was no longer here. I waited for them to depart too.

"Go and look for Archil," the abbot said to Benedict, who disappeared into the darkness.

"We might have been worried about you." Father Michael's voice was calm now. I remembered the tone of voice they'd used when they had spoken to me that morning.

"You might have been worried in case there was any unpleasantness because of me. But I knew there wouldn't be."

"Now you're making fun of us." Father Michael sounded surprised. Up till now I'd always spoken to him with respect.

"I'm sorry, it's just that I want to go."

He stood there, looking somewhat at a loss.

"I really want you to tell me what's wrong." Judging by his tone of voice he'd given a little smile. "I demand an explanation."

And I laughed: He no longer had any authority over me.

"Come on, have some supper and tell me where you've been." His voice even betrayed a touch of dependence. "Or did someone offend you? Perhaps Benedict insulted you?" As if Father Michael couldn't! "Why do you remain silent?"

"It's just that I've nothing to say."

"All the more reason to have supper. Let's go. I can't very well take you by the hand."

I found it hard to go on squabbling like this. At the same time I was afraid I'd burst out crying. I was desperate to get away.

"Forgive me, Father Michael, it's very hard for me to talk to you just now. I'll answer all your questions tomorrow."

"Perhaps it's . . . literature?" This was his word for any kind of emotion.

"Perhaps. Good night." He turned and went off without replying.

I bolted the door and closed the window shutters. I said a brief prayer in front of the icon of the Mother of God and snuffed out the candle. It was quite dark at first, then the crack at the side of the shutter turned a dark blue. A fine film of polyethylene separated me from the night and the forest. The blackness outside suddenly took on menacing proportions.

I GOT UNDRESSED, and as soon as I lay down I saw myself on the grass on the precipice and as if in a dream began to sink slowly into that same state—of desolation after hours of weeping, followed by a merciful sensation of light.

I woke up full of alarm. I lay listening to the darkness. I could only hear the dull thump of my heart beating. I thought someone was standing behind the door. I didn't know how long I'd slept, whether for a few minutes or for hours. I didn't dare light a candle and got dressed silently in the dark.

I gropingly lifted the icon down and, clutching it to my chest, knelt down. Until daybreak I prayed to the Mother of God for myself, for the abbot and Benedict, asking her "to protect us from all evil by her honorable veil."

The next day Archil didn't waken me. I missed Matins and went down for breakfast. I met Shalva, one of the restorers, by the fountain. A black stubble was growing on his shaven head and he was ashamed of it. Guram and he had gone to the farm to look for me the day before. They'd gone even farther, to the abandoned village, and I begged their forgiveness for causing all the alarm.

"I've been wanting to talk to you about your faith for some time now," Shalva said.

"I'm afraid we'll hardly have time. Anyway, why talk to me? It's better to talk about God with someone who's given himself totally to him. . . . Speak to the abbot." It turned out that Father Michael and he had once burned the midnight oil sitting in the glade. Afterward the abbot gave Shalva a catechesis, while Eli got a book about the mystical meaning of the liturgy.

I'd noticed that they'd all begun attending the service more often: Guram and Shalva stood in the church, while Eli and Nona stayed in the doorway. The soul is "by its very nature Christian," it recognizes the Truth, if only we come close enough to it.

The abbot was sitting in the next room to the refectory. He looked at me expectantly. Before coming in I asked his blessing and went out to heat up some breakfast. Before it was over, Mitya arrived back with the car—the women had waited a day more. He was shy of being affectionate in the abbot's presence, but forgot this in his joy and kissed me on the cheek. My dear boy had come back, praise God. . . .

While we were all still sitting in the refectory Mitya told us about the wonderful time at Sioni with twelve archpriests taking part—not to mention the whole Georgian episcopate. They'd consecrated a thirteenth bishop, a friend of our abbot who was the same age as him. Mitya had worn a long, wide-sleeved deacon's alb, and he'd presented his anthem, emerging afterward with a candle, and offered the patriarch the *dikirion,* or double candle, held by him during the blessing.

"Yes, Mom, the patriarch asked how we liked Dzhvari and blessed our stay here till the end of summer. . . ." My son was filled with such joy, whereas I was crushed by what I was about to tell him.

After dinner Mitya was glad to stretch out on his bunk. He was really tired after these two days of ceremonial festivities. Just the same, he kept on describing in vivid detail the service that had become so meaningful to us. I hadn't the heart to stop him— there was still plenty of time before morning.

I was sitting by the open door when its green and yellow space was filled by the dark figure of the abbot. He did not usually come to see us, and so his appearance augured something important.

"Veronica, I must speak to you."

"Come in, Father Michael."

"No, I won't. Would you mind coming out here?"

I threw my coat over my sundress and knotted my scarf at the back of my neck. We made our way slowly down the hill.

We sat on the slope where Father Michael had cut grass the night we'd arrived. I'd wanted to sit there with him and with Mitya that time, but here we were now, just the two of us. Our abandoned tent stood farther down the cliff, scorching in the sun. The glade below was thick with grass once more. Beyond it on the left we could make out a white house with a wide balcony. Benedict was walking there and could see us quite well. The pale mass of the church arose in front of us, while the mountains in the distance shimmered in the heat.

There wasn't a cloud in the sky. But the clear blue and the light were merging and dissolving in the wide expanse of heaven, in a kind of continuous upheaval. You could only long to go on gazing into this living chasm.

"Veronica . . . I told you that I got baptized only six years ago." The abbot had started speaking with some difficulty but he was quiet now. "As a young man I had a free life-style. No matter what a man brings into a monastery with him, he is tormented even more by the remnants of his past. You asked me what was the hardest part of being a monk. At one time I used to be sent all manner of people for confession—young women, girls, the lot. I begged the patriarch not to give his blessing to anyone else."

His hands around his knees, he sat up straight, looking ahead, speaking in an even, hard tone. His familiar black cap was perched forward over his forehead.

"So you see, your presence here causes me pain . . . pain in my soul."

This strange confession of his was so unexpected I couldn't believe it. I even thought at first he was adopting someone else's sin so as to conceal it with his own.

"I hinted about it to you several times. But you evaded the issue . . . or you just didn't understand."

"For some reason or other I just didn't connect these innuendos with you personally. In fact there was nobody here I could really apply them to. I suppose I took it as a sort of abstract conversation . . . about the dangers of spiritual communion."

"Whereas I was talking about it quite openly: There's no way you and I can enjoy spiritual intimacy. There are other cases too. Take my relationship with David—that precludes any feelings on my part for his wife. . . ."

"I suppose I thought that your relationship with me meant such things were kept out." I was trying to hold myself in check, but the words that came out were totally unexpected, and untrue. How could I have failed to notice what was obvious to him? This question receded into the depths of my consciousness, blocked out by our recent exchange.

"Of course they're excluded," he said. "We both know it. But human beings are made of flesh and of passions: You may not sin in deed, but you will in your thoughts. The monastic life is an invisible struggle with one's passionate nature. 'The Word of God is a two-edged sword, piercing to the division of soul and spirit, of joints and marrow,' as the apostle says—and it judges the thoughts and intentions of the heart. 'To the division of soul and spirit'—do you follow me?—how fearful . . . and how painful this can be?"

I understood now. I'd experienced this pain myself previously, but I'd almost consigned it to oblivion.

"I'm not ashamed to tell you all this," he began in a quieter, softer voice. "There's nothing hidden from God, everything is laid bare before his eyes. What could I say now in answer if he were to ask: 'Adam, where are you?' I'd most likely want to hide in the thicket too, because I forgot about him yesterday."

I didn't answer. And then he asked: "Does this confession flatter you?"

"Why should it? I think you wanted to wound me till it hurt, yes, with this confession."

"Maybe, maybe." He laughed, never once looking at me, just straight ahead or within himself. "I wanted to put it more brusquely—it's easier that way. That comes from pride too . . . We are very proud people, and there's nothing harder to acquire on our way to God than a humble awareness of one's own weaknesses . . . that, and repentance itself. But I don't want to go into detail about my feelings for you. Who can know what is or is not important?"

I had sensed, after my confession in church, something hidden deep within him. Now I heard it once more echo forcefully in his measured tone.

"Perhaps the secret lies in the makeup of our souls. . . . I never thought—it's the first time it's even happened in my eventful lifetime—I could feel so close to a woman from whom I'm fated to be so far apart—Thus it was, and is, and indeed is to be. We are scarcely going to meet each other in eternity. Even to be saved is so difficult that I can scarcely believe I will manage it. 'I will die soon, and my accursed soul will descend to Hades.' I only wish you a kinder fate." The more his earlier posing and teasing fell away, the more tense the atmosphere between us became.

"All the same, I know that this flame . . ." he said the words quietly, "can leap from me to you—and then it will sweep all barriers away."

The pain I sensed beneath the even tones of his

voice pierced my heart. I thought, I know nothing of his past or of his present. What *were* those persistent passions of his? Surely it is everything that a person has not fully loved, everything the soul has not experienced, until it is separated by the sword of death from the body or from the passionless spirit. . . .

"You'll be waiting for me to tell you that we're leaving?"

"What other way is left to us?" he replied. "We can't live side by side. Not least after this conversation we've had . . . I didn't want it; I kept putting it off until the very last. Yesterday, when you came back at last, that's when I wanted to talk to you. I'd have said it all differently."

It was his last comment that gave me the clue. "So it was you who came back . . . later?"

He leaned on his elbows, then lay flat on the grass, as if the spring that had held him erect and firm had snapped. He threw his hands behind his head, and lay there looking at the blue sky above us. "Yes, it was me." In the silence that followed he broke off a dry stalk and started to chew it. Barely turning around, I saw his face without its habitual shield of irony, his eyes reflecting the blue light. "How do you know? You couldn't have seen me, or even heard me."

"I just sensed your presence."

"Ah, so that's it." He gave a little laugh. "So my confession was for nothing. Anyway, it's all one now, Ve-ro-ni-ca . . . I was coming to you for confession."

"It must have been quite late?"

"I suppose so . . . I don't remember noticing the time. All I knew was that there would be no other

time for us. That's the way it is—something's born
in you, it ferments, expands . . . and suddenly—it's
all over. . . . What kept you all day? Where on earth
did you bury yourself?"

"By the river."

"What were you doing? Swimming?"

"No, crying."

He lowered his hand carefully onto the grass,
where it lay pointing in my direction.

"What were you crying about?"

"That everything has finished so quickly for me
. . . in Dzhvari."

"A-ah. . . ." He let out a breath, as though he'd
expected something else. He lay still, shading his
eyes. He opened them slowly, sat up, folding his
hands on his knees. He started talking, and you could
still feel the previous day's emotion: "As twilight fell
I was too upset by your disappearance. In these remote mountains of ours you're afraid to meet man or
beast. In winter the wolves come close to the monastery, their tracks clear in the snow. A human being
that has lost God is more fearful than a wolf. . . . We
were all in a terrible state because of you."

"Forgive me."

"Archil took Muria and ran off through the forest
to find you. He said: 'It's me that's upset her and she's
gone off.' I too . . . was in real torment. All the same, I
couldn't bring myself to call you when I didn't see a
light. Sorry, I don't mean to justify myself."

"Nor do I wish to blame you for anything. My
strength is not up to carrying your cross, and I've no
right to judge you. Anyway, Mitya and I have taken
you too much into our hearts."

"Why are you telling me this, Veronica?" A shadow crossed his face.

"Why? So as to tell the truth? But is it really possible, to tell the whole truth, to capture all that lies furthest within, deepest down, to capture something living in a web of words?"

In the outermost layer of what I was going through just then was a long-felt weariness with words of any sort, of my life being burdened by words. This weariness came from my lack of freedom—even from the tense way I was sitting on the hillside, half-facing the abbot, leaning on my outstretched hand so that the marks of the dry stalks were embedded in my reddened palm. It was hot under the awkward coat; I wanted to take it off and be just in my dress, to feel the sun on my arms, get rid of the head scarf. Oh, just to stretch out on the grass as Father Michael had been doing, and gaze into the expanse of blue.

One day, not in the immediate future, I'd ask him what his life had been like, right from the beginning, when he was a child. Did his mother love him? What did he like doing then? And what happened after? He'd tell me about everything and I'd get to know the kind of person he'd been, and what it cost him to enter the monastery. And as time passed, the gap between us would gradually fill up with trust and kindness . . . and the desire for tenderness.

But in reality none of this would ever happen.

What's more, looking now at the abbot's open face, released from its former tension—this face that I knew so well, whose concentration and deep sorrow I was seeing for the first time—I began to understand at last why we ought not to have drawn so close to each other. But recognizing yourself in someone else is more far-reaching and penetrating—an unconfessed recognition that goes beyond words and events, to the heart of things, to the main point—destiny, to its pain. . . .

I felt this now; he had before. When had he felt it? When he gave me the black scarf with its faded flowers? Or was it the night we left Eli's—the sickle moon reflected in the dark water of the swimming pool with its reflection broken by the abbot's stone—that the first thought came, light and clear? Or was it the night I went to confession in the little church and we'd talked about God and love and he had laid his head wearily on the crucifix?

But it wasn't only these twenty days in Dzhvari that had united us. The linking process had begun much earlier, maybe even in our noncontemporary childhoods, in the loneliness, the weariness at everything that promised to satisfy the soul, yet did not.

I still felt an immense sorrow at our earthly portion, in which God's Word—the flaming sword of the cherubim—separated us from the Tree of Life that stands in the middle of Paradise. We can no longer see God, and time has fallen out of eternity to the extinction of its beneficial light. And so a deadly bitterness spreads through the air, through the fruit that satisfies our hunger, through the water; and the immortal Spirit in each of us weeps and prays with inexpressible sighs as it calls: "Abba, Father!"

Nothing of this could be spoken aloud. Instead I said: "Well then, so we're off tomorrow morning."

He replied at once, speaking very quietly: "Why wait till tomorrow? You could leave today, now.

The car that Mitya came in is still here. I asked the driver, he was planning to spend the night here."

Amazing . . . he'd already found out the driver's plans. I'd counted on being able to put Mitya in the picture, let him have a rest. But if we don't go on foot, I'll tell him *en route*.

"Why put it off?" he kept insisting. "The sooner the better."

For the first time we looked each other in the eye. And perhaps this long look said everything that neither he nor I could say in any other way.

"We've no time left, Father Michael."

"Nor should there have been any. You see, I departed from our ancient statutes and . . . got punished at once. But they say it's good for a monk to undergo temptation."

"To him that loves God all things are profitable."

"To him that loves God . . ." he repeated the words carefully. "Yes, there is only one love that has no limits or set periods, and that's our love for God. For God's love we have to abandon all other love, anything that's of the world. Life ought to be compressed into a single dot, so that all radiuses join at the center of the circle. And this central point of life is God."

IT TURNED OUT, however, that we were not to get away. When Father Michael and I came into the refectory, Archil said that the driver had intended to spend the night here but, sitting alone on the bench by the well, he'd got bored and decided to leave.

He'd be back by dinnertime the next day, with the restorers.

"So there we are . . ." said the abbot somewhat vaguely, clearly not wanting to accept the situation. "Well, maybe it's better this way. We'll say the office tomorrow a bit earlier. You'll have your breakfast, make your general farewells. So be it, if it cannot be otherwise."

Mitya was lying on his bunk, still in his cassock and reading. He got up when I came in: "What were you talking to the abbot about for so long?"

"About having to leave."

"When?"

"Tomorrow."

"You really mean tomorrow?"

"It's just as well it wasn't today."

"And why's that?"

"I'll tell you . . . later. Meanwhile, let's get packed."

Mitya took his monk's cap from the table. "I was given this, so naturally I'm going to take it with me."

"Are you surprised?"

Cap in hand he stopped, propping himself up against the door. Outside it was green and light, the birds were chirping.

"You know, not really, I'm sad it's so soon and unexpected. But I'm not really surprised."

"Why's that?"

"It was a miracle we landed up here in Dzhvari . . . and that we've been living here. It's strange that we're leaving." He smiled, though his lips trembled at the corners. "God has given, God has taken away. Blessed be the name of the Lord."

I stood looking at my son. His hair had grown and was bleached a glistening gold by the sun. His face too was sunburned. A firmness etched the tender features I loved. His glance was light and firm.

"The most unexpected things have happened to us since we've come to faith. That festival in Sioni, that I attended by some miracle, has only just finished. It was all quite unpredictable and at the same time—I felt this quite recently—it happens in that unique way that it can only happen . . . the way that God leads us. It's the way a river flows, you can't change its course—it's all so deep, nothing happens by chance, everything has a meaning."

He sat on the threshold. "Some years back I read in a magazine about the enthronement of the Catholicos-Patriarch of all Georgia, Ilya the Second, and saw his photograph. I still remember it vividly. The patriarch stood in front of the open royal doors and blessed the people with the *dikirion* and *trikirion*. I looked at his photograph for ages, and I thought that, even if I ever got to Georgia, I'd never see him close at hand. But we arrived there, went into the cathedral . . . I saw the patriarch before the liturgy took place, when he personally gave each one the Communion bread. He gave it to me too and blessed me in Russian."

Mitya fingered the edges of his monk's cap. A still light shone evenly in his eyes. "Then we came to Dzhvari. Father Michael blessed my writing an anthem. Goodness, you and I haven't talked about it yet—so much has happened. But it was really strange how I wrote it. When I used to compose music, I'd sit for ages at the piano squeezing it out of myself . . . I ought to compose, I wanted to compose, I made a huge effort, drove myself. But there was nothing like that this time. He gave his blessing—and I wrote it. It was like music pouring out by itself. It was like the desire to sing—and I sang, the desire to pray—and I prayed. Do you remember? The abbot said: 'Let it come through you like something that doesn't belong to you.' "

That's the way we ought to write, I thought.

"And then at the altar of Sioni Church I was dressed in a red alb during the all-night vigil. There were twelve archpriests. His Holiness sat on his high-backed, carved wooden throne. Archbishop Thaddaeus, who'd written the anthem, led me up. I knelt down and offered the patriarch my present. All through the service the other sub-deacons and I held the patriarch's staff or stood at the royal doors with the *primikirion*—it's a huge candle. I was asked, in Georgian, to do something, and I did everything properly because I know the liturgy, and some of them didn't even guess that I don't know the language."

We fell silent. Then he said: "So let's thank God for everything."

The abbot didn't come to supper. After the evening office he asked me to give everyone tea. Archil and Benedict exchanged glances and refused tea, while Mitya of course came with me.

The kerosene lamp was lit. The abbot got out the fig preserves and bread himself. The warm night closed in on us from the open window. With that same parting intensity I saw his movements, our table, the rough wooden bench, the window grille. The storm we'd just had seemed so beautiful to me now.

"I don't want to sleep. It's our last night," Mitya said, giving Father Michael a timid, hopeful glance.

"What do you want, Dmitri?" He almost managed a smile.

"To have a talk . . . you never know when we'll meet again."

"What about?"

"About the monastic life." Mitya pronounced the words quietly and rather sadly. "What is it really like?"

"And what do you want to know?"

"Well, everybody lives . . . different life-styles, of course, but they live a normal life. Then suddenly you leave it altogether, forever . . . why?"

Something trembled in my heart at the underlying seriousness of his question, as though a shadow of foreboding lay in its depth.

"The ways of the Lord are unsearchable," sighed the abbot.

We made some tea and poured it into enamel mugs. A slight steam misted up the glass of the lamp. Father Michael moved the lamp, then took it right away from the table and stuck it in the wall-bracket. Its light became softer, more even.

"The fact is, God has a plan for every soul," said the abbot thoughtfully. "We don't know what it is, and we go around with our eyes shut. When we get close to God's plan we feel better, but when we're far away from it, things go badly. A lot of people live the wrong sort of life until the end of their days, never guessing they should be doing something else. They work hard, but they're never quite themselves; everything falls apart. . . . Nobody told them they had to find their own selves—and if you don't do that, you lose everything." He took off his clerical hat and took a sip of tea. "God's plan—or if we narrow the concept, his calling—includes our talents: music, for example. You've been learning the violin for eight years. Could you spend the rest of your life doing that?"

"I don't think so. I used to like listening to music, feeling it and playing. But a professional has to be a virtuoso. I'd be bored if I had to spend months polishing a piece. I thought composing would be more interesting, kind of broader, higher."

"And perhaps something higher still?"

"I don't know," said Mitya, thinking it over. "I haven't found anything higher for myself yet."

"But I know. Life in God—that's the highest thing of all. This is the highest creation because we're creating our very self, not something external. We create our own soul. 'Be perfect, as your heavenly Father is perfect.' What could be higher than the idea of holiness? Only God himself."

"But this isn't for everyone, it's kind of exceptional. How are we supposed to know whether God is calling us or not?"

"Father Lavrenti used to say, if someone comes to a monastery and likes everything there, and if the longer he's there the more he likes it, that means he has a calling. If everything seems strange, oppressive, annoying—then there's no calling."

"Is that how it was for you?"

"For me? Well, Dmitri, maybe it's best if you don't know anything about me. It's embarrassing if people hear something bad about a priest. Yes, and that's why your Mom keeps you away from the bad side of life. She wants to keep you from knowing."

He barely glanced in my direction.

"No, I'm more in favor of sound knowledge. . . ."

The abbot shifted into the shadow and leaned against the wall, clasping his hands around his knees and looking past us, beyond the window grating. A moth fluttered around the lamp.

"Have you ever smoked?" Father Michael asked Mitya, still without looking at him.

"No, never." For some reason I answered for my son.

"Not even once?" the abbot asked, amazed, turning around for a moment with an amused smile.

Mitya laughed and lowered his eyes.

"Okay, you tried it once, and then you forgot. Well, I can remember quite well: I didn't smoke, but when I was fifteen I started taking drugs. I mixed with a bad crowd: wine, drugs, fighting, all the usual things. I could tell you more"—he glanced straight at me—"or is that enough?"

I nodded silently.

"My mother was an English teacher. She liked to go out and about, mix with people: professors, doctors, you know. She was ashamed of me. She put me in a rehab clinic, but it didn't help. I came off drugs slowly—really only when I went to prison." He said all this evenly, as he had done that morning on the hillside, as though he had decided to tell the whole truth—and I felt that he was saying it for himself as much as for Mitya. "Well, I want you to get hold of this and never forget it: I'm not a typical monk, more like a sorry sort of exception among my illustrious brothers. You've read the lives of the saints: They've nearly all had pious parents and were fed with the pure milk of the faith from their earliest years—that's so important! It's the royal route to monasticism: from purity to holiness. Of course, it's impossible not to have a few falls—but some are worse than others. People nowadays are totally crippled, full of vice, turned inside out . . . I've gone though hell, my dears, and I still carry this hell inside me. So, remember this, in case I make you view other clergy in the same dark mold. D'you hear me, Dmitri?"

"Yes," Mitya said, quietly.

"The first time I called on God it was from the abyss, and I'm still there, calling from the abyss even now." He took a few more sips of tea and then set his mug aside. "They put us in prison after we'd been fighting—a whole gang of us. One of our lot knifed someone from another gang. I was twenty-five. We all got five years. What happened next, you couldn't imagine in your wildest dreams, . . . I wouldn't do what anyone wanted, and so I was put in the punishment cell. I wouldn't submit, because I just wasn't used to obeying anyone. I hadn't knifed anyone, so I didn't think I was guilty, and I took my revenge. The whole prison camp system is out to oppress and not correct, but I didn't want to be crushed. What is a punishment cell? It's made of cement. It's freezing. There's no window and you get bread and water once a day. You can't be kept there for more than fifteen days. I was let out on the sixteenth and on the seventeenth they put me back again. I began to cough blood a year later and the doctors signed me off all work.

"There was another Georgian there," the abbot went on. "He'd been well known once, a famous theater producer. He married a great beauty—and that was his downfall. He was put in prison for murder, killing out of jealousy. Well, somehow or other he came up to me. 'Let's swap. You give me your illness and I'll give you my sentence.' 'No,' I told him. 'I can't agree. They've promised me there's only one way I'll get out: in my grave.' He waved that away. 'You're not really ill. I'd soon shake it off.'

"He taught me yoga breathing exercises and postures. I had a choice: get better or die. I did deep breathing for several months and got better. As well as having TB I'd dislocated my spinal cord. When I was sixteen I'd made a parachute jump, the highest one you could, and I'd been a sports champion. Proud people always want to overachieve. . . . The doctors said I'd always have to wear a corset—but I wouldn't, of course. Well, I got better. I could tuck my leg right around my head. My spine straightened out. The X rays didn't show any more dark spots, so they let me out. The doctors couldn't believe their eyes!

"As you know, prison is the pits. To be on top you've got to become even crueler than all the others. When I returned to the world I hated everyone. But I had to go on living. I could have gone back to the polytechnic where I'd already studied six years, and couldn't get finished because of boredom—but this had lost all meaning now.

"A woman artist friend had a big library on yoga, so I made use of it. I already had the idea that yoga was a kind of religion, that we haven't plumbed the depth of our human potential. We can in fact learn everything—even how to materialize objects out of air and walk on water. But why?

"I came across a book of Lodyzhensky's about Christianity. I was really surprised—what's it all about? Yogis are . . ." The abbot straightened his shoulders, stood up, his chest expanded in a deep sigh, and his face took on a serious, distant expression, "Yogis are . . . healthy, strong, pure . . . and it's all so cold. Christians are quite the opposite: humble and meek. The yogi is always taken up with himself, his body, he's always washing himself, and not only his body, mouth, nose, ears but even his stomach. But these Christian hermits exhaust the body in every way they can, dig themselves into caves like living sacrifices. And at the same time you feel a great warmth. . . . Yes, I didn't know what it was, except that it was something warm and I'd never come across it before.

"Then I read through the Gospel, and was shaken to the core. But to say that is to say almost nothing. What did this mean for me at that time? It was a bit like coming out of prison. But only a bit. After all, even when I was free I still remained the same sort of person I'd been in prison. I still had a prison mentality. I was soaked in it: hatred, filth, the memory of human degradation and shame, and all this vileness tore at me from within, rising in my throat.

"Suddenly . . . suddenly . . . or 'straightway' as the holy evangelist Mark says, I read the Gospel and understood Pilate's words, 'Behold the man.' I understood the great majesty of our predestination looming over my former life of ugliness. And this man—was me too.

"That very day or maybe it was during one of my endless sleepless cycles at night, as well as reading the Gospel I read the conversation of St. Serafim of Sarov with the Simbirsk merchant Motovilov, whom the saint cured of paralysis. There they were, sitting in a white forest glade, the snow falling . . . Motovilov kept asking what the grace of the Holy Spirit was. St. Serafim revealed himself to the man in a special light, just as Christ showed himself to the apostles at the Transfiguration. And this young courtier, until recently condemned to death by his illness and yet healed, saw the saint's face shining as if with bright sunlight. He experienced a deep fear, but also an unspeakable joy. It was something he'd never known and could not even envisage. A deep, deep peace, blessedness and warmth, a fragrance, a sweetness—a transfiguration, a resurrection of the soul, a satisfying of all desires and feelings. And Serafim of Sarov said to him that this was the living presence of the grace of the Holy Spirit, the Kingdom of God was being revealed to him. . . .

"This was the first day of happiness I'd ever known. I now knew what I had to live for. Perhaps I'd felt the same thing as Motovilov, but on a different level—I'd only found out it exists. And I believed—at once, no conditions, no doubts. I believed with my whole heart, which had been dead and now was alive again.

"I got baptized there and then, and a few days later I went off to the Odessa seminary. I didn't even dare think about the priesthood. It never even entered my head that that's what the seminary was all about. I simply had to get a full understanding, get to the heart of the matter—to receive systematic knowledge of Christianity. . . .

"Well, to go on . . . I came to Odessa and saw the inspector. As usual I had had a bit too much to drink; one thing didn't seem to have excluded the other, only my intellect—the pinnacle of life—had been transformed while everything material remained unchanged. The inspector sighed and looked away; he didn't once look me in the face. He sent me to the housemaster to ask for a job in the kitchen or the community garden. The housemaster greeted me more warmly, but when he heard about my past he said that all the work was done by the seminarians. He told me to come back next year. And what would happen to the seminarians next year? I wondered.

"I realized it was very unlikely that I'd get into the seminary, I had another drink, bought a secondhand book about Lao-Tse, went to the station, settled down on a bench among all the luggage, and started reading. I left a note at home to say that I'd gone off for a long time and didn't intend to come back.

"A small red-haired peasant was sitting on the bench opposite. He was reading an old book too, and obviously wasn't in a hurry to leave. 'That looks interesting,' I thought. 'What kind of book is it?' It turned out to be the Acts of the Apostles. He even read a bit aloud, quite enthusiastically—it was really interesting! He had a look at my book too, but gave it back at once. 'Hey you,' he said, 'chuck this Chinese stuff—leave it for the Chinese to read. Do you think you'll find the truth if you keep looking all over the place, trying to grab it anywhere and everywhere? Truth is One. Aren't you a Christian?' 'Yes, I've been baptized. . . .' 'Do you wear a cross?' 'No, but I will. Do you know, I wanted to enter the seminary but they wouldn't even let me into the kitchen.'

"He didn't show any sympathy: and okay, that was fine.

"'Go off to the monastery. They'll teach you all you need to know.' He told me the address. 'I'm going in that direction myself tomorrow. We can go together if you like. Only don't drink anymore—you'll stink of wine.'

"So there he was: an ugly little peasant with a knapsack and clumpy boots. He only came up to my chest, yet here he was saying 'Truth is One,' and 'You stink of wine'! I was astonished, and I felt quite offended, but I went to the station next day. 'Bought your cross?' he asked. 'Yes.' 'Got it on?' 'Yes.' 'Show me.'

"I showed him a little copper cross and he looked pleased. It turned out he was going to the monastery, only he hadn't wanted to tell me—he was sizing me up. So we went together. He explained it all in the train: all the whys and wherefores. He taught me how to approach the novice master: I had to say, 'I've come to pray and if you bless me I'll stay and do whatever task you want.'

"We came to the monastery, where they knew my fellow traveler already. He introduced me to the novice master . . . 'Don't worry about his face, Father. He wants to live like an Orthodox Christian.'

"I was taken aback once more. What kind of face did I have?

"Well, they gave me my first job in the refectory. Three of us laid tables for about a hundred, cleared away, washed up, set the tables again. I kept saying to the novice master: 'I want to read books.' He'd shrug his shoulders and turn away without answering. The other monks didn't worry either. They'd pray after their meal and go away. 'What kind of people are these?' I thought. I was soon appointed senior novice in the refectory. Things went from bad to worse. I tried very hard to please the monks but I lost the state of mind I'd had at the beginning. I don't know what to call it. . . . It was a kind of cooling-off period. I talked about it to my spiritual father, old archimandrite Lavrenti. He said, 'This isn't right. You see, you're too proud. We'll transfer you to the cave, where the saint's remains are.'

"That was a good act of obedience. You stand in front of the saint's remains all day. People crowd around to see them. The cave was small. There were lots of people and no air. I started coughing again. Father Lavrenti could hardly see, even with glasses. So they said to him, 'You can't see, but your novice has gone quite yellow. He's not well.'

"Then I was given the keys to the store. I opened it, shut it, sat in the fresh air, and that's how I managed to get through a lot of books. . . . When my lungs got bad again I was let off monastic duties and spent several months getting well. They cooked special buds and herbs for me. I'd thought they hadn't bothered about me, but now I felt their kindness.

"You have to go through with this. . . . Here you both are, looking for peace and solitude, but really you both have to experience this life lived in community. The fact that you've lived in hostels or communal apartments doesn't count. It's totally different. But previously that's the way things were done—all in due order. At first you'd be placed outside the actual monastery boundaries. After that, you'd be given a special duty, and a few years after that you'd receive the tonsure and be allowed to wear a waist-length cassock, which gives you the right to wear monastic dress. And when you've learned to live in the monastic way you are allowed to wear the *mantiya*—that's when the monk makes his final vows. You're allowed to receive the blessing to become a hermit only when you're really mature, after many years of communal life in the monastery. A monk doesn't leave the world because people annoy him or because he doesn't want to have anything to do with them, or doesn't know how to get along with other people. Quite the reverse, he has to learn to love everyone all over again. Then he can go into complete seclusion with that love because he's got other business that's even more important. . . .

"Nowadays you get someone who's had no real experience of true monastic life becoming a bishop and running a diocese. So they've thought up a new word, *manager,* which makes him sound like some sort of a boss of a collective farm. The church and clergy are becoming secularized. God's Spirit in the monk is being replaced by some sort of blueprint for management, with terrible results: loss of faith, compromises and quarrels within the Church. . . . When there were disputes about Gregory the Divine being archbishop of Constantinople, he said, 'I'm not greater than Jonah. If this storm is because of me, throw me into the sea so that it will become calm again.' Depriving him of his office doesn't deprive him of God. And that's what Christianity is about—not a struggle for power and mutual recriminations.

"But I got carried away. . . . Here's the rest of my story. Our subprior attended an interchurch conference with a Georgian archbishop and happened to say, 'We've got a Georgian in our monastery too.' 'Send him to Patriarch Ilya,' he said. 'We need monks.' And so Father Lavrenti sent me back to Georgia with his blessing. They collected money for me to live in the mountains so that my lungs could get healed. And so I had a complete break for two months, and then I went off to the patriarch.

" 'What do you want?' he asked. I told him I wanted to live in a monastery. 'Find someone else who's ready to be tonsured and go and have a look at Dzhvari.'

"I'd already decided I didn't want to look at a monastery, but the patriarch insisted. Hilarion and I came here at the end of September—the best time of year in these parts. I can't tell how I felt about Dzhvari. You can guess some of it, I know, but only a part. Your whole past has been so different. . . . I told the patriarch I had two conditions: I would never leave the monastery again and would never become a priest.

"A monk is a person who repents and weeps for his sins, who tries to carry out the commandments with all his strength. A priest has no right not to obey the commandments and I thought he had to be someone who was worthy of the office. The clergy ought to be spiritual and those in holy office ought to be holy. The priestly life and the monastic life are really two different ways of serving God. There's nothing higher than celebrating the liturgy, but a monk only takes part in it, while a priest celebrates. It's not quite the same thing. There were about five thousand monks in the Egyptian monastery caves in the fifth century but Savva was the only one who decided to become a priest—and this was such an event that he became known as Savva the Holy.

"A priest is obliged to shoulder the care of his flock, speak to people, and enter into their lives. I wanted to be alone with God. But the patriarch said, 'No.' I said, 'No,' too, and went off to my monastery. But Father Lavrenti convinced me that I wasn't right to impose conditions on the patriarch, so I went back to agree to the conditions the patriarch wanted to put upon me. He told me, 'A hieromonk bears a very heavy cross, but you must take it—for the sake of others. The monastery can't exist without services.'

"So I took the tonsure at the age of thirty-two and became an abbot. But if I'd had my own way I'd have stayed a simple brother forever."

THE SKY WAS lightening beyond the window grille. The lamp had burned out, probably because the paraffin was finished. I watched the figure of the abbot

9:16 AM -
Harriet + George
dinner Sea World

Julie Zafeiris

Gregory Theopistos
671-1837

as he leaned wearily against the wall in the soft light of early dawn. Mitya had settled down on the trestle bed long since, covering himself with his cassock. He was sitting very quietly, afraid a careless movement might interrupt Father Michael.

The abbot was silent for some time, then he started to talk about the different ways that had led so many people to the monastery over the years. He said how nice it was here in the winter—when everything was covered with snow and there was so much light and brightness, and the road was blocked so no one could get up to the monastery: no restorers, tourists, pilgrims. That was when the real life of fasting and prayer began.

The soul was freed from outside things and plunged into quietness and prayer. . . .

I remembered how I used to repeat the words, *Cogito ergo sum*—"I think, therefore I am." Then life taught me another definition, "I suffer, therefore I live." As my faith deepened I began to discover the force of the words, "as long as we keep loving—we live." And quite recently, I'd read one of our contemporary writers who said, "as long I keep praying—I live. Outside of this, everything is flawed. Something is lacking."

Father Michael replied that prayer is the school of love also, because prayer is the way to God and is communion, union with him. We cannot love anything or anybody outside God.

THE ABBOT SENT us off for some sleep about two hours before the liturgy, with the promise that Archil would wake us up. It was warm and quiet inside our little house and there was even a light smell of drying grasses and cones. Mitya groaned, stretching out on his bed without getting undressed. "Well, you know, Mom, I'll never forget Father Michael and everything he said tonight here in Dzhvari. Why do you think he told us all that, and why have we got to leave?"

I explained as best as I could and he took what he could understand and accepted it. Then he fell asleep and I lay with my eyes shut. The abbot's words still rang in my memory, my heart was full of him and of his destiny. I still wanted to think over the "why" that had come up at the beginning of our explanation: Why had I not realized what was plain to everyone else? Why had the earthly distance between us not grown less, either, after the explanation or after his story? And why could it never decrease?

This distance between us—or rather within us—was the distance between the world and the church, our lifelong cross.

There is life without faith, a secular life that drags us in its wake and constantly builds and destroys Towers of Babel, exposing their inability to reach up to heaven. It promises instant happiness. You just stretch out your hand and your past and your present become of no account as you try to achieve this beautiful, imaginary thing. This life seduces, excites, attracts you, swallows your soul and heart but never fulfills them, though it promises endless satisfaction—tomorrow.

There are not reliable supports in this world; the skeleton had been removed. There is no supreme meaning that would justify everything, or precise boundaries between good and evil, or any real heart. And therefore its dragging, inconstant flesh is empty, shimmering with vague reflections of something else. Thrown into this aimless world, we become a sacrifice to our very freedom, guided only by common sense, desires, and passions—and we too are empty. Refined reason tries to snatch some sort of existence out of this emptiness, some kind of being, but it invariably slips away.

Perhaps the chief illness of our sick time, not least our permissive society, is our inability to be, because meaningful existence is in God, who gave us the first revelation of his Name in the Old Testament: "I am that I am—" the very essence of existence, and existence itself.

Communion with this existence is realized in the sacraments of the Church, where everything is totally opposite to the norms of the world. There is an exact system of coordinates, weights and measures, commandments. Everything is conditioned by a higher meaning.

God is Truth, whose reflection in the world is Beauty. The fulfillment of his purposes is Good. This is the foundation of all philosophy, aesthetics, and ethics, by which the concept of the Holy is introduced into life. And so the sanctuary that lay people may not enter is separated in church from the area open to everyone. The abbot was sanctified, and always would be, separated off by the barrier of the sanctuary.

✵

THEY CELEBRATED OUR last liturgy. The lamps were burning in the seven-branched candlestick in the sanctuary. Archil, Benedict, and Mitya sang the "Hymn of the Cherubim," which they had just learned: "Let us who mystically represent the Cherubim chant the Thrice Holy hymn to the Life-giving Trinity. Let us forget, let us lay aside all our earthly sorrow and come before God as the Cherubim in the secret, heavenly Eucharist, singing: Holy God, Holy and Mighty, Holy Immortal, have mercy on us." Through my tears I saw the yellow flames of the lamps in the seven-branched candlestick and the two tall candles burning beside the cross on the altar.

Then the abbot in his golden chasuble offered the Holy Gifts in the shape of the cross—and I wanted this last service in Dzhvari to last forever, but the liturgy came to an end, the royal doors were closed. The abbot came out of the sanctuary and silently put a silk cord with a small cross set in a wooden frame around my neck. I lifted the cross carefully on my palm.

"It's made of Georgian enamel that has been specially segmented," said Benedict. "There's a cross like that, shaped in a circle, carved above the portal here. It may be the emblem of Dzhvari."

I glanced toward the abbot as he walked away down the path, and Benedict continued, "Do you see this fine golden thread? It traces right around the cross and divides it from the dark lilac of the background. Our ancient crosses and icons are executed with this segmented enamel. You can't find anything like it anywhere else in the world. Your cross isn't old, but it's been made with the same technique by someone who's discovered the secret."

Archil came up as well. Mitya touched the edge of the cross with his fingers, bowing over it, and turning it toward himself. It was very beautiful: the golden colored enamel of this cross whose ends were all of equal length was exquisitely bound around with gold thread against its dark lilac background.

"A few days ago, Father Michael asked me to make a finely carved simple wooden frame, but I didn't know it was for you. Will you wear it?"

"Of course I will! Thank you, Father Benedict."

"I carved Dzhvari in Georgian on its reverse side," said Benedict, with a smile I had not seen on his face for a long time. "Thank God we are parting on such good terms! Let's pray for each other."

"Don't you want to come to us for good, Dmitri?" asked Archil, kindly, lowering his lashes on the damp luster of his eyes. "We'll have you."

Mitya looked at them with happiness in his eyes, but couldn't speak.

As a way of saying good-bye, Benedict showed us the Virgin Mary he'd been carving: The abbot hadn't had time to take it to the patriarch. The deacon took it out of the breast pocket of his old cassock and unwrapped the white cloth. It was a small, finely carved oval icon of Our Lady of Tenderness—the Most Pure Mother raising her hands in prayer for all of us sinners on earth who seek our heavenly home.

AFTER BREAKFAST THE abbot and I went for a walk in the clearing around the church. I touched the rough warm walls with my palm. I bowed to the graves of the *startsy* of Mount Athos and asked for their holy prayers. We sat in the meager shadow of the walnut tree beside the graves for a while.

"Well, then . . . forgive me . . ." the abbot began.

"God forgives. Forgive me too," I replied in the monastic style of farewell.

For a few moments I found it hard to breathe, as I had in church when he put the cross around my neck. "I'm leaving with nothing but gratitude. . . ."

"What for?" he asked, and I sensed a hidden shyness in his smile. Why had I never seen him smile like that before? And he wanted to know what for!

"For every day I've spent in your monastery; every day that shouldn't have happened; for this cross, and because of the kind of person you are; for your love of God; and because of the simple way we can talk now, at last . . ."

"At last—yes, it's become possible."

"May I write to you sometime? A year from now?"

"No," but there was light in the way he smiled. "It's one thing to chop off my hand with one fell swoop, it's another to saw it away more slowly: I wouldn't have the strength for that." He fell silent, looking at the foliage. "Look at this chestnut. The leaves are turning yellow. They're not necessary now the fruit has ripened. Have you noticed how the persimmon ripens? The leaves fall off completely, only the fruit remains. Autumn draws in, then the first time of cold begins and still the fruit isn't picked, because people wait for them to ripen properly. The tree stands bare, without leaves, covered with heavy orange fruit."

A quiet noise sounded above us, a puff of wind—

and a big leaf, barely tinged with yellow, fell on the dark granite of the tombstone.

"You and I have talked a lot about fasting, prayer, the ascetic life, about denial . . . But these are just leaves, necessary for the ripening fruit. When we get there"—he pointed up above the church—"no one will ask us how much we've fasted, what we've denied ourselves, what kind of offerings we've brought. But by our fruits they will know us."

I asked a question that was almost impossible to answer: Did he know the taste of these fruits already?

He answered as best he could. "I know only that these four years in the monastery have been the best in my life. One great hero of the faith could say this about himself: 'The one who has tasted mercy despises all passions and does not value life itself, because Divine Love is dearer than life.' "

Mitya came up, and somehow we both decided there and then that we wouldn't wait for the car. It was better to go on foot. Where had we to hurry to now? Our belongings weren't exactly heavy: a holdall and a travel bag. We wanted to take our time in leaving, so that we could still see Dzhvari from the other side of the gorge, and then catch a last glimpse of it from the ridge. We said good-bye to our cell and carried a pile of unread books back to the refectory.

WE CAME OUT to the spring—the abbot, Benedict, and Archil were sitting on the bench, patiently waiting. We said our last good-byes, passing on our good wishes to the restorers. Then Father Michael came up to me and made a slow sign of the cross over me. "May the Lord bless you."

I wanted to kiss the hand that blessed me, but he placed both his palms on my head only for an instant, blessing my son in the same way. "Will you come to us, Dmitri?"

"Yes, I'll come, I'll come," said Mitya quietly, and we left.

We turned around a few steps later—the abbot, Benedict, and Archil were standing in the monastery gateway together, watching us as we went away. Behind them, behind the half-ruined stone barrier, the ancient church raised its cross to heaven and the sun shone on it like gold.

Called, Chosen, and Faithful

God is light.
1 John 1:5
Believe in the light, that you may become children of light.
John 12:36
. . . You are a chosen race, a royal priesthood, a holy nation,
God's own people, that you may declare the wonderful deeds of him
who called you out of darkness into his marvelous light.
1 Peter 2:9

THANK YOU, LORD, that you created the sea. . . .

I was on holiday in Southern Georgia, staying in a
two-storied house with a garden, the home of Metropolitan Azariah. The bishop had invited me to stay
while he was working in the cathedral in Tbilisi. The
house was empty, so I took the first-floor guest
room. Usually occupied by visiting clergy, it had a
spacious refectory hung with icons and portraits of
former bishops. The windows looked out onto a
glass-roofed veranda, with a broad staircase leading
down from it. The veranda windows were wide
open, and you could see a stone wall and an orchard
overgrown with small white rosebushes. Lime trees
with clipped tops lined the road beyond the gates. I
could make out the courtyard of an old house with
wooden balconies and a patched roof. The garden
was fenced on two sides; the third was enclosed by
the brick wall of the old house, its single window
barely above ground level.

I spent my mornings and evenings at the beach,
swimming beyond the buoys, far out along the path
of the setting sun. Reddish light poured under my
closed eyelids. My sunburned body was thankful for

the blissful cool and freshness of the water. I wanted to swim until I was totally exhausted, wrapped in semi-oblivion, like a dolphin at one with the playful sea. I plunged underwater and opened my eyes. The same light still poured through the sea, paled now to green. I caught sight of my reflection on the surface of the water, fragmented by rays of light that seemed to come from the very depths. Coming to the surface, I floated on my back, scattering bubbles, my hands spread out—now sinking, now resurfacing—looking at wispy clouds lit up by the setting sun. Bathed in joy, absorbing the light, the air, the sea with my eyes, my skin, I felt no tiredness.

THANK YOU, LORD, that you created the land.

REFRESHED BY MY swim, I returned along tree-lined avenues. I was wearing a cotton-print sundress and sandals.

Gravel crunched underfoot. Huge magnolias opened their cups, their glossy leaves shining. The evening air was filled with their sweet fragrance, mingled with the scent of pines and the sea. Little lamps shone in the branches, orange and blue, their shadows making patterns on the gravel. The trees cast shadows like canopies over benches where courting couples sat entwined.

Evenings like these were made for love; and in the name of love, you, Lord, created this flowering, fruitful land, full of trees, grasses, grain. We receive this world from you as a gift, to be enjoyed to the full, to be absorbed, that we may observe your beauty, poured out for us, and love you and one another with gratitude. Every living creature mounts the steps of love from its least expression to the heights of love for you.

Beside the darkened sea, elegant people strolled along a brightly lit avenue covered with a layer of pine needles. Open-air cafés were islands of light and music snatched from the dark.

Completing the panorama was the square with its fountains, built at the beginning of the century with an expansive freedom of form that has not survived in our impoverished age. Water jetted from a multitude of pipes in alternating fountains, changing the pattern and flow, creating instant designs. Sometimes the water hit the rim of the basin, then rose up high in arch-formation. The column of water sparkled as it fell; the upturned watery cup reflected the lights and the crowd round about. The lights on the embankment seemed washed by different colors.

Everyone appeared to be going somewhere, catching someone up, longing for the holiday of their life. I passed through the crowd feeling a selfless joy in my loneliness.

The avenue, the lights, the fountains were like the designs and chapter headings of the secret book of life in which everything is about you, Lord, and about me.

I would gladly have lived like this for the whole month, bringing fresh vegetables and tomatoes, soft Georgian bread, home from the market—swimming, lying on sun-drenched pebbles, and swimming again. But when I came down to breakfast on the fourth day, there was Vera, the warden, who sold candles in the church. She often stoped by on her way home after Vespers, sometimes spending the night.

"Goderdi's coming tomorrow," she told me.

"Who's that?" I asked indifferently.

"Father Anthony."

"Is he going to live here? If so, I'll move down to the housekeeper's rooms on the ground floor."

"No. You're to go to the monastery with him."

"I'm to go with him?" I couldn't believe it.

"You'd never find your way to Gudarekhi: you go by train and it's five kilometers from there through the mountains," Vera told me, sitting at the table in her overall, a head scarf tied in a knot under her double chin, as she drank the last drops of a cup of tea. Her features were as impassive as carved wood. I felt rather awkward, revealing my total ignorance about a matter that concerned me so closely, so I questioned her further.

"Who told you about this?"

"Dumb Faina."

Well—a fine conversationalist God had sent!

The phone rang. Vera rushed at full speed into the room next door. I went to my own room without waiting for her and, when I came down again, Vera had gone. The lock was hanging on the chain between the iron bars of the gates.

I didn't know Dumb Faina. I couldn't understand how she'd managed to say anything—not least about me, since we'd never met. I didn't understand. Was Goderi—or was it Goderdi—one and the same person as Father Anthony? Why had it occurred to him to go to Gudarekhi, or whatever it was called, with me? I'd never heard of a monastery in these mountains. I had just come from a monastery, and I did not want to go to another one at all. Perhaps the uncommunicative Vera had got a bit mixed up when Dumb Faina had explained it all on her fingers. Well, no doubt things would work out.

I'd grown very tired over these last years, and I simply wanted to do nothing for a while in this house by the sea. I yearned for peace, greenery, light, and water.

No one appeared the next day, and so another morning passed satisfactorily. But when I came back from the beach I found Vera in the kitchen once more. An unknown woman sat opposite her at the table, dressed like her in overalls and head scarf, and an old sweater torn at the shoulder.

As soon as I appeared she got up, nodded to me. Her dark eyes flashed as though she felt a little afraid—I knew it was Dumb Faina.

"You can speak—she's able to hear," Vera explained.

Faina brushed crumbs from the oilcloth with a towel, got sugar out of the cupboard, poured some tea, and cut a piece of bread, which she pushed toward me, offering everything there was. She made an inviting gesture with both hands. She moved lightly, quickly, without any fuss.

Soon after, we found ourselves alone and I asked about the monastery. She nodded, brought a pen and paper, and, leaning on the table, began to give me an answer. She wrote quickly in big letters—two or

three words to a line. She'd break off midsentence
when the sense was plain, but she expressed her
thoughts clearly and freely.

I soon got the drift of things.

Metropolitan Azariah has the amazing custom of
receiving all his guests at the patriarchate in his study
at the same time. Someone comes in and receives a
blessing, then sits down on one of the free chairs
placed along the three walls. Along the fourth wall,
facing the exit, the metropolitan himself, wearing
a wide Greek-style cassock, sits behind a massive
table, his yellow-gray hair brushed back from his
temples. The table is chockablock with piles of
stuff—a candlestick with an angel, books, magazines,
a marble paperweight, a telephone, souvenirs for visitors . . . The silver knob of his black staff shines
beside the wall.

The person who is already talking about his problem greets the person who has just come in and car-
ries on talking, sitting with the rest, or coming
forward from the end of the table—depending on age
and temperament. The others who are waiting discuss the matter with great interest, offering advice
from their own experience with real-life examples.
They joke and express their sympathy and feelings,
even if it's only by interjections and nods. Sometimes
these interviews last all day. If you are not in a hurry
you can quite easily find yourself spending an hour
or two there, whereas people in a hurry (not least the
clergy) are released at once with a rumble of ap-
proval. The bishop's kindly manner creates and fos-
ters this fatherly approach.

Faina had obviously been present in the study

when the metropolitan was talking to the abbot of Gudarekhi monastery and happened to mention me. (The year before last, Metropolitan Azariah had been in Moscow with our friend Father Georgi and had dropped in to see us. From our talks, the bishop had assumed that I would want to visit a monastery in his large diocese and he suggested that Father Anthony should go with me.) Faina wanted to go to the monastery too, and received a blessing for this. So now we both had to wait for "Goderdi." (This ancient Georgian name had apparently been Father Anthony's before he had taken his final vows.)

I remembered Father Georgi greeting a tall monk as we'd left the bishop's office. They'd embraced formally, kissed each other on the hand, then on the cheek, and had begun an animated conversation. I'd noticed the new cowl, worn slightly askew as though the wearer weren't used to it. I'd noticed too the monk's broad smile and radiant eyes. Perhaps this had been Goderdi, receiving his first greetings as a monk.

Another day went by—still Goderdi didn't turn up. Faina suddenly went off to East Georgia for the festival of a patron saint.

"Will she be gone for long?" I asked Vera.

"Maybe she'll be back tomorrow—maybe not at all."

"Who is she, exactly?"

"How do I know? A pilgrim."

So, to my relief, I found myself alone again. I'd gotten so used to solitude these last years that the constant presence of anyone else had begun to feel irksome. And who wasn't "anyone else"? Only my son. But he was not with me anymore.

I SHUT THE gates and remained alone in the empty house. The stone wall cast a dark shadow across the garden. Down below were rosebushes; a light shone in the window between them. Snatches of music and talking came from the other side of the fence. Then the light was put out and the voices died away. The southern night, smells of the cooling earth . . . silence—I absorbed all this with the same blissful intensity as when I'd plunged into the water.

I dined on tomato salad, liberally sprinkled with dill and coriander, and then I went out onto the terrace. A tall monk dressed in a black habit was coming toward me along the path with its carpet of red flowers. This was so unexpected that I did not even have time to wonder how he'd gotten through the locked gates.

"Give me your blessing, Father Anthony. . . ." I asked, and he blessed me, smiling broadly.

"I didn't want to knock or shout up and down the street, so I climbed the fence."

I went back to the refectory with him. He went up to the icon of St. Nicholas, crossed himself, kissed the icon, lit a candle, and then the lamps in front of all the icons. The room was filled with a living light, which shone into the dead world.

"I remember you, Veronica," said Goderdi, turning to me with a candle in his hand. "You came to Dzhvari with your son. You're looking older. . . ."

Here indeed was a "Nathanael in whom there was no guile" (to use Christ's words)! I was sad, of course, that I'd aged over the six years since that visit to Dzhvari, but I was glad about this unexpected encounter.

"You'll be living in my room. When I was ordained deacon I lived here while I worked in a church in town."

"Would you like me to move?"

"No, of course not. . . . The whole house is empty."

"Would you like some supper? Some tea?"

"I don't need anything. I've already eaten. They're always drinking tea in Dzhvari, but I drink water. There's lovely water in Gudarekhi—straight out of a spring. You've never tasted anything like it." He sat down, wearily resting his hands on the table. I settled down at the window opposite.

"Where's your son?"

"He's in a monastery. He's become a hieromonk."

"Mitya?" Father Anthony sounded very surprised. "But how old is he?"

"Almost twenty-two. He took monastic vows when he was twenty. He was ordained deacon next day, and he became a hieromonk two months later on the Feast of the Transfiguration—my favorite festival, so full of light."

"I waited six years for my ordination. I'm thirty-seven now. I was ordained a month ago."

"Congratulations. . . . It's the greatest thing that can happen to anyone."

"On earth," he corrected for some reason. "Thank you."

Or perhaps something had happened to him in heaven as well.

He had a nice smile, and seemed almost ashamed at

the joy that filled him as he recalled his priesthood—as though he wanted to restrain it, but it burst
through, lighting his face and shining in his eyes.
Yes, this must be the man whom Georgi had greeted.
He had a high forehead, straight nose; his skin was
stretched tightly across his cheekbones; his eyes
shone with a strangely deep look that seemed to penetrate right into the depths of your very being. His
small curly beard accentuated his sunken cheeks. His
wavy hair was cut in a straight line at the back, and
that shy smile of his . . .

I remembered having seen him among the young
people who'd come to Dzhvari, and once since then,
at a crossing on Rustaveli Avenue when we were
coming back from Vespers, Goderdi had called to
Mitya from the stream of passers-by and stopped for
a minute. He'd been carrying rounds of local unleav-
ened bread—*lavash*—in his upturned palms. "I'm going to Dzhvari tomorrow morning. I've managed to
buy some bread for the monastery. It's still warm,"
he'd said. Mitya had spent two months in Sioni Cathedral and he knew everyone.

I told Father Anthony it had been our dream for
Mitya to be ordained and sent to a parish where I
could be with him. We'd hoped there'd be a house
beside the church, fields, forests, and lakes all around.
Mitya would serve and I would read in the choir,
kindle the stove, and do all that needed to be done
around the house and church.

"That would be very nice," Father Anthony replied with feeling.

"But he received the tonsure and remained in the
monastery."

"That means God wanted it to be like that. It's good for a new monk to live in a monastery for a bit: He's got to learn everything, how to celebrate the liturgy, hear confession, and, above all, learn obedience."

"I always used to ask God for my son and me to serve him together. But then Mitya said, 'You'd better not pray like that just now. I like it in the monastery. I never thought life could be so full.' I don't ask anymore, although I miss him."

"What about you becoming a nun?"

"No. I'd be in a convent, and he'd be in a monastery and we'd never be together."

"You may not be asking in words, but your heart is still weeping and begging."

"Yes, it weeps and begs."

"That's the most powerful way of praying—especially when it's a mother's prayer."

"What else is there for me to do?"

"You don't need to do anything. The Lord will do all that's best for you both. Only we must be obedient to his will. We pray, 'Your will be done,' but in fact we always expect God to do what we want. We see the short term, but what do we know about the future, about our eternal destiny?"

"I want to be with my son in eternity."

"Have you ever been in his monastery?"

"Of course. When he took his vows and when he was ordained. Those were the greatest events of our lives, but in the last three months I've only had long-distance phone calls to him."

In the morning, I sent Mitya a telegram with the phone number of the clergy house and asked to be rung after twelve when it is easier to get through. I was longing to hear his voice again.

At twelve o'clock we went down to the ground floor to the telephone table. Father Anthony pulled a little wooden box out of his knapsack that he'd wanted to fix under the little box that contained water and oils for baptisms. There wasn't enough room for the vial with the holy myrrh and he cut out a round cavity inside the lid, taking care not to chisel right through.

"It's a miracle that your son was ordained so quickly. There's no doubt he's received God's special blessing. . . . Before I took my vows I served the church for six years without pay as a psalm-reader. At night I was a laborer in a team working on the construction of the metro, and by day I worked in the church."

"But surely you found time to sleep as well, didn't you?"

"To tell the truth, there just wasn't time for it— three or four hours in the afternoon between services. And if I was on day shift in the metro I took a couple of hours off in the morning, went to church, then to work, and from work straight back for the evening service. I didn't miss a single service for six years. Oddly enough, no one at work seemed to notice when I was missing. Perhaps it was because I always worked very hard. But once I couldn't get off. The shift foreman came up all of a sudden and asked, 'Where's Goderdi?' 'Here,' I said. 'Where have you got to go to? I've been sitting here all morning as though something's drumming in my head, telling me, Let Goderdi go. I can't think of anything else!

Off you go, then, wherever it is . . .' So off I went!"

It was stuffy, although the door was wide open. Darkness closed in. I checked the phone receiver.

"You could see my church from where I worked—it was on a hilltop. At night I'd come out onto the square. I'd see the dome; there'd be fires burning beyond it. I couldn't imagine life without that church." He laughed. 'Then they drove me away. I kept on shouting, 'Truth, truth . . . purity, purity . . .' I shouted myself hoarse. The dean said, 'That's enough, Goderdi, you needn't bother coming back.' I was terribly upset. I asked, 'Has anyone been complaining about me?' I'd put my whole soul into that church, and more often than not believers would come to me with questions rather than to the priest. The dean wouldn't answer. I went back one more time. 'What have I done wrong? I'll be left feeling really bad if I have to leave. . . .' But he still didn't say anything: 'Let's go our separate ways in silence like men.' So we had to part . . ."

The clock hand moved to half-past one. My son still hadn't phoned.

What's happened, Lord? Mitya knows I always wait for his call, and that I get upset. He couldn't simply not call. Could he be ill?

"Why are you so upset?" Goderdi asked, not looking up. "Perhaps he's gone off somewhere, to the parish for instance, or maybe there's a patronal festival."

"No, it's not a saint's day today. . . ."

"Telegrams often arrive late. We'll wait a bit longer."

I sat at the table, my head in my hands, watching

him as he made fine shavings with his knife. We sat in silence for a while—but that was worse still.

"I expect you were brought up to go to church from your earliest childhood," I said.

"I was brought up to work. I was put into the care of my grandfather from the age of six and I had to do everything he said. He was very strict. He said, 'I'm an old man. I need someone to help me.' So my parents sent me away to help him. My granny used to wake me at four every morning. We filled basketsful of vegetables from the garden—potatoes, greens—and drove a cart to the market in town. It was a hill resort, a thousand meters above sea level. We arrived while it was still dark; the market was open, the wind blew through the empty stalls. I'd try to get warm behind the bags, but my grandmother would pinch me—it really hurt. 'I can't bear to see someone sitting doing nothing. Go and water the greens,' she'd say, and I'd run for water."

He'd already chiseled out a small circle in the lid. The vial of myrrh fitted exactly. "My granny's eighty-seven now. Last winter I went to the country. She was ill. She showed me her hands. 'Did you ever see my hands as white as this, Goderdi?' she asked. 'They were always black from working. . . . What do I have to live for now?'"

The last light went out in the house opposite.

"I didn't go to the Orthodox Church when I was young. Instead I found myself by chance among Baptists. Young people nowadays are such spiritual gypsies. People long ago used to believe in something: victory in war, a better future . . . Nowadays there's nothing left; on the face of it there's nothing to strive for. In a way that's fine—it means that lots of people have begun to look deeply into religion. But it's terrible as well—they just as easily get into the deep things of Satan. There are the followers of Steiner, Buddhists, theosophists, adherents of yoga—I could reel them all off . . ." He fell silent, as if he weren't sure whether or not to continue.

"Once I was sitting with the Baptists and I put my head in my hands. Just like you now, I was very tired—I was always very tired. . . . I was listening, but I didn't understand a thing. Suddenly it was as if somebody said to me, 'Look at your right hand.' I thought I'd dozed off, and didn't pay any attention, but again, and a third time, 'Look at your right hand.' 'What's all this?' I thought. I looked, and there was a saint's picture right there on my palm."

"What kind of picture? How did he appear?"

"I don't know . . . it was very faint, just like this, covering the whole of my hand. It was there for three days, though it gradually faded. I just walked about holding my hand to my heart. I was afraid to touch anything."

"Had you seen the saint before?"

"No." He smiled almost guiltily and said, speaking with an effort, "I saw him again after I'd made my vows. . . . I was alone in the church, as monks usually are the first night. I'd been given a candle, a psalter, and I'd been taken off to the choir stalls. That's where I saw him. On the wall hung an ancient icon of Anthony the Great, in honor of whom I'd just been named. I recognized him at once. I spent all night face-to-face with him. Do you know the life of St. Anthony?"

"Well, in outline. He's recognized as the founder of the solitary desert way of life."

"Yes. That's the ideal, the true monastic way. I'd already understood that the Lord had placed me face-to-face in front of him for the whole of my life, and whatever I did now, I saw it was nothing at all. Whatever may be given me, I know I've done nothing."

It was three o'clock. Father Anthony stayed on the ground floor. I went up to the room he'd had, and I asked him to give me a shout if the phone rang.

"You can't receive calls from the Baltic States here. Don't waste time fretting."

He was planning to wait for Faina until dinnertime. After that there were no trains to Gudarekhi.

"So we'll be going to the mountains right in the middle of the heat?" I was vexed. I can't stand heat at all.

"Oh, it's nothing, it's not even five kilometers. We'll get there with God's help."

Should I go or not? The question, it seemed, was no longer relevant.

THE SPEECHLESS WANDERER did not return. Father Anthony and I traveled together in a dilapidated, rattling electric train, which was only half-full. A draft blew through the upper windows, which had been left open. I dreaded to think what it would be like in the hills in a temperature of ninety-five degrees. Our considerable luggage lay on the seats: a trunk with my things; twelve loaves—*lavash* bread dusted with fine flour, crusty white bread, dark caraway bread—

all stuffed into a zipped travel bag; a knapsack filled with new potatoes, cucumbers, tomatoes, and egg-plants, and two more bags.

The Petertide fast had just begun, and everything in the market was very expensive: tomatoes cost six rubles, cucumbers five, and potatoes two.

"But what can we do?" Father Anthony had kept repeating as we walked through the steaming damp of the covered market between rows of tomatoes, cucumbers, parsley, coriander, mint, and *tarkhun*. "Fifty kopecks for five tiny bunches of dill! When my granny and I used to have our stall in the bazaar we charged five kopecks for a whole armful of dill, three rubles for a bucket of tomatoes. How are we to feed the monastery now?"

The sea disappeared beyond the hills. Green val-leys spread up to the foothills dotted with two-story stone houses with red-tiled roofs and deep terraces wound about with vines and all kinds of greenery. Small plum trees blazed with dark purple fruit.

A river curved, sparkling in the sun, and again we saw fields of corn, valleys, with herds and flocks on the slopes—an idyllic landscape, enclosed in the dis-tance by chains of densely forested mountains. Life in the villages here—grandparents and grandchildren living together; the daily cycle of work on the land; the silky manes of the young corncobs; wine stored in large casks in the cellars; cows, goats . . . cock-crow at dawn—might well be mysterious and inac-cessible. But people who have never lived in the country, only in hostels, communal apartments, five-story buildings echoing with the sound of other peo-ple's lives, reading rooms, state offices, and public buildings—are damaged, stunted representatives of civilization, with hypertrophic head, consumptive lungs, impoverished heart. People like this forget that there's something called space, that there are sunrises and sunsets, don't know that the shoot comes through soil that has swollen from the spring rains. They live with illusions, phantom ideas, passions, vanity, the conventions of art . . .

Reason, given so that we might know the One, plunges into a thousand details. The world splinters like a shattered mirror and reflects nothing. We study what has passed long since; we dream about what will never be, but we don't know how to live today. We know something about the patterns of molecules and the temperature of the moon, but we don't know the meaning of our own lives and we can't understand why we have to suffer as long as our heart keeps beating.

We'd had no time for breakfast and Father Anthony fortified himself with a piece of bread.

He told me what had happened after he'd seen the picture on his hand. "I began to think: This is the picture of a saint, although the Baptists don't recognize saints. . . ."

"Did your grandfather believe in God?"

"Of course. He grew up before the Revolution, after all. I never saw anyone prepare for prayer the way my grandfather did. He would wash carefully, smooth his hair with his hand, tuck his shirt into his belt. He would even put on a dignified air and straighten his shoulders. Only then would he stand in front of the icon."

Father Anthony smiled as though he could still see

his dead grandfather. He sat opposite me, spoke unhurriedly, quietly, and I had to bend forward to catch
everything he said, what with the rattling of the car
and the clack of the wheels. His jacket was hanging
on a hook beside the window. His habit was hitched
into his belt. In the distance it looked like a black
shirt with a stand-up collar—you didn't notice at first
that Goderdi belonged to another world. The other
passengers took no notice. There were only the two
of us, just as it had been the previous day.

"You can't tear out your roots at a stroke. Georgia
recently celebrated fifteen hundred years of Christianity, remember. In the country, people still held to
the old Christian ways and observed the fasts strictly.
From my childhood I got into the way of not touching meat products on Wednesdays and Fridays. On
Saturdays Grandfather would look at his watch.
'Time to stop work, it's midday.' Once, on a Sunday, I climbed a cherry tree to pick the fruit. I fell and
broke my collarbone. So I learned for all time that
you shouldn't work on Sunday."

He felt his collarbone, as though he were checking
whether it had knitted properly. I noticed that his
right shoulder was a bit higher than his left.

"Even today morals are purer in the country than
in the towns—especially big towns, although deprav
ity is found everywhere. But there isn't that lostness
in the villages. You still find the fear of God there,
conscience, . . . They're still alive there."

The whole world is gripped by this reaction to its
collapse and the further it moves away from its essence—God—the more quickly it perishes. When the
sanctuary within us is killed, everything that is holy

dies. The soul is made desolate: marriage, the family, honor—everything begins to fall apart. The bonds we make dissolve under their own weight.

I asked Father Anthony where he'd studied.

"At night school, after work. I thought of going to the Institute of Foreign Languages. I'd studied German at school, but I liked French and I mastered it quickly. Learning languages isn't difficult for me, but the only people who got into the Institute were the children of KGB workers and responsible officials—and they did it by paying huge bribes. When I found that out I didn't even try to get in. So God saved me from trying to have a career."

There was almost no one left in the car. An old peasant had stretched himself out on the bench next to us, his head on his basket. Nobody got on at the stop.

Father Anthony went on: "But from about the age of eleven I loved to dance more than anything else. My ballet school teacher would say, 'You're a born dancer. What legs!' "

So, there it is, I thought. There was still something different about the way he walked—grace, a lightness.

"So I didn't get into the Church right away when I stopped going to the Baptist church. I went to the theater, to ballet . . . It's the funniest thing—I can't understand it to this day—how I found myself in a church for the first time. I was going somewhere quite different and suddenly I found myself in front of icons, standing there full of tears and praying, as if someone had put me there despite myself. From then on I went of my own free will, but the first time— that I can't understand."

I thought, here I am going to Gudarekhi in spite of myself—as though the Lord had taken me by the hand and led me. Would it be for long, and why? God alone knew. Perhaps I'd understand later.

WE UNLOADED OUR luggage onto the platform by ourselves. Father Anthony stood looking at the mountains. "The monastery's up there, at the top of the mountains. You can see the cypress from here."

On a bench under the shadow of an elm, I put on a white scarf. Father Anthony adjusted the luggage—the knapsack on his back, the red bag slung in front tied to the knapsack straps, and a bag in each hand. We set off.

A village I'd noticed from the train opened up beyond the bridge. The road ran out and the space between the garden fences bristled with great ruts filled with dust and dirt. Geese waddled toward us, stretching their necks, hissing, cackling. A strong old man in a hat was watching us from an open door set within silver-painted gates.

"People are really wild here. I've never met anything like it in the whole of Georgia. . . ." Father Anthony lowered his voice as though the old man who was standing three houses back might overhear. "Once, when Father Avel was on his way to the monastery, local women attacked him. 'Why was he a priest?' They threw stones at him, even tore his cassock. He never came back again. We'd better not stay around either."

I looked around cautiously. The old man was still standing in the gateway, following us with his stare.

There was no one else among the houses—only the geese moved off, and a dog ran by, its tongue hanging out.

"But you said, traditions, roots . . ."

"That's exactly it. What other roots are there here? This is an Adjar village, the people here are Muslims, so they don't go to the monastery or help in any way, unless you pay them a lot. I don't even buy bread here, although they all bake their own."

The sun went right through us. The air was heavy with a dry heat. Father Anthony didn't linger. We were about fifteen meters apart and the gap remained constant, as though he felt we were less of a target for these hostile people of another faith if we stayed apart.

We crossed a small wooden bridge over the river that had flooded the streets, leaving a layer of mud. We left the last houses behind us in the gorge. The road rose up ever more steeply.

The blood rushed to my face. My lips felt dry. My heart beat harder and began to ache a little. The case became heavier and heavier. Around the bend in a patch of shade I stopped with relief, dropped the case, broke off a stalk of unusually dark wild strawberry, and tried to quench my thirst. But Father Anthony said that the berries were poisonous. He stood still for a while without setting down his burden, just dropping the bags for a moment, and all too soon bent down to pick them up again. "Let's go. There's a lot of work to be done in the monastery, and we haven't come two kilometers yet."

So on again and up, under the beating sun, trying to snatch the most infinitesimal patch of shade. I would have liked to look around at the tall, broad-leafed forest on the slopes, but I couldn't take anything in. My head burned, as if I had a fever. My companion's brown knapsack bobbed far ahead.

Father Anthony waited for me, pointing upward again. "The monastery is beyond this mountain. There'll be some shade soon, and a stream."

"So, how about the ballet?" I reminded him, trying to detain him for a moment.

"The ballet ended when the Church began," he said, already walking on. "No more dancing."

I dragged myself to the spring with a last feverish gasp. Father Anthony took off his knapsack and bent down to the flow of water gushing out of a cleft in the hill, set about with stone. I drank and simply could not slake my thirst.

We went around several more bends. On one, a tractor was chugging and roadmen, bare-chested in orange jackets, were smoking.

"They're building a road to Gudarekhi. All our monasteries are getting roads now." Father Anthony sounded a bit vexed.

"Is that really so bad?"

"Groups of picnickers and tourists will come screaming along in their cars. There'll be no peace: bonfires, *shashliks*, transistors. I would have destroyed the road completely, like St. Seraphim of Sarov, who prayed and an oak fell across the path."

"Yes, but believers will come too, won't they?"

"A believer will get here even through the forest."

"Somebody once said that if you really seek the truth, whatever road you travel, sooner or later you come to God."

"Yes, but not by car along tarmacadamed roads—with cognac and loose women."

I stopped in the middle of a green glade outside the monastery gates. The space enclosed me, bursting with sunlight and the sound of the cicadas. The sound was high and even, as if the golden light itself was echoing the cicadas' song.

The hundred-year-old cypress towered above the church, like a pyramid-shaped belfry; in the shadow of its branches several gravestones were sunk into the ground. Lime trees stood in black clumps with a mass of green foliage outlined against the sky. On the edge of a clearing beyond stood three little houses, seemingly stuck together with tin or plywood under piebald roofs of red and brown tile.

Not a leaf stirred, not a bird called—everything was lost in a midday doze. Only a tethered brown calf moved its thin legs and munched the juicy grass.

I went around the church. Built midcentury in place of an older, ruined one, it was a dark, cube-shaped building with a disproportionately narrow tower and the typical Georgian pyramidlike dome. These primitive shapes had none of the harmonious simplicity and power of the early basilicas, nor the luxurious refinements of Georgian medieval architecture with its many-sided arched towers, its rich decor, its inimitable stone sculptured crosses on the eastern facade, the special style of window frames.

Where has all such beauty gone in this utilitarian age of ours?

Father Anthony unlocked the church and we entered the cool semidark: Just one lamp was lit in front of the icon of the Mother of God.

Crossing himself in a broad, well-defined gesture, Father Anthony bowed to the ground before the icon and went into the sanctuary.

I bowed, then stood in the middle of the church, and as I looked I felt the poverty of its furnishings awake in me an ache, a longing. The icons were pathetically provincial and dated from the period of the decay of icon-painting. The picture of the Mother of God with Child above the sanctuary, filling the whole space under the dome, was coarse and taste-less. The linen icon-screen with scarcely distinguish-able faces was faded and torn. Above it, the ends of rough planks stuck out, like an unfinished fence.

Oh, how the beauty of the Church has been tram-pled on, to what state poverty has reduced it! What sharp contrast with the luxuriousness of God's world around it! I've witnessed this impoverishment every-where in what was once Holy Russia, with a pain that has become almost dulled by familiarity. All this after a thousand years of Christianity, after the saintly Andrey Rublyov, the churches of the Kremlin, of Vladimir, Suzdal, and the North, and the ancient monasteries . . .

You go through village after village, each with its church—cross torn down, plasterwork chipped, cu-pola stoved in, boarded up, its windows like dead eye sockets. . . . The church is deformed into repair shops, storerooms, offices, or vodka stalls, or maybe a club with a yawning, iron loudspeaker. And inside the abomination of desolation, swear words scrawled on the pale remains of ripped-down icons, the dese-crated sanctuary. Or the drunken abuse and stink of tobacco where holy words of prayer ought to be

heard and the smell of incense arise. And all around—
uninhabited villages, boarded-up houses.

Here is a fearful symbol of our times: a destroyed
and desecrated church—a picture of the human heart.

I walked the length of the walls—plastered over
with old magazine pictures, frames decorated with
cherubs and faded photos. The embroidered towels,
the flowers made of foil. When did false affectation
replace the revelations and upheavals of a living faith?
How will such wretched lack of taste ever show forth
the beauty of the imperishable world and kindle our
beggared hearts with the hope of a light-filled Eternity?

As Father Anthony came out of the sanctuary I
pointed to some planks that jutted out above the
icon-screen. "What's this?" I asked.

"I haven't sawn them off yet," he said in a penitent
voice.

"But there was an abbot here before you?"

"He used to say: 'Let people see how poor the
church is, then they'll give more.' "

"Like giving to the beggar in the church porch . . .
and do they give?"

"I haven't managed to saw them off yet!" he repeated guiltily. "I'll throw the lot out—the picture,
the trunks, the rags. I'll paint the pillars and walls
white—you'll see what a beautiful church it will be!
What can we do? There are only three old women in
the monastery—not even nuns—and one female
psalm-reader. We depend on her for housekeeping as
well as services. There aren't any parishioners. On
Sundays an occasional couple will wander in, offer

five little candles. . . . The cow and the kitchen garden feed us. It's a good thing we've got icons of sorts. . . . Twenty churches and monasteries are being opened just now in Georgia—they haven't any icons, church-plate, vestments . . . Waste land and ruins . . . as if the Antichrist has already walked the earth. Our patriarch says: 'Squeeze a handful of Georgian soil and out of it will come the blood of the martyrs.' "

"What about a handful of Russian soil?"

THREE OF US had dinner—the priest, myself, and Nonna the psalm-reader, a Georgian woman of about thirty-eight who spoke hardly any Russian. She was small and dumpy underneath her work coat of faded velvet. Her black head scarf revealed a local peasant face. Her thick brows met over the bridge of her nose; she had shining black eyes, broad cheekbones. Her loud voice almost never stopped, full of questions for the priest.

She began rattling through the prayers, while I finished them in Russian.

"Have some water first."

Father Anthony filled my glass, and I drank such spring water as I never remember drinking before. It was clear and cold with that rich taste of living water that has no name. Once you've quenched your thirst, you want to drink it drop by drop and feel its cleanness and freshness on your palate and down your throat.

Father Anthony watched me, satisfied. "And you talk about 'tea.' "

"I'm not talking about 'tea' anymore. Can I have some more water?"

Nonna looked steadily at me with benevolent interest, saying something in a lively way to the hieromonk.

"She was asking how old you are."

"I'll be fifty in nine days' time."

"She's asking if you have a family . . . I've told her about Mitya."

More about Mitya followed, with exclamations and a two-way simultaneous translation.

"She's saying you should stay here for good."

"I agree. . . ."

"Ohhh! She agrees! We'll see!" Nonna laughed loudly, shaking her fork.

On the table were new potatoes, thickly chopped tomatoes and cucumbers, and broken pieces of *lavash*. The psalm-reader ate hastily, talking incessantly, grabbing something now from one plate, now from another, dropping crumbs.

"Don't be in such a hurry," the priest said to her, a little embarrassed. "If you'd just be quiet for a moment, while you're eating." And turning to me, he said, "She was asking if you know how to milk a cow. She'll teach you."

"Well, not just now."

After the meal Father Anthony showed me the guest room, which opened onto the lobby where we'd been eating, alongside the door to Nonna's room. Two beds with their heads to the window, doors on each side, a little table, and a cupboard. Onions were scattered about under the table; there were jars of beans and a demijohn of apple vinegar.

Alone at last, I opened the window wide, pushing the vine branches aside. A blue-green distance spread out in front of me and I could see now how high we'd climbed. The valley below was cut through by a twisting river and the little town lay like a model beyond. Farther off, blue-ridged mountains stretched along the horizon. Everything could be seen picked out in detail: every tree in the valley, the outline of every roof, seemed carefully etched.

The window was on the first floor. Below was the kitchen garden, the trellising of the fence, and the slope covered with growth. Another window opened out onto a lean-to, roofed with vines. From here you could see the neighboring house, its piebald roof and a blank wall stuck over with bits of felt and tin.

I liked Gudarekhi, this airy shelter with vine foliage along the window frames, the distance beyond, and the excitable little psalm-reader—who, thank goodness, spoke only Georgian. I accepted everything there humbly and trustingly, as another way of being, which the Lord had seen fit to place me in.

That evening I got the psalter out of my case and, leafing through it, I came across this: "Whether I go or whether I stay, all my ways are known to you. Even before there is a word on my tongue, you, Lord, know it altogether. Such knowledge is too wonderful for me; it is high, I cannot attain it. Whither shall I go from thy Spirit? Or whither shall I flee from thy presence? If I ascend to heaven, you are there! If I make my bed in Sheol, you are there also. If I take the wings of the morning and dwell in the uttermost parts of the sea, even there your hand shall lead me, and your right hand shall hold me. . . .

Even the darkness is not dark to you, the night is bright as the day. . . ."

I WAS WAKENED early by sunlight and the chatter of birds. The whistling, clicking, chirping, twittering, and tender cooing—Lord, how wonderful it was. I heard each squawk and brief cry separately, a solitary faint little voice producing a triumphant chirp, and modulations and calls, far away and near at hand, right under our roof.

What a wonder, that such secret little corners are preserved, hidden by nature from mankind, where there are so many living voices. . . .

Only last summer I had this strange experience. The sun was beating down on the pine forest, the strawberries turned red on the forest's edge, the hills were carpeted with bilberries, the lakes choked with duckweed. On my third day there, however, I felt a strange sort of alarm, as if some kind of threat hung in the air of this natural woodland . . . and suddenly I was terrified—the forest had fallen silent! Not a sound, as though I'd gone deaf or the world had been bewitched into silence . . . the birds had forsaken it!

Some thirty kilometers away they'd been building a nuclear power station. Its first two sections were already functioning, but they couldn't quite sort out the third and it leaked, though no one was told. The children gathered wild strawberries, carried their baskets of mushrooms . . . but the sparrows had disappeared completely. There were hardly any other birds, only the odd swallow flitted over the water with its sad cry. There was an uncanny feeling about that silent forest, as though death had already filled every fiber and was breathing down your neck.

Yet now we had this early morning hubbub, whistling, chirping, and modulations, reminiscent of Paradise.

I TOOK BUCKETS to fetch some water from the spring. The route led past Father Anthony's house, along a cornfield to a path up the hill.

The little spring was hidden by some bushes and a bowed elm tree. The water poured out into a stone-paved hollow, and from there it flowed out in a quiet stream. I washed my face, arms, and shoulders in the cold water and drank it using my hands.

Then I came back with two more buckets. It was hard to get up the steep slope, so I took them up one by one, brushing against the nettles and slopping the water.

The heat grew intense. Father Anthony, in a cherry-colored habit all stained and covered with shavings, was building a bathhouse by the fence above the precipice. He'd chopped down six tree trunks, which we carried across the cornfield. He'd stripped the bark with his ax and dug holes for the uprights. The storeroom—right under my floor—provided roof and wall slates. Father Anthony fixed them onto the upright pillars while I held the slate at the right height and gave him the ax, hammer, and nails. My heart still ached but I tried not to listen to it.

Nonna had been shoveling earth down from the precipice. She leaned against the newly planed trunk now dug into its place, watching the priest at work. Her scarf had fallen onto her shoulders, but her work coat was pinned around her neck and she was wearing galoshes and woolen stockings. She said something heatedly, Father Anthony laughed and nodded. He said to me: "I've repaired the roof somehow— and she shouted: 'Oh, I've remembered something!' 'What did you remember?' She said that five years ago, before we knew each other, she often saw me in her sleep. And so she came up to me and found out it was indeed me she'd dreamed of. She's told me about it several times already, and now she's telling me again. She's been dreaming again about a large cornfield with the two of us working in it—as always."

The remaining female inhabitants of the monastery did not take part in our work on account of their age. Domna and Glikeriya were over eighty, they were both lay-sisters who wore the *rasso*, or cloak, had worked together in the patriarch's kitchen, and now occupied adjoining houses. Behind them lived Melanie, who was about five years younger. Domna was Georgian, whereas Melanie and Glikeriya were Russian. This was the total complement of our neglected cloister.

THE THREE OF US sat on gravestones by the cypress. Above us was the dark shadow of the branches and the bluish black sky spattered with countless stars. Every so often, the momentary flight of fireflies would cut through the surrounding dark. There were so many of them scurrying in different directions that they seemed to leave twisting ribbons of light in the darkness. The night was filled with their patterns, giving it an inner light.

The hieromonk sat with his hands clasping his knees, casting a shadow on the next gravestone. Nonna was talking away excitedly. Throwing my head back, I looked for familiar constellations.

Catching the pause, Father Anthony turned to me—as I could tell from his voice: "When I was a child, I liked to pray at night in the garden or in the forest."

"Do you mean to say you . . . prayed before you entered the Church?"

"Naturally . . . I always prayed as a child, because I suffered a lot. One night I went off into the forest, sank to my knees, prayed, and wept. I said: 'Lord, you know what lies before me. Other children run about and play. And you have taken everything from me. Please take me to yourself.' "

Nonna, tired with the day's work, put her head on my lap and fell silent.

"There was a village up in the hills, just like here. A leafy forest, pine trees . . . But I liked nighttime and the stars I didn't enjoy being with children of my own age. I was different . . . I liked to be by myself. If anyone came too close to me, I got terribly upset and even cried. I would ask. 'Lord, take him away, I can't stand him,' "

The man lived among people, but he was different. He didn't know this himself, he wanted to be like everyone else, he tried to adapt . . . it didn't work.

"I on the other hand had always wanted to share my life and soul with someone, to the uttermost, with nothing left over. It was not to be. But later the Lord granted me a son, and I had twenty years of sheer joy."

"My parents were peasants. Now I understand that they lived just like everyone else, working from dawn to dusk. I've never been able to sleep at dawn, when the whole world is waking and reveling in the light. My parents always got up at dawn too. They tried to live an honest life: that is, to have a house, cattle, their own bread. No one ever puts so much effort into producing anything as into his own plot of land that feeds him."

As we'd traveled along in the train, he'd pointed out from the window: "This is the *kolkhoz* corn—two inches high, and there's a private crop—it's as tall as I am." His agitation was clear to see.

"Yes, they lived like other people . . . sometimes they celebrated, sometimes they cursed. But I thought that was no way to live, and I myself would never live like that. And that's how it worked out. From my youth onward I had neither house nor property. I stayed where I could, ate what I could find . . . right till now."

I thought Nonna had gone to sleep. I sat without moving, afraid lest she wake up and start talking, thus silencing Goderdi. Something made me listen to him attentively, as if I'd guessed at some secret behind his words which held a promise of disclosure.

"When I was seven—what did I understand then? But once I bowed right down to the ground to the Lord Jesus Christ and said: 'I will never drink, smoke, or swear . . . I will never eat meat, as long as

. . . as long as you don't leave me . . . as long as I have your goodwill.' "

"And did you fulfill this vow?"

"I've tried. . . ."

A dog appeared silently out of the dark, circled around, heaved a sigh, and curled up at the priest's feet. Fireflies burst out of the darkness in sparks; they'd suddenly shoot up beside us and then disappear.

"When I was small I used to say to God, 'I've got nothing, let me see what's really inside people.' And I began to see what's inside us. A man would come up to me in the market and I already knew who he was and what he'd say . . . I even knew how much money he had in his purse, how much he'd want for the things he was selling. This made me suffer even more: It's better not to see what's inside us. Now I'm afraid to look anyone straight in the face, because I see their intentions. I see people's sins."

I'd noticed that he would sometimes speak looking above my head, or below it, or, if we happened to exchange glances, that a momentary shadow seemed to cross his face. . . .

"Are you giving me a warning, by any chance? I'm not afraid. I'll have to make my confession to you just the same. Look, if I forget something you'll be able to remind me. Isn't that why you were driven out of the church?" I enquired. "It's not everyone that wants to be seen through and through. Perhaps they didn't pay you because they wanted you to leave."

He laughed. "Some things are better left unsaid."

So—it wasn't because he had nothing to do that he'd kept repeating, "cleanliness, cleanliness!"

"Now I know; monks aren't made—they're born. . . . In those far-off years I used to feel such a warmth in my heart, as if the Lord were holding me close to his breast. I wanted to be alone, because then I was united to the Lord."

The meaning of the word *monk* has to do with being alone or lonely. So a monk is a person for whom the only things that exist in the world are himself and God. Now I understood. "And then you saw the light?"

"Yes, yes, all the time! All these years . . . How did you know?"

"Blessed is the person you have chosen and brought near. . . ."

"How did you know?" he repeated. "These things can't be spoken about openly. I've never talked to anyone about this: Father Avel only learned about it by accident. Some people refuse to believe all this, others will think it's some kind of enticement, a temptation."

"I'll believe and I won't make any judgment."

"I know, but all the same, you just can't say: It's not right in the Lord's eyes. Will you forgive me that I haven't been able to keep this buried within me and say nothing about it? I'll tell you something else, to finish the whole story. When I was small two angels appeared in front of me and put a crown on my head."

"What were they like?"

"A little body, just like a child's; wings . . . only completely made out of light. That was thirty years ago, and the angels have never put a crown on me since."

An owl hooted somewhere in the forest. A life we could not see was going on within this darkness pierced with lights: tiny sparks and bigger lights, making the night seem even more secretive and dense.

Dogs started to bark beside the monastery fence. Our dog went hurtling toward the sound. Nonna got up and asked what the time was.

"Let's see what's happened," said the priest, disappearing into the dark. The psalm-reader stared motionless after him, while the dogs still barked at the top of their voices, almost choking. I suddenly felt how defenseless our little houses were in the midst of these mountains and forests.

"Are you frightened?" Nonna asked, voicing my thoughts. "Don't be afraid . . . the Lord's watching over us."

Father Anthony came back. "They'd attacked a little hedgehog—that's what all the fuss was about. I carried it off to the forest." The dog reappeared and the barking stopped.

"Bedtime!" ordered Nonna. "There's work tomorrow."

Back in my room, I stood at the window for a long time without lighting the paraffin lamp. The valley beneath me was iridescent, sparkling, shot about with handfuls of fire. The river gleamed black and the mountains were black on the horizon. The shadows of the trees unfolded silently beyond the fence. A firebrand lit up the garden under my window, its smoldering cold flame enfolding the cloud of fireflies.

The immense starry sky enclosed all this darkness and light, all our lives, covering them with silence. On the other side of the wall Nonna was reading the evening prayers. I couldn't pray. The priest's words were still echoing in my mind, and this shining night—there wasn't room in my soul for anything else.

EVERY MORNING I wakened to bird song and sunshine and went out to the spring. I brought seven or eight buckets of water to the kitchen, and Nonna took one across the clearing to Mother Domna, while Glikeriya took two buckets to her hut. I went for water at night as well.

Mother Glikeriya, in a long, knitted jacket and a black skirt to her ankles, appeared in the kitchen in the morning and spent the whole day peeling, cutting, grinding, cooking on the propane gas stove. She carried frying pans from the kitchen to her cell and back again.

"That's enough, that's enough, dearie, don't overdo it," she'd say in her sweet voice every time I put the last bucket on the shelf.

But from time to time a piercing shriek would echo from the kitchen—this would be Glikeriya and Nonna talking. Glikeriya knew some colloquial Georgian, which she'd acquired in the course of her kitchen work, and she larded her speech with these idioms. Nonna could understand these simple words in Russian too, but basically they'd each shout in their own language so they never really understood each other, getting uptight and steaming over nothing.

"They're both so small, yet they make such a noise. . . ." Father Anthony would say in amazement. "Why can't they live in peace? Glikeriya and Domna still have slanging matches every day, too, though they worked together for fifteen years. That's why they were both sent here—into exile. Now they're living together, but they hardly ever talk, and they always eat separately."

Glikeriya and Nonna would make up just as suddenly as they'd fallen out, and I'd hear a sweet voice through the door urging the psalm-reader to try something.

Or before the liturgy was celebrated the priest would tell them to forgive each other and they would bow and say, "Forgive me." And answer, "God forgives and I forgive." Then a long silence would follow, but it was clear that there wasn't enough friendly contact. And Glikeriya obviously placed her vain hopes on me.

FATHER ANTHONY SAT on the roof, banging in the nails to hold the last slates. Nonna was leaning on her spade, looking up at him.

Under the awning the new bath shone white, as the priest and a watchman installed it with the necessary mountings. All that was needed was to pipe in water from the spring. Father Anthony came down and unlocked the door next to the storeroom: Behind it was a semibasement, filled ceiling-high with logs.

"If it's not too hard for you, get all the logs out and stack them up. Then we'll flatten out the earth floor with a spade and transfer everything from the store. After that the storeroom can be turned into a summer kitchen, and we'll get three more beds into your entrance hall."

"Are you expecting a rush of visitors?"

"Not at the moment . . ." He was a bit embarrassed that I'd guessed his rather obvious purpose. "Well, there'll be people coming to Gudarekhi. . . ."

I began throwing rough-hewn birch logs out of the doorway. On first impression it looked as if it would take two days. But the work went easily. You bend down once—and there's two logs out; bend down again. . . . It wasn't hot and everything smelled damp and of rotten bark.

By midday I'd emptied the cellar, and the logs were scattered in the sun, drying out.

"Nonna said about you: Look at this townie working like a peasant." But the priest spoke encouragingly as he put in the bathhouse door.

"I don't know how long I can endure this."

"You should endure it till the end of your life." Once Saint Anthony the Great prayed the Lord to show him the way to salvation. He had a vision of a man working fervently, and praying just as hard. If we act like that, then we'll be saved. . . .

"Easier said than done. . . ."

"Of course. Generally speaking, it's very difficult to be saved. St. Anthony spent eighty-five years in the desert—he was a hermit and performed great acts of faith. . . . Now people are careless—they think spiritual feats and even plain hard work don't matter.

But work without prayer—it's just like a body without its soul. . . ."

"And prayer without works—is that like the soul without its body?"

"Prayer without works—that's for the age to come. There the soul will be free from the body and will live in the endless joy of communion with God. And while it's on earth, the spirit must fight with the flesh, otherwise the flesh will swallow it up. Why did the ascetics wear the body out? So that the spirit might be free to rise to heaven. . . ."

So I tried to make stacking logs an act of prayer. But every few minutes I found my thoughts all over the place, and certainly not in heaven.

"You've done a lot today, an awful lot. . . ." Father Anthony said to me toward evening.

"If it's logs you mean . . . As far as prayer goes—a round nothing, the day's been spent in vain."

Neither spiritual feats nor works nor prayer—Lord, there's nothing for me to hope for, except your great mercy. . . .

LATE EVENING. DARKNESS hid the church's earthly poverty. Only the lamps and candles in front of the icon-screen and the Mother of God were lit. Two lecterns stood in front of a pillar—along with the reader and me.

The priest blessed me to begin the Vespers, and I read the introductory psalm of David on the creation of the world. My voice filled the church and echoed in the dome.

Bless the Lord, O my soul; O Lord, my God,

you are wonderfully great; clothed in honor and majesty. . . . You clothe yourself in light as with a garment. You have stretched out the heavens like a tent,
and laid the beams of your chambers on the waters.
You make the clouds your chariots and ride on the
wings of the wind. You set the earth on its foundations so that it should never be shaken, until you
yourself dissolve the elements, and wrap up the heavens like a scroll that has been read. You created the
earth with all its majesty, covered it with a light-
bearing deep, as with a garment. How manifold are
your works, O Lord. The earth and the sea are full of
your creatures. You open your hand and they are
filled, you hide your face and they are in confusion.
And when you take away their breath they die and
return to their dust. You look on the earth and it
shakes. You touch the mountains and they
smoke. . . .

May your name be kept holy, for you have given
me life and the ability to reflect these profound depths
of dark and light, as well as the beauty in which you,
the invisible and unknowable one, are seen and recognized. You have left me one task: to search for
you, the Life-giving Truth and the unfading Light,
to speak to you or about you. Bless me, help me,
yourself complete all things through me, if it be your
will, for this surpasses my strength. . . .

Who am I, who have nothing either in earth or in
heaven, that I should speak of you? People have been
crucifying you in themselves and in others for two
thousand years. And your Blood is on us and on our
children. And so our hearts are dying, "because in-
iquity abounds" love dries up, and reason deprived

of grace is unable to distinguish good from evil. And the plundered, crippled, and poisoned world perishes with us, though it was created by you for us like the garden of Paradise.

I have been dying since the day I was born, suffocating among living shadows. I called you with all my being, even though I did not yet know you. This soul, created in your image, prayed to you.

I thank you that you brought my soul out of hell, and since then your hand has led me—from death to life—through all the fateful events of my life, brought about by my suffering for the Truth. There is not a single chance link in the long way of the cross to you, in which every day, a tiny circle in the circle of Eternity, is a meeting with you and after is a day of judgment.

Father Anthony stood in front of the royal doors saying the prayer of the Great Litany—for the salvation of our souls and our earth, which has forgotten God, and for the abundance of its fruits, for all those who are sorrowing, suffering, trapped by evil and perishing in it. He took the censer around the church, filling it with the aroma of burning incense. An old blue chasuble sat crookedly on him—one shoulder a bit higher than the other; his stole was the wrong color. But he took the service so sincerely, without any doubts, making our prayer a joint offering to God. After all, the life of the soul is nothing if not its grateful, total turning to God, when it breathes in his immensity as it fills up with light and is transfigured. . . .

WE SAT ON dried-out grass under a little fig tree on the hilltop. Young pear trees, figs, and *tkemali* plums were scattered thinly over the slope below, where the monastery orchard had once stood. Gray-and-blue-colored birds moved so sedately they almost seemed to saunter between the tree trunks on the gently sloping ledges of the hillside, calling to each other and fluttering up to the branches.

From our very first moment at Gudarekhi, before we'd even quenched our thirst, I'd wanted to come straight up here and look at the world around. But Glikeriya had made such a fuss: "Where are you off to? What's this? Our Father Anthony's dead tired. You shouldn't travel during a fast." So in a spirit of appeasement the priest promised that we could go on Sunday, after the service of Holy Communion when we couldn't do any work in any case.

And so, as dawn broke, we had Matins and then celebrated the Eucharist straight afterward. We'd passed half the night without sleep, and now felt tired, but elated and purified. Father Anthony lay propped on one elbow, his boots showing beneath his cherry-colored cassock. I leaned against a tree trunk and the broad fig leaves cast their shadows around us.

The ledges beneath us had once been artificial terracing on which the vine dressers had set out their vines. I'd first seen them when I'd been going to Vardzia, an ancient monastery of caves in eastern Georgia that Mitya and I had visited six years before.

A fantastic view opened out beyond the slow waters of the broad river, beyond the trees on the far bank. A huge mountain rose up above the hilly valley whose grass had withered in the heat, a yellow-brown cleft with exposed seams of rock. Through this cleft, layers of caves stretched in tiers for a mile around the hill.

We crossed the river by a bridge, looking down at the reflection of the mountain.

Once upon a time this whole monastery complex had a single four-storied facade, flights of steps (now half-destroyed) and arched passageways made of smoothly hewn stone. We caught our breath as we walked through the loggias and terraces with caved-in ceilings, trying to keep close to the walls (the narrow passageways had caved in and there were piles of rock everywhere).

A great silence surrounded the neglected, desolate monastery. In the church of the Dormition of the Most Holy Virgin we spent a long time looking at icon frescoes dating from the twelfth century. In the sanctuary, winged archangels protected the Mother of God and Child. This monastery had been built in the time of the Empress Tamara, who stood crowned and resplendent in regal Byzantine vestments, turning her face (which I now recognized) toward us, and holding a model of a Georgian church.

How wonderful it was to see the simplicity with which the icon painter long ago had captured our earthly and heavenly worlds, to see his majestic fluidity of line—row upon row of saints and martyrs mounting to a heaven peopled by angels with weightless wings—a perfect harmony of paint and form. The soul, borne briefly into these high star blue spheres, felt great loss as it came back to everyday reality.

A tunnel led from the Church of the Dormition—the largest of fifteen underground churches—to a pool of clear water. There were many other tunnels and passages driven through the rock that linked the inhabited parts of the caves (the refectories, storerooms, secret hiding places, and concealed exits), and a three-kilometer conduit guaranteed water in the event of a long siege.

The monastery in that brilliant period was both fortress and spiritual center. Five thousand monks in underground churches and five hundred caves made a way for the burdened human soul to enter the realm of the pure Spirit. It was they who kept and copied the sacred books for those who came after them. Here the hieromonks of old blessed young monks, preparing them for the conflict with the unseen forces of evil—the spiritual powers of earthly darkness. From here Tsaritsa Tamara sent her armies on triumphant campaigns against the infidels who troubled the frontiers.

Everywhere among the ravines and sun-baked slopes of the hills around the monastery the small dark caves of the hermits could be seen.

We climbed up to one of these caves. It was hollowed like an arch out of the dry sandstone at the top of the mountain. With a feeling of deep awe and timidity I entered this holy dwelling . . . there were recesses for the lamps and icons, a hearth, and a shallow ledge. There was a niche for the humble church vessels, containing all the monk's earthly possessions. From the semicircular flattened platform in front of the cave an expansive view opened out, with the mountains on the far horizon. A solitary tree spread its broad-leafed canopy to protect the cave entrance.

Lower down, in the shaded margin of the gorge where the clefts in the mountains met, we came across another little cave hidden under the sparkling screen of a noisy waterfall. We took it in turns to bathe under the cool flow of water with its blinding splashes of light. Then we went back to the cave and for a long time sat in silence on a stone at its entrance.

It seemed that nothing had changed over the centuries—the height and distance, the solitude, the heat, and withered grass. The tree still cast its patterned shadow, protecting the hermit's dwelling from the sun's burning rays. The waterfall still rushed down, as it had when the monk went there each morning to fetch water in his clay jug. You could say it was just sheer chance that we had not found him at home; or maybe he was hiding because he'd spotted us from the ravine. . . . It was as if there were no dividing thickness of time, or perhaps we had entered its unchanging heart—full of light—in whose unchanging nature other ages find their due place.

What have we discovered since those days, and what have we lost? We've piled things up on the outside, but we've lost something at the heart. The shell is still intact but inside there's nothing but dust. Yes, and even the shell has cracked; it's about to crumble into pieces, as dead casing does

Terraced hills on both sides of the road to Vardzia; they had once been covered in vines but now were deserted. It would seem that eight centuries before the whole land had been one large monastery and garden.

We left feeling sad that we'd never hear the Vard-
zian monks sing, or walk through their vineyard that
had known streams of God's grace because of their
prayers, or taste its fruits.

This sorrow was alive in me as I looked down on
the white church far below us, its sheet-iron roof
sparkling. I saw patched houses on the edge of the
open clearing and a cypress towering over them.

Farther on, hills unfolded in green waves. An immense valley filled a third of the horizon, with a
winding dark blue river and a scattered little white
town, the whole enveloped by a heat haze.

Nonna, hands around her knees, sat between me
and the priest, but a little higher up. I didn't see her,
I only heard the unending torrents of speech in his
direction—they didn't bother me as I didn't understand them.

"Just be quiet for a bit. . . ." The priest raised his
head, smiling protectively in Nonna's direction, as if
speaking to a child. "She's got a pathological need to
talk, you can't make her stop."

Nonna carried on with fresh inspiration, desperate
to express something even more important.

"All right, now be quiet. . . ." He raised his voice
a fraction and Nonna fell silent. "You know, she
only began to walk and talk when she was five, so
she can never say enough. Her mother didn't want
the child, and even tried to get an abortion by jumping out of a tree. So even before she was born the
Enemy was fighting with Nonna, knowing she'd be
working for the Church. God be praised that she
came here. How would I have managed on my
own?"

"Where did she come from?"

"She'd been a reader in another monastery that was even poorer than ours. She left because of difficult temptations. . . . She's had a hard life, I couldn't begin to tell you about it. We knew each other just for a day: She saw me, trusted me, and came here. She left her house, her mother . . . Another thing that draws us together is that we're from the same area: like other places we have our own local characteristics."

Nonna had gotten up and was wandering about beside us, gathering some sort of grass.

"Some people won't believe that we don't have sexual relations, that a young monk can be chaste. Without a spiritual life, I'm sure that would be impossible. But can there be purity of spirit without purity of body?"

If he was saying all this for my benefit—about the reader and himself—he need not have done. I did not have a single bad thought about the man. Purity can be just as obvious as impurity. I'd even supposed the Lord had kept him pure and chaste since childhood. Besides, Nonna could hardly be said to be an enticing prospect.

"You can lead people into error, of course, but God can't be deceived. . . ." he began with secret inspiration. "We are transparent to him—every movement of the soul, every thought . . . What a fearful thing it is to be a priest! There's no higher service. . . . When a priest stands at the altar, he stands by the fire. . . . Do you remember when a disciple of St. Sergius of Radonezh saw a flame enter the holy chalice, while the saint was celebrating?

Even now this fire descends on the Lord's grave on Easter Saturday and the patriarch of Jerusalem lights the candles from it! And remember the Book of Exodus—Mount Sinai smoked because the Lord had come down upon it with thunder and lightning. . . . God told Moses to draw a line around the mountain: The people were not to break through to see God, lest they perish. And the priests, whom he himself had called, had to purify and sanctify themselves, so that the Lord should not smite them. We are standing on Sinai, at this same fire! The prophet Isaiah wrote: 'Which of us can abide this devouring fire? What one of us can live in the eternal flame?'

"This same fire, unseen, always descends into the holy chalice during the Eucharist! The Savior spoke of it when he said: 'I have come to bring fire down upon the earth, and how I wish it were already kindled!' We receive from it each time we have Communion. Help me, Lord!" He crossed himself. "It's not just that there ought not to be sinful thoughts, there oughtn't to be any kind of trivial ones at all. . . . Maybe the lamps go out, and you think, where can I get some oil? Or the censer doesn't catch light. Or you're saying the deacon's litany and in the pauses, while they're singing 'Lord, have mercy!' or 'Grant, O Lord!' you blow on the coals as hard as you can—doing the sexton's job. Or the reader gets stuck in the *troparion* . . . a thousand details can distract you. Of course we ought to have a deacon, a server, a reader, a choir, but there's no one here!"

For a few minutes we were plunged into a silence filled with heat, heightened by the sound of the cicadas. We heard only the occasional calls and chatter of birds. Cloud shadows floated over the valley.

"You see, the Lord doesn't simply see—his right hand holds you! I told you how I turned up in church that first time, well, that's how it always is," said Father Anthony, as if he hadn't interrupted the conversation we'd begun a few days before. "I go somewhere, suggest something, and this hand lifts me and puts me somewhere else entirely."

To show me how it would happen he tore a handful of dry grass, lifted it above the ground, and dropped it firmly on the other side. As he did so his expression was full of wonder and humility.

"For instance, when I was young I wanted to get married."

"You?" I asked in amazement.

"Did you think I'd been born a hieromonk?"

"You said yourself that monks are born, not made."

"Yes, but I didn't mean from birth itself. You don't give your consent straightaway. I fought against it for a long time. I really wanted to get married. . . ." He laughed, blushing. "I think that's how it is for lots of people who have a difficult childhood: afterward you want to raise your own family, to have love in it. In actual fact, there were three different times when I planned to get married. In spite of the fact that I'm not handsome, some very good girls agreed."

He looked at me quizzically, a bit embarrassed.

I did not contradict, though he did not seem ugly. His face no longer held my attention: I looked within all the time, guessing at the face beneath the appearance.

"One time, the wedding day had even been set. I was still working on the construction of the metro. A week before the wedding, a train driver was moving a concrete slab. He went into reverse by mistake, and my foot fell between the edges of the slab. I screamed so much that the driver thought he'd crushed me to death, and all but lost consciousness. Another driver jumped into the cabin and dragged the slab away. Just imagine, one sharp edge of a concrete slab is brought forcibly against the sharp edge of another, what chance is there for a bone to survive between them? He dragged the slab back, and I saw that my foot was whole! I mean, blood was pouring out everywhere, the flesh was torn, but the bone was whole. . . . I started jumping on the other foot and laughing with joy—they thought I was out of my mind. The engine driver was unconscious, and I was laughing. I couldn't believe my eyes . . . my leg was strapped up and an ambulance was called. I clambered to the edge of the slab and felt it with my hands. My leg had fallen into a small cavity (a bit chipped off, several centimeters long), just big enough to shield a bone."

"What about the wedding?"

"The wedding . . . The very same thing happened as with the two previous ones: a serious illness, or series of critical events, that made it impossible to carry out our plans. I spent two months in the hospital. My fiancée was transferred to Siberia; she wrote twice, and then a third letter said she'd met someone she'd known at school and was going to get married.

In the hospital I kept having the same dream: I was all in black, and someone was saying to me, 'You're a monk. You're a monk.' I often had this dream. Well, if I'd wanted to become a monk there and then . . . but it was not to be! It was several years before I entered the Church. It became clear that I didn't have God's consent to my getting married. But even when I'd grasped that, do you think I accepted it at once? Not a bit, I kept on resisting. I couldn't have accepted this as God's will until . . ."

"What do you mean, 'until'?" I couldn't bear his long pause.

His flow of words seemed suddenly to have run up against an inner barrier, and turned deep within him.

"Nothing else . . . that's all just now. . . ." Father Anthony laughed and sat down, looking at me with a direct concentration. "What interests me, is why this is so important to you, why I am telling you all this."

Why didn't he answer? Surprise at our contact was only superficial, even for him. And that was precisely the point: There is a different kind of measure, and by that we both knew with certainty what united us.

IN THE COURSE of these few days Hieromonk Anthony had become for me a messenger, a living and true witness. From the time when it was first revealed to me that God is the Way, the Truth, and the Life, right to this very day, his ambassadors have come to me. And when I find a new book by a Holy Father, or somebody comes into my house dressed as a priest, I know that this is a messenger. I concentrate vision and hearing, and store his words in my heart.

A strong invisible thread stretches from one messenger to another. A seed cast into the earth (whether five or twenty years before) suddenly, in the course of days, grows into a branching tree, flowers, and produces much-needed fruit. Life discloses the secret interaction of the love of God and my own freedom.

Two years ago, Metropolitan Azariah came into the apartment I shared with Mitya. He'd been in Italy with Father Georgi at celebrations in honor of Francis of Assisi. On the way out, Father Georgi had left behind their winter clothes and the money and documents they had not wanted to take abroad with them, promising to call in on their way back.

A metropolitan had never visited our humble dwelling before. The car stopped at the entrance to our apartment, and Father Georgi got out in his clerical cloak, then the metropolitan, also wearing a cloak and a skull cap, and carrying a silver-topped crozier.

When they sat down at the table—which I'd have considered beautifully laid till then—I was horrified at its poverty. The main thing lacking was wine. They'd arrived at the height of the anti-alcohol campaign, when wine shops were besieged by crowds of Soviet citizens black with rage at their own powerlessness and barely restrained by ranks of militia. Their cursing echoed far beyond the trouble spots. What kind of table was this for guests from Georgia, with Father Georgi unable even to pronounce one of the flowery toasts that had enhanced our meals in Tbilisi?

But my high-ranking guests ate dumplings with

soft white cheese, drank tea, and praised everything so sincerely that I soon stopped feeling embarrassed.

Metropolitan Azariah told me about his childhood. He'd become seriously ill when he'd been about seven. It was winter and the mountain village was blocked with snow—there was no doctor or medicine. His temperature had stayed at nearly 104 degrees for several days. A neighbor who'd buried her own children came in and said he wasn't going to make it. His mother sat at his bedside, wept and prayed, and suddenly he saw a shining cross in front of him. It seemed to be silver but it was alive. . . .

"I shouted, 'Mama, look, God's here!' My mother couldn't see anything; she thought I was delirious. The cross disappeared, and next morning I was well again."

He'd often been ill when he was a child, and he recalled two other episodes of miraculous healing.

"Once I woke up at night because I'd seen a light. A small shining cloud had flown into my room, although the window was shut. It slowly came closer, stopping just above my head, but not touching me. It departed again just as slowly. Another time it was summer. We were all sitting around the table in the garden. There was a shining cloud again, only much bigger. It began to come down, right above my head, and I shouted, 'Look, do you see it now?' As soon as I shouted, the cloud disappeared, and no one else had seen it that time either. I remember that I felt an unusual joy and love toward everyone. I just loved everyone: my mother, father, the children in the yard, even complete strangers! I wanted to weep for joy when I saw them. It was just a reflection of the joy of Paradise. . . . And I still knew—just as on the night when I'd seen the cross—that God was here."

He fell silent, and drank the rest of his cold tea.

"I've had a lot of miraculous experiences, but much persecution too. I didn't become a priest until I was forty—quite late in life. I was a forester until then, going around tens of hectares of forest on horseback or on foot. Sometimes I wouldn't be home for weeks on end. I would go around the forests and spend the night in old hunting lodges. The first night I stayed in one, I felt afraid because there was such a noise above the ceiling. In the morning I climbed up to the attic and saw that squirrels were living there. Dried herbs were hanging under the roof, there were rowans and Cornelian cherries. The previous forester had used them for making tea, and the squirrels were sitting there. I went a long time without meeting a soul. There wasn't a house or village for miles, only birds and animals.

"One time I came close to death. . . . I'd dismounted, left the road, and wandered into a quagmire. The more I tried to get out, the deeper I sank. There was nothing to grab hold of, no one to call. I sank up to my waist, then to my chest—oh, Lord, what a terrible way to die—alone at night, in a bog, without repentance, Communion . . . You know, there's a psalm . . . how does it go in Russian? 'Save me, O Lord, the waters have come over my soul. I sink in a deep mire where there is no foothold. I'm worn out with crying. My throat is parched. . . . Hear me, O Lord, don't let the abyss swallow me; don't let the pit close its mouth over me. . . .' For years after that I couldn't read that psalm without tears. How I prayed then!"

The metropolitan's eyes filled with tears. He looked at the icon of the Savior and made the sign of the cross, sighing deeply. "Suddenly my horse came up quite close, and turned its tail to me. I grabbed it, twisted it around my hand, and the horse pulled me out. It was my favorite horse! We came back earlier than usual and the first thing I did was to give the horse a drink, and a piece of black bread and salt— and only then had something to eat myself. I owed my life to it. How we got back to the lodge I don't know. I was unconscious, holding the reins, and the horse led me. I think I may have slept for days, and when I got back to the village I discovered my hair had turned quite gray. So I've had gray hair since I was thirty-six, only it's yellow now."

At that time he'd been married, bringing up two boys. His wife died and he went off to serve God.

"The priest was twenty-five, and I was over forty, and here I was, his deacon. He would give me twenty kopecks at the end of the service. 'Here, take this, you haven't earned any more.' I'd take it and say, 'God save you.' Now I'm metropolitan, he's retired and comes and asks *me* for help. I always help him, and never remind him about those twenty kopecks. I've seen a lot of evil, but I've forgiven everyone."

"Did you still see that shining cloud once you were a priest?"

"Once, when I was already archbishop. I went out to bless the people at the point in the service where one says: 'Look down from heaven, O God, and see and visit this vineyard.' At that moment I saw myself engulfed in a flame. . . . It happened afterward as well. I don't know why the Lord is so merciful to me. I don't perform any great spiritual feats. I'm bad at fasting. I'm often ashamed of myself, and I feel worse than everyone else."

I remembered from the Desert Fathers how Father Ammon had come to Father Anthony and asked, "I see that I work more than you, and do more spiritual tasks. Why does God give you more glory?" Father Anthony replied, "Because I love him more."

So Metropolitan Azariah talked about himself without a trace of pride or any desire to impress us, and without making it sound as if it were of earth-shattering importance: It was just the way it had happened. He was unassuming, simple, and clear. He didn't seem to realize how exceptional his story was; he simply put it all down to the unfathomable mercy of God.

We sat for a long time, not wanting to break up our fellowship around the table without good food and wine. I spoke about my own life: how I wanted to live until my son became a priest and we had our church and house.

"So be it! Everything will be this way." The metropolitan looked at Mitya joyfully. "It's God speaking through your mother . . . and you'll remain a good son, not like other boys."

Then the metropolitan met me in Tbilisi in the same simple, kindly way as when Father Georgi and I had called upon him. He rejoiced from the heart that my son was already a hieromonk: "He was just a boy when we came! God grant he becomes a real priest. . . ." He asked where Mitya was and how he was getting on. Then he asked where I'd spend my holidays and offered to put me up at his seaside residence.

A few days later he asked Father Anthony to show me the monastery: so yet another messenger came.

"I saw myself engulfed in a flame. . . ." the metropolitan had said. I've been pondering this mystery for several years.

Moses fled from the land of slavery, and in the desert an angel appeared to him in a burning bush. Moses went to see why the bush was on fire and yet was not burned. God called to him from the fire: "I have heard the cry of my people and I have chosen you to lead them out of the land of slavery into the promised land." Moses hid his face, afraid to look at God, and asked: "What is your name, so that I may tell the people?" "I am that I am," said the Lord.

He is the One who exists from the beginning and lives forever, Being itself and the very Essence of being, Life and the First Cause of life.

Then came thunder and lightning, a cloud over Sinai, a blaring sound. The glory of the Lord overshadowed Mount Sinai, and the children of Israel saw it on the summit like a devouring flame.

The Bible appears to have said everything, and yet everything is a deep secret. What is this flame that set the thornbush on fire but did not burn it up? Why did an angel appear, but God called and Moses was afraid to look at God's face? What beams of light lit the face of the prophet as he came down the mountain after talking with God? What was the fiery pillar of cloud with which the Lord went ahead of the people in the desert?

And what is the glory of the Lord that is like "a devouring flame"?

Years were to pass before I received any answers from the Holy Scriptures and the works of the Holy Fathers, but it soon became clear that if they half reveal the secret, then it is explained by means of other mysteries.

And all of them together, just like the mystery of my own life, are rooted in the all-embracing Secret—in God.

But since the time I had been arrested by this single Secret everything in the world had become a revelation of it. Life acquired meaning and completion. Chaos was transformed into cosmos, which in Greek means beauty.

NEXT MORNING FATHER Anthony got ready to chop poles in the forest to support the beans. It was time for the long shoots to be stretched up instead of spreading over the ground. The evening before, we'd agreed that I would help him, but when I woke up he'd already gone.

"Where's Father Anthony?" I asked Nonna.

She was dragging a reluctant calf on a rope and didn't look around.

As I was bringing water back from the spring I heard the ring of an ax somewhere up the mountain and set off in the direction of the noise. I climbed the terraces to the clearing where we'd been the day before, gazing again at the valley spread below me, but not pausing. I could not see Father Anthony and the noise of chopping was now echoing from below.

A large pig with striped piglets was rooting on the terraced hillside in front of the fence. I went around carefully because I wasn't sure whether it was a boar or a sow.

Nonna came to meet me, a switch in her hand.

"Where's Father Anthony?" I asked again.

"Don't know," she answered sulkily. She was frowning crossly; her black eyes stared straight past me.

"We're going to work. We're putting sticks in for the beans." It seemed to me that everything was quite straightforward, but she didn't want to understand for some reason, and just shrugged her shoulders. "To work," I repeated. She knew this word already.

"The priest's working. Why should you?" she said, and walked on, though it had seemed as if she'd come this way specially to meet me. I looked at her: black coat, faded galoshes, the brushwood switch drooping from her hand . . .

Not long afterward, I found them both in the kitchen garden. Father Anthony was digging a small hole and knocking in a pole. Nonna was scattering earth into the hole. They were working together just as she'd seen in her dream. There was nothing for me to do here.

"What am I to do today?" I asked, when the priest had put his ax aside and blessed me.

He seemed a bit embarrassed that my place had been taken. "Perhaps you could pick some cherries."

A tall tree laden with dark red cherries grew behind the church at the far end of the cornfield. Father Anthony said the watchman had picked a lot and had taken them all home.

The priest went into the church to fetch a bamboo ladder, which had been resting against the scaffolding under the dome. He set it among dense branches and tied it in place.

Can there be better work than cherry picking, in the morning, in the mountains? I climbed to the third section. It was terrible looking down, but I had a fine view all around me. I was dazzled by the huge cherries. Bending the branch, I picked them with my hands, with my lips—and cool, dark red juice flowed out. The sky was darkening through the foliage as if a storm were brewing. Everything filled me with joy, like the feeling of being up high.

Rain started to pour down so hard that the steady noise beat above my head as I went down the slippery bamboo rungs. Soaked through, I ran into the kitchen and put my bowl of cherries on the table.

Nonna and Father Anthony had just come in from the field. "Don't spill them." He steadied my hand. "I'll take them to the metropolitan."

"Won't you taste them?"

I wasn't averse to tasting the cherries either, back on firm ground, enjoying them unhurriedly. While I'd been up the tree I hadn't been quite sure I'd get down in one piece.

"He always wants to give everything away rather than eat it himself." Glikeriya looked into the bowl. "Oh, I'd make such fine dumplings with these cherries!"

But he didn't give in to temptation.

The day darkened. Rain streamed down the windows, shrouding the dull panes, and the top of the oak tree rocked and creaked, shedding its leaves.

"Oh dear, there's so little work left and I really wanted to get it finished today." Father Anthony pressed his forehead to the glass. "I'll have to go for bread again tomorrow and the beans are suffering terribly."

Toward evening, squally bursts of rain were replaced by a steady downpour. Glikeriya placed steaming potatoes on the table, but no one sat down. The priest suddenly flung the door wide open to the raw cold, threw off his shoes, tucked up his trousers, and disappeared out of the door, shouting something to the reader. Nonna ran after him, thrusting her arms into her padded jacket.

They came back half an hour later, soaked through and filthy. Water streamed down Nonna's hair, but her flushed face held no trace of the morning's sullenness.

THE RAIN WENT on and on.

Before going to town in the morning the priest called me to see which of his garments needed to be mended.

There was only a little table in the half-empty entrance hall under a mirror hanging at an angle that had been left by his predecessor. Father Anthony spread out a piece of tarpaulin, laying out bundles and packages, which I sorted. The colorful heap of varied objects from the priest's vestments sparkled with beads and silver brocade thread.

We pulled out a stole and a worn alb from one bundle—this inheritance had been considered unnecessary and had been left behind by his predecessor too. From another we extracted a chasuble of dark violet velvet, with a circle of crosses stitched on it; the golden thread on the crosses was worn, but the old chasuble was still beautiful.

"It's a present from my spiritual father. He's over ninety and he can't stand in such a heavy chasuble, so I've got it for the winter. Don't you think this green one would do for the summer?"

We found a big hole in the shoulder of the chasuble. "The rats have been at it," the priest said, vexed.

We couldn't find one single garment intact out of the whole bundle. But they all had to be washed and darned just the same, in order to find something suitable. I'd never handled consecrated garments before, and now I had the kind of feeling I'd had once at Easter, when I'd stood at the choir stalls and through a side door saw the whole altar covered with red brocade on fire.

He said quietly, "I won't be back for two or three days. You may find some unexpected difficulty with Nonna and Glikeriya. Please, I really beg you, don't leave on their account. Not a day passes here without temptations. The Devil fights with God here. There's a particular sort of battle in monasteries. I give you my blessing not to give Melanie any money, and try not to have any contact with her, if possible. If local men turn up, go to your room at once. Do nothing without prayer. . . ."

"Would you look in at the metropolitan's residence, and see if there's any mail for me? You won't forget?"

Sunday was the anniversary of the day my son made his vows, which by a miracle had coincided with my forty-ninth birthday. But now I was fifty and the next day would be my name day—I was sure there would be letters to mark all these festivals.

Back in my room I spread out the vestments and began on the least pressing work first: stitching crosses on the velvet chasuble.

I soon heard Glikeriya shout from the kitchen: "Vasiliy! Come and eat!" And the watchman replied at once.

When Father Anthony left, the watchman, Vasiliy, came up from the village beyond the mountain, bringing his hunting gun, so we wouldn't be left unprotected. He was a big strapping fellow of about seventy-five, with a shaven head and gray whiskers. During the hot weather he wore a cotton hat with a fringe, and I'd often see this hat above the cornstalks that had still not reached their full height.

The watchman was a Tartar. He'd settled in an Adzhar village and pretended to be a Georgian. He'd been in Gudarekhi for eighteen years. A previous priest had threatened not to let him into the monastery unless he got baptized. He agreed and became Vasya, but he had not been to church once for a long time or put his fingers to his forehead to make the sign of the cross. He did watchman's duties several times a month, for which the priest gave him sixty rubles. But these days he was weeding the cornfield, digging Melanie's kitchen garden, repairing her roof

and getting thirty rubles a day for any work he did.
She got him to make a lot of wooden storage chests
for the church—which Father Anthony would have
loved to throw out. What's more, each chest cost
thirty rubles.

"Where does she get so much money from?" I was
surprised as I remembered Melanie's distorted figure
wandering alone among the lime trees in the evening.

"She's always got some garden produce to sell at
market—pomegranates, flowers." The priest was reluctant to answer. "She sells young corn at the beach:
a ruble a cob. She goes around the churches and people give her money for the monastery. She brings
cabbages, curtain lace . . . the rest she invests in the
watchman. It's a mystery to me why she does it. She
and Glikeriya are rivals, seeing who'll give most.
Glikeriya sends him to the spring for water, counting
aloud: 'I gave him ten. . . . He's brought two buckets, he's due one more.' They're ready to give the
watchman the whole monastery."

It turned out that the pig and its piglets I'd thought
were wild belonged to Vasya. Two cows of his
grazed outside the gates; Nonna was making some
kind of swill for them from meal and peelings. Sometimes the watchman's son, Teimuraz, age about
thirty-five, came with him—tall and also broad-
boned but still slim. He'd finished technical school,
but recently he'd been working with a restaurant
band—calling himself a singer. He and his father often sat in the cornfield, or the singer would appear at
the kitchen door with a lazy, limp expression and ask
a single question: "Any leftovers?"

The watchman didn't eat in the kitchen when the

priest was present, but now Glikeriya fed him like an honored guest and, once he was in her domain, they chattered endlessly.

"Vasya, how many cows have you got?"

"Four cows."

"And bullocks?"

"Three bullocks . . ." he answered, pausing to chew, or count up his bullocks.

"Why three bullocks for four cows?"

"No, there's only one bull, and three bullocks."

"So they're young ones, waiting to be slaughtered?"

"For the slaughterhouse . . ."

"Vasya, why did Teimuraz's wife leave him? He's so attractive . . . I'd say, a very attractive young man! What's more, she ran off with the children."

"She didn't like work."

"Oh well, four cows, three bullocks . . . and you've got some pigs too, and some sheep. . . . Did you say about five sheep?"

"About five pigs. About seven sheep . . ." the watchman counted slowly.

"And haven't you got piglets too? Eat up, eat these tomatoes. Shall I bring you some cheese? We don't drink milk during the fast, it all goes to make cheese. A piece of cheese?"

"All right, bring me some cheese."

The watchman finished his dinner, and silence reigned.

Melanie, the watchman, and Donna hoped to drive the priest and the reader out of the monastery. They lived here with their kitchen garden, like old peasant women in the village down the mountainside, took their corn to market, melted wax, sold the tourists candles and paper icons. The watchman meant more to them than Father Superior.

Father Anthony's predecessor had only ever come to the patronal festival. On that day—the birth of the Virgin—the peasants from neighboring Georgian villages usually gather, driving their lambs along, bringing chickens. The church is full, the heat melts the candles, a discordant crowd sings in the choir stalls, everyone doing their own thing. When it gets dark they light bonfires, roast lamb, drink wine . . . in the morning the previous superior would drive up in a truck, catch the sacrificial chickens and lambs, and go off to the next patronal festival with his clucking, bleating load.

"The gardens belong to the monastery, we've got to work them together, to restore the structure of communal living. . . . And we have our Sunday service, and on Fridays Melanie goes off to market. What are we to do? Young people don't come to the monastery anymore, they're more like Teimuraz: between the cattle shed and the restaurant. Where are we to expect the breath of the Spirit to come from?" Father Anthony said longingly. " 'The Spirit blows where it wills. . . .' Serafim of Sarov used to say that faith would be reborn in Russia.

"Will we live to see the day? Perhaps those who come after us will. If indeed there is anything after. Yes, don't put your trust in earthly things—the realm of the Spirit is not of this world. . . ."

There was a gloomy, overcast bluish sky. Outside the open window the vine leaves shook under the force of the rain. Raindrops trembled in the hollows of the leaves, highlighting their fine veins, along which flowed green, life-giving sap, hanging on the edges of the leaves, reflecting green and blue. Matt clusters, which had barely started to fill with juice, were being washed by the rain, which pulled them downward.

"Don't touch it, it's a vine," the priest said, resting his hand on the trunk as I was clearing stones from a plot of ground and throwing them over the fence. He squeezed the juice out of the grapes to make Communion wine.

This vine grew profusely in Palestine, and God compared his chosen people to its branches. It became a holy symbol: "I am the vine, and you are the branches; he who dwells in me, and I in him, will bear much fruit; for without me you can do nothing. He who does not remain in me, will be cast out like a branch; and these branches are gathered, thrown into the fire, and burned. . . ."

Blessed is he who abides in you, whom you have chosen and brought near you. But what is the state of being chosen? I'd always been struck by the Apostle Paul's words on this, and I looked them up to reread them.

". . . To those who love God, chosen by his will, all things work together for good. For those whom he has foreknown, these he has predestined to be like the image of his Son. . . . And those he has predestined, he has also called, and those he has called he has also justified, and those he has justified he has also glorified."

He has predestined! He has called. He himself has justified and glorified. . . .

So from the beginning of time he called Goderdi, a six-year-old boy. From the same beginning of time he left me. "Why have you rejected me from your face, O undimmed light? And a strange darkness has covered me. . . ."

And the apostle goes on: "So it was with Rebecca, when she conceived twins from Isaac our father. For when they were still unborn, having done neither good nor ill (so that God's will in choosing might come, not from works, but from the One who calls), it was said to her: Jacob have I loved, while Esau I have hated."

They were not yet born, but the Lord loved Jacob, and hated Esau!—that the choice might not come from works.

And, anticipating and answering my question, the apostle said: "What shall we say? Does God lie? In no way. For he said to Moses: I will show mercy to whom I show mercy; I will have pity on whom I have pity. And so, God's mercy depends, not on the person wanting it, but on God who grants us his mercy. For the Scripture says to Pharaoh: for this very reason I have placed you to show my power over you and that my name might be proclaimed through all the earth. And so, he has mercy on those he wants to; and he hardens those whom he will. Will you say to me: 'What do you still blame me for? For who will resist your will?' And who are you, O man, to contend with God? Will the pot say to its maker: 'Why have you made me thus?' What then, if God, wishing to show his wrath and reveal his might, in his long suffering has spared the vessels of wrath, which were ready for destruction, so as to show the riches of his glory over the vessels of his mercy, which he has prepared for his glory? . . ."

To me his reply was not enough. Yes, I was happy to think of Father Anthony as a vessel prepared to receive his glory. But I could not believe that the Lord in his long suffering had spared me only as long as I sought him blindly and without him was dying—he is merciful.

"Perhaps you were looking not for him but for something else?" Goderdi sounded doubtful but he was probably right. I was looking for something that would ease my sufferings, I longed for perfect love, and couldn't quench my thirst. I read thick tomes to find the Truth that would answer the eternal questions of being, and I crossed three oceans in the pursuit of beauty. But still I did not know that all this was you: the easing of suffering and blessing, unending Love, absolute Truth, and perfect Beauty—are all different names for you.

And so, without loving you—I loved you; or, without looking for you—all my life I've been looking for you alone.

"Who is to blame that he is blind, him or his parents?" the disciples asked the Savior about the man born blind. And the Lord answered: "Neither him nor his parents but this has happened so that the works of God might be seen in him."

You predestined me to endure the lot of the generations that rejected you, and were struck down with the plagues of Egypt and with darkness—to endure the fate of the generation that has lost you and so is lost itself. You made me drink the bitter cup to the drops, the cup prepared by the fathers, so that I'd no longer want this poisoned drink, either for myself or for my son.

Those who have seen you—did not want to see you.

We were born blind—so that we might see.

And so the works of God have been revealed in every generation.

Having forgiven me and received me into your house, as you received the prodigal son, you baptized me with the Holy Spirit and with fire.

"The seal of the gift of the Holy Spirit . . ." the priest replied, sealing my forehead, eyelids, and lips in oil with the sign of the cross. "The seal of the gift of the Holy Spirit . . ." And he signed me on my breast, my hands . . .

And so you sealed me with this same Spirit, who hovered over the water when the earth was still form-less and void, and you transformed chaos into cos-mos. This was how I was called—in the mystery of baptism, which is accessible to us all.

However, "Many are called, but few are cho-sen. . . ."

The sun peeped out. I washed the vestments, but soon had to take them all down again because of the rain, and now they were hanging dripping all around the kitchen and in my room. I sewed little decorative threads onto the damp sleeves and turned them inside out to iron them, heating up an old iron on the stove.

The bent figure of Melanie appeared in the door-way—one shoulder thrust forward lower than the other. She was wearing a thick woolen shawl, a long prewar jacket, and long skirt.

"Hello, Veronica. . . ." She spoke with real emphasis, looking at me attentively, with a cunning smile.

Her face was pitted with pockmarks, and she looked as though she wanted to find fault with me, but was biding her time. She'd come for a pot but sat holding it on the little settee, telling me how she'd settled here twenty years ago alongside the empty church—she'd previously worked on the railway as a switch operator. She wasn't just gossiping for the sake of it: She wanted me to be her ally in her struggle with Father Anthony and the reader.

Glikeriya appeared and began her usual conversation about where the produce had gone. "Could the earth have swallowed it up, by chance? The papers were full of natural disasters, floods, drought, failed harvests, storms. One couldn't get away from the weather. It hadn't been that long since the stalls in the vegetable shops had been bursting with fruit and vegetables. As for the grapes—green ones, pink, blue— any flavor you liked, fresh and dried figs, apricots, quince, pears . . . Yesterday, so they say, an Uzbek was selling young figs at the bazaar, three for a ruble. Have you heard the like of that? Before they reformed the money, apricots cost one and a half rubles per kilo—that's fifteen kopecks, new style. No one can remember now what prices used to be like. Or has earth stopped producing fruit under the Soviet regime?"

"A watchman in Sioni used to quote the Psalms: 'God turns the rivers into desert and fertile land into salt because of the wickedness of those living in it. . . .' Do you remember watchman Nikita?" I asked.

"Well, of course . . . a fine figure of a man—about fifty. They say he was even a doctor of science, a chemist?"

"Not quite a doctor, he never finished his thesis. He took too much out of himself over it, so that his wife asked for psychiatric help: He wasn't responsible for his actions, kept shouting out various formulas. It was only in the hospital he came to himself, and he remembered nothing. After the hospital he dropped chemistry and went to the mountains. He started going to church in Tbilisi. It was the first time ever. He talked to Father Georgi about the meaning of life. Then they went to the monastery, to Dzhvari together. He settled there for six months.

"Just think!" Mother Glikeriya was excited. "They took him some borshcht—beet soup—from our kitchen, joking—clever watchman he is, writing a book . . ."

"It's called *Confessions of a Former Atheist.*"

"Was it printed?"

"Typed, in *samizdat*—self-published."

"Nikita's wife, who was a doctor of science as well, came for him. Then she left, while he stayed. They say he's in Dzhvari now."

Father Georgi had told me of a chance meeting in the mountains: He wasn't a priest then, he'd only just stopped being a film critic to go and work in the patriarch's office. The patriarch asked him to go around to far-flung neglected churches with his friend to photograph and describe them. They'd stopped for a minute on an overgrown slope, in front of the last place you cross to get to the monastery they were visiting, and suddenly heard someone coming along singing. The person came closer, and the strains of "Virgin, Maid, rejoice! . . ." became audible. The pilgrim soon came into view: He was barefoot, with a staff, a linen bag on his shoulder—it was Nikita.

I could well imagine the way he walked along the forest trail to the deserted monastery, gathering nuts and berries. I was only sorry that I myself couldn't go from monastery to monastery like that. In any case, how few monasteries are left in holy Russia! At the end of the last century there were still more than a thousand. That was the time to go around to them.

Mother Glikeriya made *shchi* (cabbage soup) from three-year-old pickled cabbage and was waxing eloquent on her other favorite theme. In earlier times, if a noble lady wished to enter a monastery, she sold her estate, made a contribution to the communal chest, and was given a cell. Now they send old women like Domna here, and who's going to earn their keep?

Because of these conversations about who owes what, Melanie and Domna lived off their own produce, "from their own table."

They got their spiritual food too "from their own table." Mother Domna sat on the bench under the lime all day with her rosary, but whether she prayed or dozed not even the spiritual father of the monastery knew.

Glikeriya's talk of contributions to the common purse were slanted at me too. I gave Father Anthony money for my keep, but Glikeriya didn't know this and kept hinting and instructing me, a habit acquired through living among a kitchenful of people. What's more, Glikeriya and Melanie each considered herself to be the real housewife.

Nonna went through the kitchen in weary silence. She would wash the dishes, milk the cow, performing her duties mechanically. Or she'd suddenly start tossing pots from shelf to shelf to show they weren't in their proper place: "It's always me who has to clear up!" All the light of life seemed to drain from her appearance when the priest went away. When he was around she seemed to float through the air, and was always beside or around him. She'd clean the candlesticks under the oak opposite his window when he was in the house. She did her washing beside the bridge above the ditch while he was working there with his ax. If he was in the sanctuary she'd find work to do in the church. Her face would be alight and flushed.

She got up at dawn, went to bed at dusk, and the burden of her labors was eased only by the fact that he saw them. Then she had a letter from her mother: She was ill, her children had scattered, her young brother was in prison. Nonna should have made a trip home, but it was unthinkable to leave the monastery and Father Anthony untended.

"The priest is alone—someone has to look after him. . . ."

The rain kept on and on.

The priest didn't come back on the third day, as he'd thought he would. By evening Nonna was beside herself, and disappeared for quite a while.

"She's gone to check the road," Glikeriya explained.

At dusk they didn't sit down to supper, they waited. We ate later, and the reader disappeared again.

When the paraffin lamp was lit, Nonna sat on the couch, clasping her hands in a spirit of gloomy concentration. She kept looking at the doorway, her eyes seemed hot and feverish. Mother Domna came by and the reader started talking nervously in Georgian, repeating the name "Avel." I guessed she was recalling how Father Avel had been attacked in the village, and was feeling upset.

On the morning of the fourth day, neither the priest nor Nonna was to be seen.

At dusk I saw a tiny figure in a broad tarpaulin coat with a hood, wandering in the rain. I didn't guess at first that it was the reader dragging heavy bags—of course, Father Anthony had passed through earlier with the remaining load.

He soon appeared in our little kitchen, tired, smiling, his hair wet.

"No letter for you," he said to me from the threshold.

"Did you look on the dresser? Did you ask Vera?"

"I looked everywhere, asked everyone. The letter hasn't come so far."

I was truly vexed.

"I'll more than likely be back in town on Saturday. . . ." Father Anthony joined the conversation. "I'll have to find an artist there. . . ."

Nonna heated up some beans and cut some bread vigor had returned to her movements, life to her appearance.

"We had lots of trouble with the cherries," Father Anthony said, sitting in his place between the dresser and the window. "The metropolitan didn't return: ill, they say. I'd intended giving Vera the cherries, but she didn't call by. I took them to the artist . . . he promised to paint a new icon of the Mother of God above the altar. I thought that if he wasn't there, his wife or children would be at home—same story, no one in. What was I to do?"

"In your place I'd have eaten them long since."

"I went to the other end of the town to a certain church member. He's helped us a lot here in Gudarekhi . . . he's got three children. Thank goodness they were all in. They ate your cherries with great pleasure, and quickly at that."

So that was whom the Lord had destined them for.

"Don't talk." A radiant Nonna turned to me. "He's eating." And immediately started talking animatedly herself.

"She's been standing under the tree on the road since morning." The priest shook his head. "She'd gone at least three kilometers down the road . . . But why?"

And when Nonna ran off after the cow, he asked: "Didn't she attack you? I'm surprised, she is so small and proud. Once when I wasn't here she threw herself at Glikeriya, grabbed her just like this . . ." he crushed his cassock onto his chest with both hands and shook it. "She threatened to throw her right out of the gates."

I said Glikeriya had asked me to pick some parsley, and Nonna had wondered where I'd gotten it. It turned out Glikeriya had sent me to Nonna's kitchen garden.

"Why don't you use your own parsley?" the reader had demanded angrily.

"Mine hasn't grown yet!" Glikeriya replied.

"It's the hardest thing of all being a clergyman in a female monastery. It's easier carrying knapsacks than sorting things out with them. But how can I go away, if the Lord has put me here?"

He ate little, as always, drank water, and then stopped, resting against the window.

"Nonna has loved the Church since childhood. She has visions, too. A man stopped me in town one night: 'Why have you got a beard? Why are you a monk?' He hit me in the face but immediately shouted: 'A-a-a! Forgive me, you see I was a Christian myself.' Thank God, for this reminder. . . . And when I returned to Gudarekhi, Nonna said: 'Yesterday I had such a strange vision: as though someone had beaten you up . . .' And she named the street where it had happened straightaway. She even sees a soul. . . ."

I'm sure it's Father Anthony's soul: If you concentrate completely on someone like that, you can see their soul. I spoke carefully about this and he answered me, blushing.

"Do you think I need all this? Do you think I find this easy?"

I returned the bread to the dresser. It had been wrapped so carefully it had stayed dry, although the bag was sodden. A chunk had been torn out of the middle of one loaf: Nonna feeding her dog or calf. What use is it if she sees Father Anthony's soul, but doesn't feel for all his labors? But perhaps she can even see a calf's soul and knows how much it likes soft bread.

The next day Domna will take two or three loaves, Glikeriya the same again: two or three will just disappear, maybe the calf or the watchman will eat them.

"Is the bread all finished?" Father Anthony would say in surprise. "I brought twelve loaves—where have they all gone?"

Darkness fell. The paraffin lamp was lit, and the windowpane glowed from cascades of rain. The reader was sitting opposite the priest, writing out the Canon of St. Shio Mgvimsky.

Georgi's brother, Father David, had taken Mitya and me to Shio Mgvimsky monastery. There had been an earthquake in the valley shortly before we arrived; it didn't destroy anything, but the rock of the ancient monastery cave split off from the valley where the student camp was—a cleft opened up between them.

On the way back we called in at Zedaizeni. A landscape that gripped my spirit opened up beyond the fortress wall. There was a ravine, overgrown with juniper and blackberries, and mountains beyond, with the ancient city of Mtskheta in the distance and a church high above the confluence of the Araagva and Kura rivers.

Father David had lit candles on a stone ledge of the altar in the empty, echoing church, and said the office. Mitya sang "Our Father" in old Georgian, and swallows, disturbed by our service, flew in and out of the window frames.

Father David told us how a lonely old priest had worked in the church several years back. However, a crowd of drunks who'd come into the fortress for a midnight picnic, bonfires and all, locked him in the church. It was late autumn, the church was unheated;

the priest spent a week behind the stone walls without food and with almost no water, and became seriously ill. After his time no one else would serve there.

Long, long ago, in the sixth century, several monks came to Georgia from Syria—John of Zedaizeni, Shio of Mgvimi, David of Garedzhi. Their followers spread out through the mountains and deserts, founded monasteries, built wonderful churches, wrote sacred texts. Fourteen centuries later that self-satisfied contemporary of ours sacked the monasteries, destroyed the churches, smashed, burned, broke up everything he'd managed to wreck, violated the shrines and the clergy, scrawled their names on the walls, barbecued lamb, got drunk—and drove off to conquer new heights. Each period has its own heroes.

May we yet hope that one day a bridge will be thrown across the gulf between the two layers of centuries?

We talked about this. Then Father Anthony, looking through the wet pane at the darkness, asked, for no apparent reason, whether I knew hieromonk Avel.

"Yes, I do . . and have you been to see him?"

"Yes." He smiled. "We've visited each other at different times . . . when there was nowhere else to go. I lived with him for about two months. He stayed a short time with us, too, a long time ago when I was still a child at grandfather's in the country. And, do you know, I've still got his exercise book with portions from the Book of Job. . . ."

"But in Georgian?"

"In Russian . . . He must have had a Russian Bible. Only you can hardly make it out."

"I'd like to look at . . . what he wrote out."

Since the time the Lord sacrificed to Satan all Job had on earth, including even his body, saying, "only spare his soul," the fate of this righteous man has remained a theme for meditation on unmerited suffering.

"I'll show it to you. How did you meet him?" Father Anthony wondered.

The whole world around consisted of the steady battering of rain. The flame guttered inside the paraffin lamp funnel. It was good to be able to sit in a warm room in bad weather, tucked up in an old blanket, and talk about anything you wanted to remember in all its unusual detail.

A BELL HAD sounded and an old woman had come out and led us into the garden. It had been a sunny day, peonies were growing in the garden, and the birds were singing.

Father Avel had soon appeared on the road, blessed everyone, and sat down beside us on the bench, while Mitya's friend Givi, who'd brought us, began speaking in Georgian. Father Avel looked at us with obvious interest, slightly raising his brows: "Mother and son together in church . . . how rarely this happens now, how nice to see it. Well, let's go inside."

A dark heavy wooden cross with a crown of thorns on its crossbeam was hanging along the wall opposite the entrance. Glass and crystal pendants of the most varied chandeliers hung from the ceiling above it and along the walls; several lamps burned—green, red, and blue, and all these transparent garlands, threads, rhomboids, ovals, crystals, and balls reflected a pale mottled light. A large icon of the Trinity hung on the wall in a silvered frame with three winged angels. Round about were icons in wooden frames protected by glass, and large and small paper ones.

Church vessels lay along the walls on wooden shelves. There were candlesticks of copper, stone, and wood, one like a clay saucer with a holder in the middle. There was a folding, wooden Transfiguration ornately carved, of which only the upper fold had survived.

We moved in silence along the shelves. That white angel with the broken-off marble wing must have stood on a grave at one time. The old clock shaped like an ancient Georgian church with its pyramid-shaped dome, faced with small, flowery, ceramic tiles, had long since ceased to tell the time. . . . No hollow echo came from the cracked bronze bell with letters around the edge, which were green with age. It was a long time since the holy vessels had been covered by the traditional *aers,* the large cloth veils that cover the holy gifts—or the smaller covers, whose pattern of golden crosses was completely threadbare. The copper jug for the ablutions of the celebrant hadn't been filled.

"I collected all these things close to churches and monasteries that had been shut," Father Avel said, moving along the shelves with us. "I'd sometimes dig up the piles of rubbish in the yard, in a corner by the fence or in the cellar, and unearth a jug like this.

Perhaps it had been standing in the sanctuary for forty years while the Holy Spirit was descending on the Holy Gifts. . . ."

"May I touch this?" I pointed to an exposed cover of cherry-colored velvet with stitching of the finest silver: a cross and chalice.

He placed the cover on my hands, and I carefully put it to my lips.

Father Avel, illuminated by the reflections in the pendants of chandeliers, broken long since, looked at us with mild dark eyes, and his face shone with quiet joy.

That was how I remembered him: a tall, full figure enveloped in a worn cassock, with a little carved icon of the Mother of God on his breast in place of a cross—a pure young face. The youthful impression the priest made was despite the fact that I could see he was nearly sixty, and that three deep wrinkles furrowed his forehead from temple to temple, following the line of his raised brows. But his thick, curly hair, tied in a knot, was totally black.

"Sometimes I've been given something priceless; none of these treasures should be sold, they're all relics of former church life. To me they're priceless, like the crucifix from the church I was baptized in . . . the church has been destroyed, the figure of Christ has gone, and I made the crown of thorns myself . . . I even put it on him—the sharp thorns really pricked my skin—how the Savior must have suffered!"

Father Avel touched the wall—a hidden panel opened. We went into "the temple of Christ's Nativity" with a grotto and figures of Mother and

Child, wrapped in swaddling clothes in a manger, the star of Bethlehem, woolly lambs.

The priest took half a lamb mold off the table: "My grandmother used to bake a lamb like this at Christmas, with big raisins for its eyes. I used to feel happy, seeing it on the table under the Christmas tree, smelling of fancy pastry, cinnamon, and vanilla. . . . What's become of all this? Why has the light of the world gone out, why has the world gone cold and flat?"

Mitya sat stroking a rolled-up lambskin.

"It's been said: unless you become like little children, you won't enter the Kingdom of Heaven." Father Avel smiled. "So I console myself with all this like a child."

We saw half-rotted monastic clothing, a knotted rosary on a thick string, made of polished glass, little pebbles that had been drilled through, a long woolen rosary rope, completely worn down . . . there were iron chains, copper and wooden crosses.

"There's another little room . . ." said Givi.

"There's nothing of interest inside," the priest remarked.

He touched the wall again. A little door half opened into a cell you could barely get into, even on your knees. It contained a cross on the wall, a lamp—a worn mat on the floor. The door half opened and shut. He didn't want us even to see it for long; that was where he prayed.

We came back to the first room. Mitya and Givi moved the things on the shelves around. Mitya had that absorbed expression I'd loved so much when he was a little boy.

Father Avel was telling us how he'd built this house with his own hands, using bits of planks and boxes, so as to have somewhere to put his accumulated treasures.

"I even constructed a dome, a dark blue one like you get in Russian churches, but the district inspector didn't like it, and told me to take the dome down. But how much of God's mercy has been revealed in all this . . . there was nothing to cover the roof with, for instance. A stranger came in, looked around, and said: 'I'm building my house and I've got some corrugated iron left over, could you use it?' And he brought the exact amount we needed. . . ."

Father Avel also said that people ought to love and forgive one another, because the image of God is to be found in each of us.

"All that's bad in us happens by chance. And, you boys, never despise people. Even when you see the kind of person we're getting more and more of— awful, dirty, drunk, using foul language. God's image is preserved even in such as these, at a depth perhaps that they themselves don't even know. This image has been fouled and muddied by the Enemy, as one might soil an icon. But if it falls into kind hands, they clean it—and it begins to glow with light. . . . It's harder to see God's image in those who degrade you, and who are the image of the Beast . . . but you should pity them even more, because their souls are condemned, perhaps irretrievably, to eternal torment. . . . How hard it is to love your enemies, oh how hard! It takes one's whole life to learn this . . . but in such love we become like the crucified God. . . ."

※

AS I TOLD Father Anthony all this he nodded in agreement, or shook his head. Then he asked: "Is this all you know about him? Didn't Givi tell you any more?"

"No, and we didn't ask—that was the total picture we got. . . ."

"I'll go and look for his notes . . ."

Nonna went off to her room, leaving the door ajar.

Father Anthony came back, holding a small, half-sized exercise book. The reader came back too.

"Going to bed?" She put it half as a question.

"Good night." He laughed—and to me, "She's so used to giving orders."

She sighed wearily and sat down again, her cheek in her hand.

I pulled up a lamp. The notebook's cover was very worn. Father Avel had probably carried it about in his pocket for a long time. It was squared paper, several strokes depicting the monastic sign of Calvary and, farther on, a tiny string of letters on both sides of the page, and words broken off because the edge of the page was torn.

"Read aloud," Father Anthony said, "and I'll tell you what I know too."

" 'If I speak, my pain is not assuaged; if I forbear, how much of it leaves me? God has given me up to the ungodly and cast me into the hands of the wicked. . . . His archers surround me; he slashes open my kidneys and spares nothing, he pours out my gall on the ground, he breaks me with breach upon breach, he runs upon me like a warrior. I have sewed sackcloth upon my skin and have laid my strength in the dust. My face is red with weeping, and on my eyelids is deep darkness; although there is no violence in my hands, and my prayer is pure. . . . For when a few years have come, I shall go the way whence I shall not return. . . . Why do you hide your face and count me as your enemy? Will you frighten a driven leaf and pursue dry chaff?' "

"You're saying it all too easily, you can probably say it off by heart. . . ." Father Anthony interjected. "Read it. I wanted to reread it for myself as well."

" 'But man is born to trouble as the sparks fly upward . . . the arrows of the Almighty are in me; my spirit drinks their poison; the terrors of God are arrayed against me. . . .

" 'Can that which is tasteless be eaten without salt? My appetite refuses to touch them; they are as food that is loathsome to me. O, that I might have my request, and that God would grant my desire! That it would please God to crush me, that he would let loose his hand and cut me off! This would be my consolation. . . .' "

I stopped to take a breath.

"Do you know what his 'loathsome food' was?" Father Anthony laughed. "It's quite apposite. . . . Avel went hungry for a long time. At night he'd go to waste ground behind the sweet factory where refuse containers stood. Sometimes they'd throw cake crumbs through his half window. When I was living with him, he'd bring in this sweet stuff, a mixture of greasy pink and yellow cream, arrange it on a plate and say, 'That really must have been a beautiful gateau.' He'd bless everything, eat it, and thank God for it afterward. I couldn't eat it. You can eat one or two cakes, but what do you do when you've got to eat this disgusting fatty artificial cream every day instead of any other kind of food . . .? We'd often sit in front of that plate, have some tea with dry black biscuits, then he'd say, 'I'm going to feed the birds, this will be a real feast for them.' "

"Do you think the birds would want to eat food like that?"

"Some of them did. Blue tits, for instance, really liked to peck at fat, crows and pigeons too."

"Why did Father Avel starve himself like that?"

"Didn't you know that he'd stopped serving as a priest?"

"Stopped serving? No, I'd never heard. Was that long ago?"

"About thirty-five years. Well, read a bit more then."

" 'What is man that you prize him so highly and pay attention to him, you visit him every morning, try him moment by moment? How long will you depart from me? If I sin, what do I do to you, watcher of men? Why do you make me your opponent? Why have I become a burden to you . . .? For now I shall lie in the earth; you will seek me, but I shall not be. . . .

" 'I loathe my life. . . . Does it seem good to you to oppress, to despise the work of your hands and favor the designs of the wicked?

" 'If I am wicked, woe to me! If I am righteous I cannot lift up my head. I am filled with disgrace and look upon my affliction, it increases. You hunt me like a lion . . . and bring fresh hosts against me.' "

Father Anthony sat leaning his elbows on the table, his fingers clasped. I waited.

"About thirty-five years ago, the year Stalin died—he died in March, and everything happened on the May Day parade—Father Avel was quite a young priest. You know the main square in Tbilisi? The podium for the government is put there for the parade. They always hung portraits of the leaders stretching up two stories on the building of the Executive Committee; at the height of the parade when the whole square was blocked with people, and a member of the government was speaking, the giant portrait of Stalin suddenly went up in flames. Father Avel had gotten into the corridor upstairs, opened the window, soaked the portrait with paraffin, and set fire to it."

"This sounds like a tall story?"

"Well, of course, it got embroidered a bit. But he certainly burned those portraits. Lenin's portrait caught fire immediately afterward. A shudder of terror went through the square. Everybody froze with fright. Silence descended. The leaders were furious, but Father Avel, leaning out of the first-floor window, preached a sermon: 'The Lord says, you will not make yourselves an idol, or any image of it. . . . "Do not bow down to them and serve them, for I am the Lord your God. You shall have no other gods before me. . . ." Come to your senses, people. Georgians have always been Christians. Don't you realize you're worshiping idols? Jesus Christ died and rose on the third day . . . but your graven statues will never rise to life; even when they were alive they were dead.' "

"I simply can't imagine that such a thing was possible. They wouldn't have let him say even five sentences."

"Well, he probably said five, maybe more. The doors to the building were locked. He'd got in through the attic beforehand and sat it out till the parade started. It's true they got him down pretty quickly. The fire brigade raced up with their ladders. . . ."

Father Anthony had been speaking with deep feeling, but now his fire turned inward.

"When they got him down the crowd threw itself at him, bursting through all the lines of soldiers. They kicked him, hit him with their rifle butts and rubber hoses, and shouted, 'Let me be the one to finish the swine off.' Every single one of them wanted to show how zealous he was by trampling the foe of the people with his own boots. The firemen dragged him away. . . ."

"Why didn't they shoot him?"

"They didn't shoot him because he was as good as dead when they carried him away. He had no face left, just a mash of blood. His head was smashed and he had seventeen fractures to his body. He didn't regain consciousness for almost a month, but they looked after him well, so that they could hold an investigation. . . . It was as though they were trying to set up a show trial—they didn't want to carry a condemned man in on a stretcher. But there was no way he could get better. He was at death's door the whole time, but he didn't actually die. That's what I was told—I was only just born at that time myself. I don't have any precise information—Avel doesn't talk about it. Either they dragged the whole affair out until the time of the Khrushchev amnesties, or they spent a long time trying to uncover a plot and wanted to drag the names of fellow conspirators out of him. Then they said he was a mental case—irresponsible for his actions: they were either helping him or it was just more convenient for the authorities to put it that way. When they let him out a few years later he was forbidden to serve as a priest.

"It wasn't just the Church—he couldn't get work anywhere for ten years. However, one good thing was that he had a house to go to, and his mother was there too, the old woman who opened the door to you . . . the pair of them lived off his pension. Because he'd been certified insane he'd been given a pension of seventeen rubles. They wouldn't even let him into private houses to do a bit of work. Everyone was scared of him. Neither he nor his mother dared go out in daylight—the neighbors would set their dogs on them. At first he'd go through the villages and work as a watchman in the vineyards or as a stoker in the churches. Then his mother became paralyzed as a result of all these frightful experiences, and he couldn't leave her. For a few years he sat in the church porch, begging. Even the priests would drive him away. Only people who didn't know him would give him anything—people who knew him would turn away, or make fun of him. . . ."

"How did you get to know him?"

"That was some years later. He was working as a watchman in our *kolkhoz* garden. He had a little hut there. By day he would go away into the forest and dig himself out a cave in the cliff like a hermit. I found this cave by chance—I told you he liked to pray in the forest—there were three boards in a corner and some old clothing, candles literally stuck to the wall, and so I just kept watch for him. He'd live with us in the autumn, helping my grandfather, chopping logs, kindling the stove . . . No one knew he was a priest. Well, and this little book of his never came out of the pocket of an old double-breasted jacket. I found it recently and I want to give it to him."

"When did you live at his place?"

"I worked as a psalm-reader when I'd finished working on the metro. They hadn't paid me at the church. I met Father Avel and he said, 'Why bother renting a room? You can live with me in the meantime.' So I lived in his room, which he'd turned into a church. I'd wake up in the morning because the birds were pecking at the window. You'd go out and he'd be sitting under a tree—just like the garden of Paradise. Boxes and packets of different colors were hanging up on the branches for the birds, and there were earthenware saucers on the ground, plates of grain—and the birds came fluttering around and pecked at them. A woodpecker perched on the palm of his hand. It had a little red triangle on its neck and white streaks on its wings.

"And, do you know, for all his simplicity I never met a man who was wiser or better read than Father Avel. He'd read a lot of the early Fathers and remembered everything, especially Isaac the Syrian. That was a difficult time for me, and Father Avel comforted me a lot, so that I wouldn't get too depressed. St. Isaac says that if you find constant peace on your way it means you're far from achieving spiritual things, and you've been forgotten by God. The more you grow spiritually, the greater the sorrows you meet. When a time of great sorrows comes it means that the soul is secretly rising to a higher level. If the soul is powerless and weak and asks God to save it from sorrows, and God hears it, then inasmuch as the soul has no strength for great suffering, so also is it insufficient for great giving. The Lord doesn't give great gifts without great sufferings, and the grace which God gives is in proportion to the sorrows sent in his Providence."

"So this is why they say we should rejoice at sorrows and thank God for them. . . ."

"Isaac the Syrian writes that we should rejoice at sorrows because we're walking the same path as all the saints. But we should beware lest we fail to endure temptation on account of our pride: More convincing temptations are then sent to us because of our proud hearts. In suffering, the soul is isolated, defenseless—and humbles itself, dies to the world. It cries to the Lord out of the depths, and the Lord will not destroy a crushed spirit."

We parted company at three in the morning.

I took Father Avel's notebook with me. The lamp was on the windowsill. I held the open page almost flat against the glass. He'd obviously taken a lot of time over these notes; often, after he'd finished a chapter, he'd go back to the beginning and pursue a new theme.

"He deprives the leaders of the nations of their reason and leaves them to wander in the desert where there is no path. The people groan and the soul wails for those who have been killed, and God does not forbid it. Among them are enemies of light who do not know his ways or walk in his paths. . . .

"God is alive who has deprived me of judgment and the Ruler of All who has grieved my soul so that as long as there is breath in me and God's Spirit is in my nostrils my mouth will not say an untruth and my tongue will not utter a lie! I am far from being able to confess you as just; until I die I will not yield in my innocence. I have held to my truth strongly and I will not let it go; my heart will not reproach me in all my days. My enemy will be like the godless one, rising against me like a lawless one. For what profit is there to the hypocrite when God will cast out his soul?"

Noted with particular care, and written separately on the page was: "Do not incline to godlessness which you have preferred to suffering. God is high in his power. . . . Who will show him his way? Who can say, 'You are dealing unjustly?' Ruler of all! we cannot comprehend him."

Toward dawn, when the rain had stopped and the edge of the sky had turned a pale green across the valley, I found the main theme in Father Avel's notes: " 'I know that my Redeemer lives and on the last day he will raise my wasted skin from the dust, and in my flesh I will see God. I will see him myself, my eyes, not the eyes of another, will see him ' "

" 'I will see him myself. . . .' The whole argument of Job with God when worn out and desiring death he cries, 'Why do I suffer so?' And the Lord answers from the whirlwind, 'Who is this, darkening Providence with senseless words? Gird up your loins like a man: I will ask you and you explain to me, where were you when I laid the foundations of the earth? Tell me if you know, if you have understanding, who determined its measurements—surely you know! Or who stretched the line upon it? On what were its bases sunk? Or who laid its cornerstone when the morning stars sang together and all the sons of God shouted for joy? Have you commanded the morning since your days began, and caused the dawn to know its place, that it might take hold of the skirts of the earth, and the wicked be shaken out of it? It is changed like clay under the seal, and it is dyed like a garment. . . .'

" 'Did you ever go down to the depths of the sea and know the abyss?' the Lord asks the person who demands an answer from him about his fate. 'Have the gates of death ever opened for you? Where is the way to the dwelling of light? Do you know the ordinances of the heavens? Can you lead out the constellations in their time?'

" 'And the Lord continued and said to Job: Shall a faultfinder contend with the Almighty? He who argues with God, let him answer it. Then Job answered the Lord: Behold, I am of small account; what shall I answer you? I lay my hand on my mouth. I have spoken once, and I will not answer; twice, but I will proceed no further. . . . I had heard of you by the hearing of the ear, but now my eye sees you. . . .'

"Why did this righteous man suffer? Was it not in order to bridge the gulf between 'I had heard of you by the hearing of the ear' and the thing that consoles all suffering, after which there is nothing left to desire: 'but now my eye sees you'?

" 'The Lord restored the fortunes of Job and blessed the latter days of Job more than his beginning. . . .' This recompense is the prototype of the resurrection of the soul, whether in our lifetime or after death—the soul which sees God."

THE CLOUDS ABOVE Gudarekhi dispersed, but the rain continued on and off.

Father Anthony was going back to town by train after the evening office. While we had dinner he told us about his last meeting with Avel.

"He'd aged, gone gray, he'd changed a great deal in his last years. It was true, he used to talk more about joy and love, because he'd borne too much grief and hatred. Now—his talk was all about repentance. He told us of one such incident: 'When I was young, I was told about a priest who drank. I didn't know him but I said: This man is unworthy to stand at the altar of the Lord. I was still living like a pagan myself and yet I dared to judge a man in holy orders! So the Lord showed me who was unworthy: I've been rejected by him for thirty-five years. I often dream that I'm offering the Holy Gifts, but it may be that I'll die without having celebrated one more liturgy.' His eyes filled with tears. Then he repeated Job's words, when he learned he had nothing left on earth: 'The Lord has given, and the Lord has taken away   Blessed be the name of the Lord!' "

"Where is he now?"

"Monasteries are opening up now; he travels around collecting money for churches. He'll probably stay at some monastery—after all, he's been a monk since his youth. I keep on praying that the Lord may still allow him to work as a priest before he dies. Although it's not right to ask in this way: God knows best. His kingdom is an endless liturgy, which everyone who is saved will celebrate with the angels."

"Who will be saved?" Nonna caught the drift of our talk.

"The one who endures to the end," he replied.

"Almighty Lord! We can never reach him. . . ." His wisdom is unsearchable and his grace is secret. Cain keeps killing Abel, and thus prepares a way for him to a blessed eternity.

But my eyes don't see you, Lord . . . You didn't come to me with unspeakable light one pure morning of life and your angels did not shadow me with invisible wings. "Why have you rejected me, O light that never goes down?" A strange darkness has covered me. Behold the weeping of my soul from the beginning of days.

From the beginning, right till this very day when I kneel in this empty church at the edge of the earth, I speak to you. I brought a candle-end and lit it in front of the icon of the Mother of God with you, the Child, in her most pure arms—the Child and Ancient of Days—with the One who spoke to Moses and declared his Name in the revelation of the New Testament. Oh, if I were righteous like Job, and could demand an answer from you, but I can only weep at your feet, as the prodigal son wept in poverty and humility, knowing that he had sinned before heaven and before you and wasn't worthy to be called your Son anymore. . . .

Why have you thrown me into this spiritually bankrupt world for forty years? And why have you spoken your Name to me so late? I hear you right beside me. Everywhere I touch the edge of your shimmering robe. Everywhere I glimpse your reflection. I know that everything in the world is a symbol, the visible sign of your invisible presence, a revelation of you and your secret cloak. I feel that as long as I take part in your endless life I live, and everything on earth lives too. The more I feel this and trust you, the more I long for you.

But I haven't seen you for so long, so unbearably long, and I haven't the right even to want to catch sight of you, for this is the portion of those who are perfect. What am I to do with this unslakeable longing and thirst? I cry out like a blind beggar beside the road you travel along, "Lord, I want to see!" And will you not answer as you did then, "Receive your sight. Your faith has saved you."?

"Blessed are those who have not seen, and who have believed," you reply. But if my faith were sufficient for blessing . . .

So what is your kingdom and glory and this unspeakable light that has been revealed to your chosen ones? What light did Goderdi see in his childhood when he prayed at night in the garden? Why did the boy who saw the shining light understand that "God is here"? What sort of shining cloud came down above his head, unseen by the others, but filling him with love?

Anthony and Avel, and Metropolitan Azariah, Job the long suffering, Moses in front of the burning bush—all these are heralds to me, living witnesses to whom the Lord has revealed his shining glory in different measure. The apostles on Mount Tabor saw Jesus Christ in this glory.

Anticipating this revelation, he promised that some of the disciples would see the kingdom of God coming in power while they were still alive. And so he went up a high hill with Peter, James, and John, in order to pray. They went up Tabor before nightfall; he went a short distance away from the disciples to pray. Night came on: Peter and his friends were heavy with sleep.

An unbearable light suddenly shone about them, awakening them. Trembling with holy terror, they saw the Son of Man in the unsearchable glory of his kingdom. His face shone like the sun in the darkness of the night. His clothes became white and shining like snow, such as no whitener on earth could make them. Peter, not knowing what to say, exclaimed, "It is good for us to be here!"

In this bright Tabor night, in the same glory, the two prophets, Moses and Elijah conversed with Christ. Moses had asked God long before, "If I have found favor in your eyes, open the way to you, I beg you, that I might know you." But the Lord replied, "I will make all my glory pass before you, but man cannot look on my face and live."

The prophet Elijah was allowed to hear your presence only in the blowing of a quiet wind after the fire and storm.

Now the desire of both the great prophets was fulfilled—they saw God face-to-face. The revelation to Moses by God in the burning bush and on Mount Sinai—is completed fifteen hundred years later on

Mount Tabor. For this it was necessary for the Babe of Bethlehem to be born of the Virgin Mary, to take our flesh upon himself in order that the eternal human desire to see God might be fulfilled.

St. John the Theologian would reveal the great secret: "God is light." Ten centuries later another witness of the holy mysteries, St. Simeon the New Theologian, uncovered the sense of these words in his Divine Hymns: "God the Trinity existed before the heavens were created, before the earth was formed, One and Only, light without beginning, uncreated light, light ineffable—immortal God, One without end, constant, eternal . . . There was neither air, nor darkness at all, nor light, nor ether, nor anything else, but there was God alone—Spirit completely bathed in light, all-powerful and insubstantial. He created the angels, cherubim and seraphim . . . after that he produced the heavens and then the earth, the water, the chasms, and the immaterial light that had no part of any of this remained within them."

We cannot see the divine light by ourselves, but God shows himself to those whom he chooses and prepares—revealing himself as and when he wills.

Inaccessible by nature, he reveals himself in love in which the impossible becomes possible.

Moses and Elijah, the apostles, Peter, James, and John, saw this glory and were living witnesses to the fact that God and his saints share one and the same glory and kingdom and light. To see him means to be in him, to see God means to dwell in him and to be part of his creating power and blessing. This is eternal life, salvation, resurrection, and paradise.

All our life on earth is realized only insofar as we take part in him who first called himself by the Name "I am that I am"; we are alive if we are in God and he is in us.

The Transfiguration of the Lord is the mystery of mysteries and the revelation of revelations; in which we find the meaning of confessing the faith, of martyrdom, of spiritual victories, of the hermit life and of monastic life, the fulfillment of holiness. . . . In it are all God's promises and the hope of faith, the justification of all our sufferings.

IT'S HARD FETCHING water in the rain: several steps had been beaten out of the slope, but the earth had swollen, our feet skidded on the clay. There was nothing to hold on to, only nettles grew along the path. It would have been good to have dug out the steps and paved them with flagstones, to have put in a few upright posts and made a handrail. And when I'd gone, the steps would remain.

The water tank under the spring had filled up after the rains. I drank my fill. Nowhere was there such tasty water as in Gudarekhi. And such peace!

The watchman was standing on the edge of the cliff in a hooded felt cloak, looking down at me as I went up with the bucket. "What are you afraid of? I'm a man. I don't bite. . . ." he said, with a kind of dark humor, but quietly, not wasting his words.

I greeted him and smiled. Perhaps he wasn't happy that I was carrying water—I might have been depriving him of some of his earnings. I asked Glikeriya about it.

"Well," she mumbled, "Vasya means more to us than you do. You came and you'll be leaving again, but he's been here for twenty years."

It was true that he meant more . . . and anyway, so what? He was their guardian and helper, even though he didn't do it quite free of charge, while I, it's true, would leave.

Suddenly I thought: Why am I here? Their life is settled, good or bad, who am I to judge? I'm just a passing stranger. Where is my resting place on earth, then? That's my misfortune: No such place is found for me. And so I travel through alien, if holy, places.

I went out into the rain again in my old coat and rubber boots.

Beyond the church, opposite the house was an awning above the steps to the side exit. I sat on the dry upper step and the rain washed my muddy boots. It flowed down off the roof, splashed in clear puddles on the grass, and the grass stems swayed under the water as though they were swimming. I felt as if I were sitting in a high chapel made of streams of light from the awning. The sky cleared although the sun hadn't come out; the streams and raindrops were full of light.

The soggy, watery glade glinted green in front of me. Rain spattered on a gravestone. A pomegranate tree covered with red flowers stood beside the grave. In the distance a damp mist swirled around the forested hillsides.

Well, let's sum up what I've made of my fifty years. I'm sitting on the doorstep of an unknown church at the end of the world, and it seems that in the whole vast expanse there's no one who would miss me. To the publishing houses I'm a lifelong member of the part-time staff—I don't think I could take being forever in one establishment, nor would one organization be able to put up with me for long. I don't have many friends—I make too many demands of them, partly because the things I want are exceptional and go beyond the bounds of our social setting, or simply because I've got a difficult nature. Everything on earth lost its value for me while I tried to get to heaven, but so far I've not found anything even there.

And all I've had on earth is the son, whom you, Lord, have given me. I've carried his soul on the palms of my hands for twenty years, feeding it with my breath, warming it with my love, repeating to him all the words you have told me. I've returned your greatest gift to you and now I'm alone again. Alone, as at the beginning of days . . . I'll stay for a bit in Gudarekhi, and then what? To my empty shell of a apartment from which all life departed the day my son left?

Perhaps this is the life of an exile, of a pilgrim, the homelessness of those who seek the heavenly city?

But the rain was shot through with sunshine; it splashed lightly at my feet, giving the grass a green shimmer. Peace spread through the valley, imperceptibly dissolving these thoughts. I sat resting my elbows on my knees, my chin in my hands looking at the little pomegranate tree, and my sad mood was touched with light. The deserted yard of the monastery, the pomegranate flowers, the damp mist on the slopes of the hills—everything echoed a quiet gratitude within me. How much I would be missing without Gudarekhi, without Anthony and Avel, this valley . . . And the Lord has brought me all this way just to see them . . . I've been granted so much, on sea and on land, along every path, all earth's roads, along which you lead me to yourself, my God. . . . Could I have really lived in any other way, or have had any more than I have now?

I looked through the rain at the earth which you have created, and I could not look enough. It occurred to me that you have given me all this to be my home in the world, spacious and free and filled with your presence.

THE RAIN STOPPED, and everything sparkled. The birds began to chirrup. I hung damp clothes among the lime trees and went back home.

Father Anthony had tied a cotton towel around him and was rolling out dough for the Communion bread. "Watch how this is done—it could be useful for you."

He was gently pressing the little round lumps with the palms of his hands. He cut the top with a seal—a cross inside a circle—and set it in like a hat. On the four sides of the cross were the Church Slavonic letters IS-KhS NI-KA—Jesus Christ conquers. The Georgian imprint on the small loaves is like a strict pattern or hieroglyph that reveals and hides a secret, both sign and symbol, like everything else in the service.

"You don't give yourself a break at all."

"My granny used to say, that's your fate. Aged six you get a big load put on you and you carry it till death. . . . Being a prior of a monastery is a big responsibility, I'll answer for it on Judgment Day."

"And when do you have time to pray?"

"At night . . ." He laughed. "I used to pray a lot, but now I work more for the Lord. It's the straight path to temptation when a young monk prays a lot. The Fathers say, if you see a novice who's rising to heaven, you must grab his feet and pull him back to earth."

"Do you read the Holy Fathers?"

"Only a little nowadays . . . Sometimes I read them and think, I've read this before."

"Isn't it said about this very thing, that God writes with his finger in faithful hearts?"

"No, someone's said this about it: The Fathers of old had great revelations and wrote about them in their books. After them came others, those who read these books and learned how to live by them. But now we buy the books and put them on our shelves."

He pulled out the griddle with the nicely browned Communion bread. He'd consecrate the loaves at the service in two days' time. The Communion bread is the firstfruits of food and a world restored to God: bread is blessed at the *litiya*—a special service during a vigil; the *artos* is a special loaf, blessed at the Easter Liturgy. The eucharistic bread and wine are transformed by the Holy Spirit, thus blessing those receiving Communion. Water, the primal element of life, is blessed on the day of Epiphany; apples, clusters of grapes, on the Transfiguration; fields at Trinity. The earth receives the blessing of the Lord, food loses its utilitarian aspect and joins us to the God who has given it, restoring the link between the particular and the universal, between the world, ourselves, and the Creator.

The priest rolled out some more Communion rolls, and gave them the imprint—Jesus Christ conquers.

I recalled the words from Revelation about the ten kings who will receive authority from the beast and wage war with the Son of God. "And the Lamb will conquer them, for he is Lord of Lords and King of Kings, and those with him are called and chosen and faithful."

Father Anthony is one of those who are chosen and faithful. . . .

Can untruth be with God—in that he predestined and called him? When he sent his disciples into the world, the Savior said to them: "You did not choose me, but I chose you that you might go and bear fruit." "I send you, like lambs among wolves . . ."— living sacrifices, like himself—the Lamb, slain voluntarily from the foundation of the world. He chose us for unending spiritual feats to his glory, for preaching, for martyrdom and persecutions. . . .

But could I agree to such a choice? And if I did, was I ready for it?

And now the Hord shows me how this sacrifice should begin. Not to eat cherries but give them to unknown children; not to bathe in the sea but take bread in my knapsack up the mountain. To work from morning till night, and to pray at night. Every day ought to become a staircase of large and small selfless deeds, and then, perhaps, toward the end of life the Lord will say: "Well done, good and faithful servant! You have been faithful in little, I will set you over much; enter into the joy of your master." And this is the joy of the grace of the Holy Spirit, visions of the Lord's glory, dwelling with him on Tabor. . . .

"What a pity, there's no one to give the Communion bread to. No one ever comes to the service."

"Don't let that upset you, you'll have everything—I'm speaking from the heart. People will come and the Lord will give you everything you need."

Father Anthony blushed: "As a child he sent me his angels, nowadays he sends people and comforts me through them." He made a broad sign of the cross. "Yes, God is always talking to us—through people and through life's events, only more often than not we don't listen to him. . . . Once I heard a voice when I was praying—I almost melted at the sound, it was like thunder. For a long time afterward I couldn't pray without crying—and I knew that the Lord is able to hear every word we speak. . . . Since then it's often been hard for me to hold back my tears during the litanies, in the prayer for the sorrowing, during the priest's secret prayers for his own sins and for human ignorance. . . ."

He covered the hot rolls with a fresh towel: "Father Avel wept at prayer as well . . . he's the only person who knows what I'm telling you now, you know. He was very surprised my spiritual life began so early. And it was he who first told me I'd become a monk, when we met in the forest when I was just a child."

And Father Anthony soon came stepping lightly through the yard in his black cassock, an empty knapsack over his shoulder.

I took the washing down from the line—it had been drying in the sun: "Perhaps you shouldn't go now, you won't get a rest before the service."

"For as long as we're alive, we mustn't rest," he said, making his usual little joke.

Faithful Nonna was waiting for him by the cypress in her black scarf and velvet coat. She was going to walk halfway with him.

Next day Father Anthony brought me a letter and a telegram. He took them out of his breast pocket with a look on his face as though it were he who'd been hoping for news from his son.

"I only found the artist yesterday. There was no one in the residence, and because of this letter I had to spend the night with neighbors."

I suspected that he'd gone to town specially for it.

In his telegram Mitya—now called Hieromonk Kirill—had sent good wishes for my name day and birthday, and said he had some very important things to write to me about.

Judging by its postmark, the letter had come this morning. I ripped the envelope open and went behind the church to read it. I sat on the same step I'd sat on the day before when I'd been sheltering from the rain, and took out the folded page of an exercise book. I read the first words— and a feeling of such warmth flooded my heart, as if the Lord had touched it. My son wrote that two weeks ago an unexpected event had occurred which he still didn't know how to react to: He'd been transferred from the monastery to a parish. He'd already moved and had just finished his first week.

"The church is small, made of wood, but in good

condition. It's dedicated to the Mother of God 'Joy of all those who sorrow.' There are some old birches, a rowan, and poplars by the fence. The priest's house is beside them. There are hills all around, fields and meadows, a mass of clover, forests, and lots of lakes.

"I've spent a year in the monastery and I've always thanked God for it. Now I've been transferred to a parish, and, I'd say, things have gotten even better. . . . I celebrated my first liturgy last Sunday. There weren't many people there, only about twenty. No choir, just me and the reader. But the main lack I felt was of you standing beside the pulpit and taking Communion along with me.

"I'm really looking forward to your arrival. The Lord has answered your prayers and I'm very happy about that now. . . ."

Through my tears I could see the shining day, the sheen of the wet grass and leaves. The pomegranate tree was ablaze with Easter flowers. My heart was so full of gratitude and love, that all I could do was sit and weep, and read over and over the words of the letter that gave purpose and meaning to the rest of my life: serving God with my son.

In the hallway Father Anthony was turning a piece of linen inside out: His new chasuble was wrapped up in it.

"Last night I called in at the church up the mountain. There's been a change of priest; the man who was an assistant priest is in charge now. He saw me and said: 'Goderdi, go into the sacristy and pick out the most beautiful vestment you fancy. No old one, mark you, a new one. . . .' Then he threw up his hands: 'Oh, forgive me! I called you Goderdi out of force of habit. . . . You're Hieromonk Anthony now!'—and he started embracing and congratulating me."

The chasuble was the pure, golden color that stands for divine light in church symbolism. There was a stole to go with it, and cuffs.

"Everyone congratulated me," Father Anthony said, a bit embarrassed at not being able to conceal his joy. "They gave me two bottles of wine, as well, and roses from the church garden. . . ."

"Where's the wine?" Glikeriya got interested. "Let's put it on the table at once!"

"The wine is made from grapes—it's for the Communion. And I had to leave the roses in the metropolitan's residence. Everything there's covered in white, bags of cement . . . The believers bring everything they've got and help paint the church. You'll see how nice it will all be. . . ."

"I won't . . . I'm going away tomorrow after the service." I told him about the letter.

He made a broad, quick sign of the cross: "Thank God . . . Thank him every day for your son, for everything God sends you. After all, it's said that the Lord fulfills the wishes of those who love him. I believed this would happen, but I never thought it would be so soon. Only don't be under any illusions: You've seen what a remote parish is like, it'll be tough going."

I knew that. But the difficulties were still in the future. For the moment I was happy.

I just couldn't get to sleep, then, at four o'clock, in the dark before daybreak, I heard the hollow echo of the church bell striking.

Glikeriya and Nonna stood on either side of the church entrance, wearing old cassocks. Nonna was reading the Six Psalms. Father Anthony came out to the pulpit in his new chasuble.

It was good to pray with them on my last night in the dark church, lit by two wreaths of freestanding candles in front of the icon-screen. In my youth, before I knew that God existed, my great expectations were not fulfilled, and I thought if I lived to be about forty, everything would get worse. But starting life in the church every day brought new discoveries and now at my fiftieth birthday I was filled with happiness as the earth is filled with moisture from merciful rains. How can I describe this feeling?

Father Anthony called me up to the lectern. "Do you want to read the Benedicite, the Praise Psalms?" Of course I did!

"Let everything that has breath praise the Lord. Praise the Lord from the heavens. Praise him in the heights. Praise belongs to you, O God. Praise him, all you his angels. Praise him, all you his hosts. . . . Praise him, sun and moon. Praise him, all stars and light. Praise him, the heaven of heavens, and the water which is above the heavens. Let them praise the Lord's Name: He spoke and they were, he commanded and they were created. . . . Let everything that has breath praise the Lord. . . ."

I read the pre-Communion prayers in my cell to the accompaniment of the dawn chorus.

And at the Last Supper, being celebrated now and

forever, Jesus Christ gave me a portion of his Body and Blood—from the hand of his chosen and faithful Hieromonk Anthony.

That same day, I said good-bye to everyone at Gudarekhi and went back to the residence.

FATHER ANTHONY'S LUXURIANT dark red roses were still on the refectory table—the color that stands for martyrdom, the color of blood. My son had worn a dark red chasuble at his ordination. The roses still smelled fresh and sweet. I changed the water in the vase and lit the lamps.

Faina and Vera were waiting downstairs. Faina was frying strips of eggplant with *adjik,* vegetables, and garlic. She was wearing the same scarf and gray sweater, darned at the shoulder. She moved the egg-plant toward me.

"What about you?"

"I've eaten," Vera replied, "and Faina takes only bread and vegetables—she doesn't even take the oil we're allowed to use during a fast."

It turned out that Metropolitan Azariah hadn't come after all: He'd been ill and was convalescing in the mountains.

"How did you like it in the monastery?" Faina wrote on a paper napkin.

I ate the eggplant, drank some tea, and began to tell them about it. When Vera left I asked Faina where she goes on pilgrimage. She brought a bundle of paper and began to write quickly. I managed to get some sort of idea about her life.

She was a year older than me, separated from her

husband and with a married daughter. Faina had
come to faith about ten years ago and started to travel
to holy places, staying wherever it seemed good for
her soul to be. She would do any kind of odd job—
for example at the archpriest's or in a priest's house-
hold—and then she'd go on again. She'd worked for
a well-known Georgian bishop, but when I asked
about him she wrote, "I know a lot of people but I
never tell anyone about them."

More often than not she travels without money,
and gets bread and water in churches, where she also
finds shelter, as she was doing here, and in return she
cleans the church building and does washing.

I'd thought from the first day that her lack of
speech was either a penance or a freely made vow,
and so was her strict fast, and I became more and
more convinced of this. She had become a pilgrim at
the call of the soul.

Faina was waiting for Father Anthony and would
go back to the monastery with him.

"Do you plan to stay there? That's a heavy cross."

"A cross isn't usually light," she replied simply,
"but you won't be saved without one."

THERE WERE NO plane tickets, nothing for it but to
go by train—in four days' time.

I could have enjoyed the sea meanwhile, but the
sea no longer gave me any pleasure: The number of
people had tripled, cutters wove along the shore,
steamers, the heavy monster-of-a-catamaran *Iveria*
bombarded the shore with songs and cruise an-

nouncements. Somehow, as I sailed along the path of the setting sun, I discovered I was counting aloud the days that remained before my departure—Tuesday, Wednesday, Thursday.

All I wanted was for Father Anthony to come again. The cement and paint had already been sent to Gudarekhi: the bus rolled up to the gates, the young people loaded up everything quickly; and now the place was being repaired.

Faina and Vera shared my isolation. Vera came up to me one evening. She had on a heavy, blue silk dress with a yellow pattern and a yellow head scarf. Her angular figure looked clumsy in an elegant dress. In spite of the heat the dress was buttoned up, with the usual long sleeves. There was a secret decisiveness in Vera's face.

"You read the Holy Fathers and visit monasteries. . . . Does that mean you believe in God, then?"

"Why do you doubt it?" I asked, surprised, and very offended.

"Oh no, I don't doubt you. I wanted to ask you about it. I've been selling candles for twenty years, you see. I cross myself, just like everyone else, but I don't know whether there's a God or not."

"Yes," I replied with relief, "there is a God who created the heavens, the earth, and ourselves."

"In all my life no one has ever explained anything to me. Yesterday a little girl came up to me in church. 'Where is God? And what's he like?' she asked. And I was just like a little ignorant child myself."

"That's just it! It's not enough to light candles and cross yourself."

"Well, that's what everyone does. They come and light candles once a month, and then they go on a drinking spree."

That's because we live in a sick society: They talked about people becoming spiritual barbarians even at the start of the century, and it's been getting worse ever since. Faith used to be simple: You learned from your grandparents, from your mother. They would take children to church, to confession, Communion: children were brought up to honor God, and the whole structure of life was defined by the cycle of festivals. Everyone fasted in Lent. They even closed theaters and vodka stalls. They brought flowers to church at Pentecost and decorated the churches with birch leaves and grass.

If the church's sacraments work on your soul from earliest childhood, your soul knows about God by itself, just as it knows about goodness and love; it doesn't need proofs. The Russian countryside—and townspeople too, before the 'educated' people of recent times—lived by the thousand-year Orthodox order, which was forcibly shattered, rooted out with barbarian cruelty, maligned, and slandered. This was total rape—and it happened at the same time as other acts of violence—civil war, collectivization, the destruction of well-to-do peasants, enforced ideology, and enforced optimism. Even nature suffered—fields, rivers, and forests. Our hearts and souls were exhausted, downtrodden, poisoned with lies and alcohol. So there's the net result of this triumphal procession against God and the human heart. And we fear the world in which we have to survive.

Religion gives inexhaustible food for the intelli-

gence; faith comes from listening, and unbelief comes
from ignorance. But how can we see the Kingdom of
God within the soul, if our souls have been turned
inside out? How can we recognize Truth if the generations of those who bear it are destroyed? Monasteries have been destroyed, burned, and books have
been taken away from libraries. Poor Vera, poor mil-
lions of wretched people whose past, present, and
eternity have been stolen!

I talked to Vera the following night too, but how
little that was to last her the whole of her life. . . .

Repairs began in the residence. The door leading
to the first floor was left wide open all the time, and
stairs were attached to the terrace windows. Two
young bare-chested men appeared in turn on the
stairs, filling the whole window space. They were
whitening the window frames and painting the walls.
One was red-haired, with a sad, pale, freckled face,
like Vera—it was her son Tolik. The other was swar-
thy, with dark eyes and long eyelashes and a sharply
etched face—Suren the Armenian. We kept bumping
into each other all day, and willy-nilly spoke to each
other.

Somehow or other they brought a melon, cut it up
on the garden bench, and called me over. Suren
started talking about astrology, which he'd learned
about from charts of days and years of birth, with the
names of the corresponding planets, which he'd copied into his exercise books when he'd been at school.

"Judging by these charts, my wife and I aren't
suited to each other, and we've started falling out.
Does that mean that astrology determines our fate?"

I told him why the Church forbids fortune-telling,

astrology, palmistry, augury, witchcraft, and extra-sensory perception—which is so fashionable now. It's all linked with the powers of darkness and it's terribly destructive.

Suren wasn't happy. For some reason or other he wanted to believe in astrology. The midday heat struck us. The bench was placed in the shade of a vine—we hadn't finished the melon—and he began talking about another religious phenomenon that was upsetting him.

"There's a house where young people meet on Saturdays. To start with, they pray for a long time . . . then they put the light out, take their clothes off, and then, well, I'm ashamed to tell you about it. And yet they're praying into the bargain—how do you figure that out?"

"It must mean they're praying to Satan or some Eastern idol that embodies debauchery. What's it got to do with Christianity? Remember the Old Testament commandment: Thou shalt not commit adultery. Christ even calls it adultery when a man looks at a woman with lust. . . . Have you read the Gospels?"

He hadn't—though, like Tolya, he reckoned he was Orthodox.

" 'If a man looks at a woman with lust . . .' " Suren laughed. "Do you mean there are men in this day and age who've been faithful to their wives all their lives?"

"Lust is what leads to family breakups, much more than astrology does."

Suren didn't try to talk to me any more about

religion. These poor children of Vera and other Russian, Armenian, and Georgian mothers, who'd grown up completely free of God, no longer knew how to distinguish Orthodoxy from astrology or astrology from debauchery.

While I was talking to Suren, Faina was frying some potatoes for the young men. She washed their dirty shirts and hung them out in the sun to dry. Having nothing, everything she did she gave to others. So it wasn't for nothing the Lord led her into my life: I speak, and do nothing, while she remains silent and does everything.

Father Anthony came on the last evening. I was very glad when I spotted him from the terrace.

"I've got boils again. . . ." he told me, somewhat vexed, from below. They'd started appearing after he'd gone out in the rain for bread. He came up, threw down his heavy knapsack, and blessed me. "You're still so brown. If I'd been swimming and sunbathing, I wouldn't have gotten boils. They're really unpleasant, you know."

"If only you'd fast a bit less and take some rest. . . ."

"If only, if only . . . I wouldn't be a monk then. I'd spend the day on the beach, by night I'd drink cognac in the Adzhariya restaurant and dance the twist with the female holiday-makers—what is it they dance nowadays?" He laughed at the thought of such an unseemly life.

All I could do was advise him to take hot baths with marigold.

"I'll have to go to Komany. I was struggling somewhat in Lent last year too, but I bathed in the spring at Komany, and I got over it. Have you been there too?"

"A long time ago."

IN THIS GODFORSAKEN place in Abkhazia, John Chrysostom, the sanctifier of Constantinople, died, worn out, en route for his place of exile. He'd been sent there by the tsaritsa, whom he'd accused of immorality. He made it on foot in a convoy to the isolated village in the mountains of a foreign land and, as he was dying, he said: "Praise God for everything." Sixteen centuries later the whole world uses the liturgy he composed.

The ruins of St. John Chrysostom's church in Komany were overgrown with birch trees and grass; a bushy burdock grew thickly around the edge of fallen-in ceilings. Nearby, in the overgrown garden stood a two-story house with wrought-iron window grilles: previously a church house, it was now a house for the mentally ill. An old shell with new contents.

Mist from the ravines wisped upward. For long afterward I could picture these ravines, especially during the *akathist* prayers for the martyrs when I heard the words of the Apostle Paul about those who were called, chosen, and faithful. Of them the whole world was unworthy. They were stoned and tortured, endured insults and imprisonment; tormented and exiled, they wandered through deserts, mountains, and ravines.

At the foot of the mountain was a spring of pure water on the spot where St. Basilisk was martyred.

Pilgrims plunged into the cold lake, looking for pebbles with red spots—"with the blood of the martyr." They took them home to heal some sick body or soul.

The Church stands on the blood of the chosen and faithful, and the liturgy is celebrated on the particles of their holy relics. . . .

FATHER ANTHONY LIT the lamps. I put peaches on the table: Their skin was soft and reddish gold. He said no, as usual, but then he took one and cut it up.

"Are you going to have supper now?"

"Later on, I think."

He was telling me how they'd been painting the church in Gudarekhi the previous day. They'd moved all the rubbish, painted the inside walls white . . . He was sad that I wouldn't see how the new paint made it look so high and light.

I suggested we should go down to the garden. He put his chair back beside the wall under the bishops' portraits.

"Look at this bishop," he said, pointing to a photograph of an old archpriest in a cowl, with a gray beard and sad eyes, and smiling at him. "He used to sleep here on these chairs so as not to pander to the flesh. I don't know about the others, how they carried their cross . . . We remember a thing or two from the lives of the great saints, but of course every spiritual warrior has his own unique relationship with God which no one else knows about."

Everyone, even the most sinful person, knows something about the world, about God, that no one else knows—and that's the reason why our own individual lives are given to us. Each person is precious in the eyes of the Lord and the soul is dearer than all the treasures of the world. If people knew this they wouldn't go on living in fear, senselessly killing one another.

THE NIGHT WAS quiet. The vine leaves that grew over the shed were black above the garden bench and stone wall. Stars twinkled through the foliage. The rosebushes shone with a pale light. A light glowed in one of the ground-floor windows, and beyond it Faina was bending over the table.

I woke up at four o'clock and went to open the window. Faina was standing on the garden path. She lifted her head and pressed her hand to her breast. She was either looking at the constellations or talking to God. Had she just gotten up, or had she simply not gone to bed?

"What's she always writing?" the priest had asked.

"She's copying out the works of the Holy Fathers. She's a pilgrim, an amazing woman. She'll be more use in Gudarekhi than me."

"You've been a great help to us. Come any time. I'll be so pleased to see you and your son. Ask him to pray for me and I'll pray for you both."

"What should we ask God for you?"

"There's only one thing to pray for: that we should all meet in his kingdom."

"It's so hard to imagine—will we recognize each other?"

"Of course it's impossible to imagine—but everyone who is saved will recognize one another, and we'll see all the saints. . . ."

"And the Lord Jesus Christ as well. We've been told so clearly about that in Revelation—there'll be no night there, no need of a lamp, or even sunlight. The Lord himself is the sun of the heavenly kingdom, and the saints dwell in his glory forever. We shall see God—like Job, Moses, and the apostles on the night of the Transfiguration."

The things we were talking about were almost impossible to put into words. But I had the feeling there was something else Father Anthony wanted to say, the most important thing of all which he simply couldn't put into words, but which always lay beneath everything he said, lighting his words from within. Then he said, looking at the dark bushes in the garden, "The Lord appeared to me once on the border of life and death. I saw every feature of his face. He was shining with the light of the Transfiguration. My flesh seemed to dissolve in him and my soul tasted the fruits of Paradise. Now I know how Christ will be all in all for each person in Eternity— the sweetest food and drink, love and the satisfaction of every longing. . . . As you know, longing that is unsatisfied is sorrow, but in his kingdom there is neither illness nor grief—only endless life. Do you remember the anthem for the Feast of the Transfiguration—it's your favorite festival, isn't it?"

" 'Up on the mountain wast thou transfigured, Christ our God,' " I quoted, recalling the words with some effort. " 'And thy disciples, insofar as they were able, beheld thy glory. . . .' "

" '. . . May thine everlasting light shine upon us

sinners.' Do you understand? The disciples saw his glory 'insofar as they were able.' That's how it is in Eternity: the Savior will see all the saints, but each of us will receive him according to the measure of our worth, faith, and love." Father Anthony fell silent. "His voice is unusually clear and pure, and in him there is no pain at all. When we speak, our pain can be heard so clearly, because we are sinners—I've been aware of this echo ever since then. Christ spoke to me, just two or three phrases which were so important, but I couldn't remember them afterward, no matter how hard I tried. Perhaps they'll come back to me when I need them: at my death, or at some time of great testing. The main thing wasn't the words, but the appearance itself."

I couldn't bring myself to ask for any more details—where had it happened? In reality, or in a dream? On this earth?

But, as though he'd understood my thoughts, Father Anthony added, "I can't explain how it happened. There aren't any words in human speech. . . . It happened eight years ago, and if I were an artist I could still draw him exactly, but I'm not; all I've been given is to understand that we must live in such a way that the light of Christ dwells in our souls all the time."

We went up onto the terrace. It was quite late. Fifteen minutes later I went into the refectory with a plate of salad, a piece of Georgian bread, and a kettle of boiling water. Father Anthony had already gone to sleep, slumped on the chairs beneath the bishops' portraits, still wearing his cassock, resting his head on his hand, sunk in the deep sleep of a weary man.

I put the salad down carefully and put out the light. The lamps were burning and so, if the priest was to wake up during the night, he would notice the supper on the table beneath the dark red roses.

Father Anthony had gone before morning, so I didn't say good-bye to him. Faina had gone with him too. She'd taken only the candles, of all the things Vera had gotten ready for her—they'd spent all the day before melting wax. Faina had left me eight slim candles, arranged so that they looked like a white leaf. I drank in their honeyed smell and thought about the church that stands somewhere in the midst of forests, lakes, and clover meadows, fenced in by old birches; thought about the inscrutable ways by which you, Lord, used these fields and meadows to lead me to yourself.

Lead me, speak to me through people close to me, through people I meet by chance; let your will be done in me, and give me strength to live in your Name, to pray, to suffer, to cleanse my soul, so that it will burn in this life and the next like a candle of pure wax lit by your ever-present Light.

Glossary

The translators would like to thank Father John, Orthodox priest in Edinburgh, for his generous help with the English explanation of many technical Orthodox terms.

adjik   Spicy Georgian sauce.
aer   Large cloth veil that covers the Holy Gifts.
ajapsandali   Georgian vegetable cutlets made of eggplant, potatoes, onions, garlic, and red peppers.
akathist   "Not seated." Famous liturgical hymn in honor of the Blessed Virgin Mary; also, in Russia, similar hymns addressed to other saints.
artos   Bread blessed at Easter and cut on the Friday after Easter.
borshcht   Beet soup with a dash of cream.
dikirion   Double candle held by the bishop, together with the *trikirion*, during the blessing, signifying the human and divine nature of Christ.
gazik   From the initials of *Gorkiy Automobil'ny Zavod*, plus the diminutive ending *ik*.
hierodeacon   Monk who is also a deacon.
hieromonk   Monk who is also a priest.
Iveria (or Iberia) Ancient name of the Caucasus.

Jesus Prayer	"Lord Jesus Christ, Son of God, have mercy on me, a sinner."
kamilavka	Cylindrical clerical headdress of Greek origin, awarded to priests as a favor; purple when worn by a priest, black when worn by a monk.
Khutsuri	Old Georgian language, used in the liturgy.
kolkhoz	State farm.
lavash	Georgian unleavened bread.
litiya	Series of prayers said during all-night vigil or a short prayer for the deceased.
mantiya	Sleeveless monastic robe or gown.
Ossetians	Caucasian people who speak an Iranian language.
panikhida	Memorial service for the dead, without Holy Communion.
paraman	Square piece of cloth depicting the cross, worn by monks on the chest or the back.
paten	Small dish that holds the bread or wafer at the Eucharist.
Petertide	June 29: lesser Orthodox fast, preceding the fast of the apostles Peter and Paul.
prosfora	Holy bread, shaped like little round loaves, with a cross impressed on the top.
rason (Russian *ryasa*)	Long, buttoned surplice with full, wide sleeves, worn over the cassock principally by Orthodox clergy.
samizdat	Self-published literature, without official Communist sanction.
shashlik	Skewered barbecued meat.
shchi	Cabbage soup.
skufya	Soft, velvet cap worn by the clergy (rarely by deacons).
staretz (plural *startsy*)	"Elder." Ascetic monk or hermit

	endowed with gifts of insightful and spiritual direction.
tarkhun	Georgian herb.
tkemali	Plums used, for instance, in a sauce for meat dishes.
trikirion	Triple candle held by the bishop together with *dikirion* during the blessing, signifying the three persons of the Trinity.
troparion	Set prayer.

Suggested Reading

Anyone unfamiliar with the tradition described in this book and curious to learn more about it may like to read the following books which were recommended by Bishop Seraphim Sigrist of Pleasantville, New York:

Anonymous. *The Way of a Pilgrim*. Translated by Olga Savin. Boston: Shambhala Publications, 1991.

———. *Writings from the Philokalia*. Translated by E. Kadloubowsky and G. E. Palmer. Winchester, MA: Faber & Faber, 1951.

Bloom, Anthony. *Beginning to Pray*. Mahwah, NJ: Paulist Press, 1982.

Climacus, John. *John Climacus: The Ladder of Divine Ascent*. Translated by Colm Lubheid. Mahwah, NJ: Paulist Press, 1982.

Colliander, Tito, ed. *The Way of the Ascetics: The Ancient Tradition of Discipline and Inner Growth*. Translated by Katharine Ferre. Crestwood, NY: St. Vladimir's Seminary Press, 1985.

Del Bene, Ron, et al. *The Breath of Life: A Simple Way to Pray*. Nashville: The Upper Room, 1991.

Evdokimov, Paul. *The Art of the Icon: A Theology of Beauty*. Translated by Steven Bigham. Torrance, CA: Oakwood Publications, 1989.

Fedotov, G. P. *The Russian Religious Mind*. Cambridge, MA: Harvard University Press, 1946.

Fudel, Sergei. *Light in the Darkness*. Translated by Sophie Loulomzin. Crestwood, NY: St. Vladimir's Seminary Press, 1988.

Gorodetzky, Nadejda. *St. Tikhon of Zadonsk: Inspirer of Dostoyevsky*. Crestwood, NY: St. Vladimir's Seminary Press, 1976.

Hackel, Sergei. *Pearl of Great Price: The Life of Mother Maria Skobtsova 1891–1945*. Crestwood, NY: St. Vladimir's Seminary Press, 1981.

Kovalevsky, Pierre. *St. Sergius and Russian Spirituality*. Translated by W. Elias Jones. Crestwood, NY: St. Vladimir's Seminary Press, 1976.

Lossky, Vladimir. *The Mystical Theology of the Eastern Church*. Translated by the Fellowship of St. Alban and St. Sergius. Crestwood, NY: St. Vladimir's Seminary Press, 1991.

Macimus the Confessor. *Macimus the Confessor: Selected Writings*. Translated by George C. Berthold. Mahwah, NJ: Paulist Press, 1985.

Meyendorff, John. *St. Gregory Palamas and Orthodox Spirituality*. Translated by Adele Fiske. Crestwood, NY: St. Vladimir's Seminary Press, 1974.

A Monk of the Eastern Church. *The Jesus Prayer*. Crestwood, NY: St. Vladimir's Seminary Press, 1987.

Palamas, Gregory. *Gregory Palamas: The Triads*. Translated by John Meyendorff. Mahwah, NJ: Paulist Press, 1985.

———. *Orthodox Spirituality: An Outline of the Orthodox Ascetical and Mystical Tradition*. Crestwood, NY: St. Vladimir's Seminary Press, 1978.

A Priest of the Byzantine Church. *Reflections on the Jesus Prayer*. Denville, NJ: Dimension Books, 1978.

Schmemann, Alexander, ed. *Ultimate Questions: An Anthology of Modern Russian Religious Thought*. Crestwood, NY: St. Vladimir's Seminary Press, 1977.

Sophrony, Archimandrite. *The Monk of Mount Athos*. Crestwood, NY: St. Vladimir's Seminary Press, 1973.

Symeon the New Theologian. *Symeon, the New Theologian: The Discourses*. Translated by C. J. De Catanzaro. Mahwah, NJ: Paulist Press, 1980.

Ware, Bishop Kallistos, ed. *The Jesus Prayer*. Crestwood, NY: St. Vladimir's Seminary Press, 1987.

——— (Timothy). *The Orthodox Church*. New York: Viking Penguin, 1964.

———. *The Orthodox Way*. Crestwood, NY: St. Vladimir's Seminary Press, 1986.

ABOUT THE AUTHOR

Valeria Alfeyeva was born in 1938 and lives in Moscow. She is a member of the Writers' Union and the Moscow Association of Writers. After graduating in journalism form Moscow University, she traveled widely in Russia and abroad. She has joined geographical expeditions to deserts and sailed the Pacific, Atlantic, and Arctic oceans on fishing trawlers, cargo vessels, and scientific research ships.

Her observation of the magnificence of creation led to a different kind of search—an inner journey that resulted in her conversion to Christianity, and a deep love of the Orthodox Church. She has made several pilgrimages to monasteries in Russia, Georgia, France, England, and the United Sates.

OTHER BELL TOWER BOOKS

The pure sound of the bell summons us into the present moment. The timeless ring of truth is expressed in many different voices, each one magnifying and illuminating the sacred. The clarity of its song resonates within us and calls us away from those things that often distract us—that which was, that which might be—to That Which Is.

Being Home: A Book of Meditations
by Gunilla Norris
An exquisite modern book of hours, a celebration
of mindfulness in everyday activities.
Hardcover 0-517-58159-0 1991

Nourishing Wisdom: A Mind/Body Approach
to Nutrition and Well-Being
by Marc David
A practical way out of dietary confusion, a book that
advocates awareness in eating and reveals how our attitude
to food reflects our attitude to life.
Hardcover 0-517-57636-8 1991
Softcover 0-517-88129-2 1994

Sanctuaries: The Northeast
A Guide to Lodgings in Monasteries, Abbeys, and
Retreats of the United States
by Jack and Marcia Kelly
The first in a series of regional guides for those in search of
renewal and a little peace.
Softcover 0-517-57727-5 1991

Grace Unfolding:
Psychotherapy in the Spirit of the
Tao-te ching
by Greg Johanson and Ron Kurtz
The interaction of client and therapist illuminated through
the gentle power and wisdom of Lao Tzu's
ancient Chinese classic.
Hardcover 0-517-58449-2 1991
Softcover 0-517-88130-6 1994

Self-Reliance: The Wisdom of Ralph Waldo Emerson
as Inspiration for Daily Living
Selected and with an introduction by Richard Whelan
A distillation of Emerson's essential spiritual writings for
contemporary readers.
Softcover 0-517-58512-X 1991

Compassion in Action:
Setting Out on the Path of Service
by Ram Dass and Mirabai Bush
Heartfelt encouragement and advice for those ready to
commit time and energy to relieving suffering in the world.
Softcover 0-517-57635-X 1992

Letters from a Wild State: Rediscovering Our True
Relationship to Nature
by James G. Cowan
A luminous interpretation of Aboriginal spiritual experience
applied to the leading issue of our time:
the care of the earth.
Hardcover 0-517-58770-X 1992

Silence, Simplicity, and Solitude:
A Guide for Spiritual Retreat
by David A. Cooper
This classic guide to meditation and other traditional
spiritual practice is required reading for anyone
contemplating a retreat.
Hardcover 0-517-58620-7 1992
Softcover 0-517-88186-1 1994

The Heart of Stillness:
The Elements of Spiritual Practice
by David A. Cooper
A primer of spiritual discipline, a comprehensive guidebook
to the basic principles of inner work.
Hardcover 0-517-58621-5 1992
Softcover 0-517-88187-X 1994

One Hundred Graces
Selected by Marcia and Jack Kelly
With calligraphy by Christopher Gausby
A collection of mealtime graces from many traditions,
beautifully inscribed in calligraphy reminiscent of the
manuscripts of medieval Europe.
Hardcover 0-517-58567-7 1992
Softcover 0-517-88230-2 1995

Sanctuaries: The West Coast and Southwest
A Guide to Lodgings in Monasteries, Abbeys, and
Retreats of the United States
by Marcia and Jack Kelly
The second volume of what the New York Times *called*
"the Michelin Guide *of the retreat set."*
Softcover 0-517-88007-5 1993

Becoming Bread:
Meditations on Loving and Transformation
by Gunilla Norris
A book linking the food of the spirit—love—with the food
of the body—bread.
Hardcover 0-517-59168-5 1993

Messengers of the Gods:
Tribal Elders Reveal the Ancient Wisdom of the Earth
by James G. Cowan
A lyrical and visionary journey through the
metaphysical landscape of Northern Australia and the
islands just beyond it.
Softcover 0-517-88078-4 1993

Sharing Silence:
Meditation Practice and Mindful Living
by Gunilla Norris
A book describing the essential conditions for meditating
in a group or on one's own.
Hardcover 0-517-59506-0 1993

Meditations for the Passages and Celebrations of Life:
A Book of Vigils
by Noela N. Evans
Articulating the unspoken emotions experienced at such
times as birth, death, and marriage.
Hardcover 0-517-59341-6 1994
Softcover 0-517-88299-X 1995

Entering the Sacred Mountain: A Mystical Odyssey
by David A. Cooper
An inspiring chronicle of one man's search for truth through
the esoteric practices of Judaism, Buddhism, and Islam.
Hardcover 0-517-59653-9 1994

The Alchemy of Illness
by Kat Duff
A luminous inquiry into the function and purpose of illness.
Softcover 0-517-88097-0 1994

A Walk Between Heaven and Earth:
A Personal Journal on Writing and
the Creative Process
by Burghild Nina Holzer
How keeping a journal focuses and expands our awareness
of ourselves and everything that touches our lives.
Softcover 0-517-88096-2 1994

Journeying In Place:
Reflections from a Country Garden
by Gunilla Norris
Another classic book of meditations illuminating the
sacredness of daily experience.
Hardcover 0-517-59762-4 1994

Chant: The Origins, Form, Practice, and
Healing Power of Gregorian Chant
by Katharine Le Mée
A book that explains the extraordinary effects
of this ancient liturgical singing.
Hardcover 0-517-70037-9 1994

Wisdom of the Jewish Sages:
A Modern Reading of Pirke Avot
by Rabbi Rami M. Shapiro
A fresh interpretation of Judaism's principle ethical scripture.
Hardcover 0-517-79966-9 1995

Bell Tower books are for sale at your local bookstore
or you may order with a credit card by calling
1-800-793-BOOK.